BIG
MIRACLES

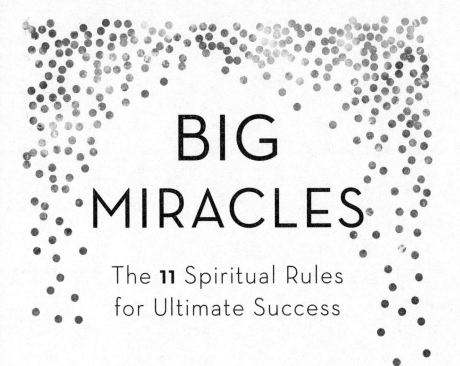

BIG
MIRACLES

The **11** Spiritual Rules
for Ultimate Success

JOANNA GARZILLI

HARPER**ELIXIR**

An Imprint of HarperCollins*Publishers*

HarperCollins books may be purchased for educational, business, or sales promotional use. For information, please email the Special Markets Department at SPsales@harpercollins.com.

FIRST EDITION

Designed by Paula Russell Szafranski

Title page art © Mutanov Daniyar/Shutterstock

Library of Congress Cataloging-in-Publication Data is available upon request.

ISBN 978–0–06245698–4

17 18 19 20 21   LSC   10 9 8 7 6 5 4 3 2 1

To my husband, Nick, and son, Dominick

Contents

Preface

YOU ARE A MIRACLE.

If you're seeking miracles, you're in the right place. I know the eleven rules in this book will support you in creating your heart's desire, because they've worked in my own life over and over. I'm living proof of a miracle, and you are too. We forget the miracles we are. We're born into the world as bright lights, but then life happens. Others tell us who we are based on their fears, and we believe it. Eventually we can't see ourselves through the clouds that fill our minds and block our ability to see the magnificence of life and the opportunities here for us now and always. A big miracle happens when we break through those barriers to manifest our heart's desire—transcending the limits of human power and experiencing Spirit's power working through us. The clouds clear and doors begin to fly open simultaneously in every area of our life from love, health, and career to finances—and we can see the light again.

I've had many breakdowns in my life as well as many breakthroughs. When I look back upon my life, I see the purpose to it all: the good, the bad, and the ugly. Sometimes I've dropped down on my knees, cried out to the heavens, "Why?!" and heard nothing back. That's because I was feeling sorry for myself. I know that I wasn't really asking, "Why?" because if I had, Spirit would've given me the answer. I secretly feared that Spirit would make a suggestion that I would not want to follow through with. Spirit always answers your prayers when you are open and willing. When I've been quiet enough and listened attentively and openly, Spirit has always guided me to a solution. As I open my heart to Spirit, I always feel it being filled with such love that I am awed by how miraculous life is.

This book is a tool to help you remember the love, power, and strength of your soul. You are a spiritual being first, and Spirit wants you to have the richest life possible. You aren't your outer identity, your clothes, your car, your zip code, your relationship status, or your level of education, although those are expressions of you. You are a soul in a body. With the tools you find in this book, you'll be able to shape your mind, body, and spirit to their ultimate expression.

If you've been praying for a solution for issues in your relationships, finances, career, or health, I promise you it's here for you in these pages. I've dug deep into my heart, stretched my soul, and confronted the perils of my ego to get these words onto these pages. Writing it has been a labor of love, and my sincere hope is that, as you turn each page, love fills your heart and you become more sensitive to Spirit. I know you're already sensitive and attuned, and I also know that a spiritual awakening is constantly unfolding for each of us from moment to moment.

If you've suffered a loss, I pray you find solace in these pages.

If you've struggled with seeing your beauty, I pray that these words can teach you to look into a mirror with love in your eyes.

Each chapter of this book provides a way for you to plug into Spirit and be lit up from the inside out. You may already be close to the electric outlet of Spirit or you may feel at a distance from it, but if you keep showing up, you'll find the energy source. You will be able to plug in, the lights will go on, and then you'll know exactly what to do to break through the barriers you're facing.

A big miracle is when you've created your ideal life, one that is bigger than you ever imagined would be possible for you. It's your vision of heaven on earth. You wake up in the morning, take in your surroundings, and you're filled with a sense of deep heartfelt gratitude—that's a big miracle breakthrough. It's as if you can hear your heart singing with joy, and every cell in your body is smiling. You have the energy necessary to create another miraculous day. Not only will your day be fun and rewarding throughout; you'll also be able to help and inspire others. Some of the people you touch with your magnanimous presence will be your loved ones, friends, and colleagues. Others will be strangers. Regardless of any challenges that arise, you'll remain open and feel enthusiastic, because you know that Spirit is always guiding you and you have faith that a positive outcome will ultimately be realized.

After a big miracle breakthrough, you no longer wake up overwhelmed and you never go to sleep plagued with anxiety. You don't dread the phone ringing for fear of a demand from a debt collector or negative words from a family member. You've moved past numerous obstacles you formerly believed were insurmountable. Because of your sacred relationship with Spirit, you always seek spiritual growth, which means that achieving breakthroughs is now a part of your daily focus. You understand that the power of miraculous transformation is yours and will be a significant factor as you continue to reach for your ideal life, whatever that means for you. As you move toward a breakthrough, self-awareness grows, allowing you to deal with often turbulent unprocessed emotions.

I began my spiritual quest to understand the meaning of life when I was six years old in my bedroom in Hampstead, London. Every night I knelt by the side of my bed and prayed for my family, because I was often overcome with a fear that I might lose them. On the one hand, I felt Spirit all around me, loving, protecting, and guiding me, and on the other hand, I felt fear of death and, in the pit of my stomach, pain and sadness. I was a very sensitive child, and I tried to soothe those feelings with food. I'm still sensitive as an adult—but now I have the tools in this book to keep me aligned and peaceful.

As a young person, I often questioned why I felt I wasn't enough. I've always been very empathetic. I feel other people's feelings just as much as my own. I went through a phase in my teens and early twenties during which I tried to drown out my sensitivity by partying hard. I didn't do drugs, but I was drawn to addicts. I made it my mission to rescue others as a way to deflect myself from confronting my own issues. I felt more comfortable around wacky people in chaos, because they made me feel normal.

I also tried to fit in and be a good worker. One day at my corporate finance job in London, while reading the spiritual novel *The Celestine Prophecy* by James Redfield during my lunch break, I realized I couldn't sustain the life I was leading. I felt I had to go to Peru, as did the characters in the book. I had to go and experience the insights the author wrote about. It was a pivotal moment for me. Within a couple of months, I'd left that job, rented out my London condo, and gone off on a global spiritual adventure. I was happy living a Spirit-driven life.

I spent many hours speaking and doing spiritual rituals with people of many indigenous cultures: from camping out in the desert by the ancient Nazca Lines to joining prayer circles at Machu Picchu in Peru; from visiting Isla del Sol (Island of the Sun) and Isla de la Luna (Island of the Moon) in Lake Titicaca, sites revered by the ancient Incas, to doing secret ceremonies in Egyptian pyramids and at various sacred sites along the Nile River. I was initiated into the Rosicrucian Order and spent time with medicine men and women from Navajo, Hopi, Chumash, and Amazonian tribes, participating with them in their prayers and dances. I went and connected with Aborigines in Australia and Maori in New Zealand and immersed myself in spiritual connection with others who were seeking or already deeply connected to Spirit. Regardless of the location, language, or kind of ritual, there were common threads in every tradition I learned about that led to the same experience of Spirit.

Spirit does not discriminate. Spirit always responds to genuine requests for guidance and supports our heartfelt intentions and desires, no matter how we express ourselves. Each person, in each culture, holds his or her own interpretation of Spirit, but fundamentally Spirit is the same for everyone. Spirit is everywhere.

Over the years, I also became a Reiki master teacher, studied tantric sexuality, taught yoga, produced a movie, hosted a television program in the United Kingdom, and began doing psychic readings. As my spiritual journey progressed, I shifted from giving psychic readings to doing spiritual coaching, because I found that holding space for others to have a breakthrough was much more powerful than telling them what they should do. Even if I can see very clearly what is blocking individuals' next best step to a miracle, I prefer to ask them the right questions, so they are more engaged and can connect to the answer directly. It means that they are more likely to follow through and take action with the answer they receive.

As I approached thirty, Spirit drew me to Hollywood, California. So many doors opened for me there that, although I have also lived in many other places around the world, Los Angeles is the place where I feel Spirit the most. These days, I love going to Malibu to host morning miracle breakfasts by the ocean, where people, usually women, come together in small groups to help each other create visions of their big miracles. No matter what I do, the most important thing to me is my relationship with Spirit, because I long ago recognized that Spirit takes care of me. If something doesn't work out the way I want, then I know I must do my best to align with Spirit. If you do only one thing that I recommend in this book, do that: align with Spirit. It is the rule that underlies all the others.

For many years, I was out of balance. I was either immersed in the material world with issues related to my job, making money, and my social status, or I had rejected materialism and meditated in nature with people who had no interest in the world of fashion, movies, or business. When I started following the eleven rules, I came into balance.

Whether you are struggling with your relationships, finances, health, weight, career, or low self-esteem, the eleven spiritual rules apply to your situation. I've had challenges with all of them. In fact, I've been in toxic codependent relationships, run up a lot of debt, engaged in emotional eating that led to weight gain, developed adrenal fatigue, been rejected for jobs, and at points experienced very low self-esteem. I also used to be good at starting projects, but could never finish them. I'm proud to say I've overcome all of those challenges by communicating directly with Spirit. Transforming my difficulties was a big miracle.

I was born into a Jewish family in England and attended Church of England schools. I married a man who has a Jewish mother and a Catholic father. We had two weddings. The first was at Mountain Gate Country Club in Bel Air, California, with a nondenominational officiant. Our second wedding was at St. Martin of Tours Church in Los Angeles with a Catholic priest. Each religion has beautiful and uplifting rituals. I love the smell of frankincense, looking up at the dove on a church ceiling, and the rainbows created by stained-glass windows. I also love the sounds of the bells in a Buddhist temple, listening to songs sung from the Torah, lighting a prayer candle, kneeling in front of a sweat lodge under a full moon, and singing Sanskrit chants and Christian hymns. I view all these practices as ways to raise our energy and get closer to Spirit, which is the whole point of spirituality. For miracles to be abundant in our lives, we need to become good at communing directly with Spirit. As I feel closer to Spirit, I'm uplifted and miracles begin to flow through me.

Before you begin reading this book, I recommend that you clearly identify what you desire this book to help you achieve. I call this setting an intention. You'll find many suggested meditation and journaling exercises in every chapter. As you work on them, go at a pace that's right for you. These rules represent my life's work and experiences. When I wrote this book, I envisioned it being with you for a long time and hoped that it would be the kind of book you'd want to share with loved ones, friends, and anyone seeking a deeper relationship with Spirit. You might voraciously devour it over a weekend, but you could also close your eyes and request that Spirit guide you to the appropriate rule to help you with whatever is challenging you at present.

If you're feeling overwhelmed, close your eyes and open the book to any page, look at a paragraph, and ask Spirit how the story, tool, or exercise being described can be applied to benefit your life now. Stick with one rule for a day, a week, a month, or even a year, and you'll see miracles happen as you put it into practice in your life. Adhere to all eleven rules, and you'll be headed for a breakthrough before you know it.

All life, all matter, is made of energy. How you use your consciousness can shift your energy. Just having this book by your side and seeing the title is a way of your saying very clearly to Spirit, "Show me the way to a big miracle. Bring it to me. Tell me what to do, and I'll do it." That can be enough to get you aligned. Miracle workers know they have the power to act and create certain results. They are alert to doorways of opportunity. If you read this book on a plane, while waiting for an appointment at the doctor or dentist, or on the beach, you're probably going to attract fellow miracle agents. So if you see someone reading this book, go and talk to her. Ask how you can help her achieve the miracles she's seeking. You could also exchange your miracle stories. That will lead you both to experience more miracles. We're all part of one community, and I'm grateful and honored that Spirit gave me the opportunity and gift of serving as a channel for this information.

Happy reading. Your big miracles await you!

BIG
MIRACLES

1

RULE 1: Align with Spirit

If I am to align with Spirit,
who must I be?

You are far more than your mind and your body. You are first and foremost a spiritual being: a mind and a body animated by Spirit. At your best, you are an expression of love and a demonstration of beauty, someone creative and inspiring. At your worst, you are an expression of your unevolved ego—a narrow bandwidth of consciousness bent solely on defending your self-interests; someone frightened, possibly abrasive or clinging. It's not that you stop being spiritual when you're driven by ego; it's that you don't recognize yourself as such. Anytime you feel joyful, peaceful, and fulfilled, you're fully expressing your true spiritual nature. Your spirit has a unique expression that it wants to put out into the world. It loves to create and contribute through your talents, gifts, character traits, and special worldview and to use these to connect with and support others. As a spiritual being, you're compassionate, sensitive, kind, and generous. Best of all, to be a spiritual being you don't need to be like anyone else; you just need to be you and stop resisting your true nature.

When you're spiritually aligned, your mind receives the energy, impulses, and desires of your spirit and puts them into action in your life. You're able to communicate your needs clearly and set yourself up to live in a harmonious environment where you are supported in every way you want and need to be. You're in the flow. You get exactly what you need, in the right way, and at the right time. Your relationships are fulfilling, your work is rewarding, your body feels healthy and wonderful, you have plenty of energy, and you have the money you need to do the things you love and pursue your dreams.

When you're in spiritual alignment, you're connected to Spirit and receiving clear guidance. You can see the direction you want to go in, and you're headed toward it. Even if there are difficulties in your life, they don't faze you, because you understand that they're part of your spiritual growth—they're making you stronger. As long as you practice patience, listen for guidance, and act upon it, you will get the breakthroughs you desire in every area of your life.

The more you focus on your spiritual alignment, the more miracles you can expect to see happening in your life. A big miracle breakthrough is the sum of a series of small miracles that have added up. Spiritual alignment is a vital necessity if you want a big miracle breakthrough, because it is the foundation for everything you think, feel, and do. If you move out of alignment, your progress won't be smooth. It will be much more difficult to reach the destinations you want to reach.

When you wake up every morning, making spiritual alignment a priority can ensure that your day goes better. Just before going to sleep is also a perfect time to check in with Spirit and make sure that you are in optimum alignment. A lot happens during the day, and if you aren't centered and grounded, it can throw you off balance.

As you progress in your spiritual growth, you'll see how beneficial it is to check in regularly with yourself and make a request to align with Spirit. No request is too big. Spirit wants you to have everything your heart desires.

How Spiritual Misalignment Happens

Spiritual misalignment can happen suddenly, through a traumatic event, or it can happen gradually over a period of months or years. Once you know how to read the signs of misalignment, you'll be able to course-correct and move from survival- to abundance-oriented, inefficient to productive, sad to happy, overwhelmed to peaceful, and so on.

In 2003, I started having heavy nosebleeds. It scared me. Intuitively I understood that my physical condition was a symptom of an underlying dissatisfaction with my relationship with my boyfriend at the time, but I kept suppressing the truth of my situation. I'd been writing entries in my journal like, *"Dear Spirit, I am scared. Take away my pain. Please stop these nosebleeds. I want to feel happy,"* yet they didn't stop.

I was approaching critical misalignment. Although I felt a constant low-grade stress and lethargy, I put on a game face to hide it. Sugary foods seemed to help alleviate my pain, as they suppressed my overwhelming feelings of unease, but I gained forty pounds and didn't notice or care about it. That's what I told myself anyway.

Even so, miracles happened.

At the time, I was working without pay in the movie industry. I had invested the last of my savings in an effort to get the production of a new movie off the ground. I didn't know how I was going to support myself, and Spirit gently nudged me to create a flyer advertising energy healing work and put it up on the notice board in a local health-food store. I'd completed all levels of Reiki training, but still viewed the healing sessions I offered primarily as a hobby, and I'd only worked with a handful of people referred to me by friends up till then.

I was surprised when I got a phone call from someone requesting a session, even though that was the purpose of the ad. I was scared the woman would think I was a fraud if she knew all the details of my life, but when we first met and she sat in front of me vulnerably sharing her pain, my fear and shame subsided. My desire to help her took the focus off me. As we met for weekly sessions, my client's life began to improve greatly, and I began to feel better too. This gave me hope, and I was finally able to break through to a new perspective. That day, instead of writing about my feelings of anger toward Spirit and my despair about my relationship and finances, I asked the question, *"Dear Spirit, why am I getting these nosebleeds?"* Instead of simply pleading for the situation to improve, I took responsibility and asked how I could change the situation. I was finally willing to face the truth. In my desire to open up to Spirit and help this woman heal, I became reacquainted with my true nature and was able to reach for better alignment in my own life.

A miraculous breakthrough unfolded over the following weeks. A lightning bolt didn't strike the ground near me. Instead, I gained increasing clarity about my relationship and realized I needed literal distance to get some perspective on it. I made a decision to leave the English countryside and visit London to stay with one of my dear friends who gave me space to breathe and think. I also took a trip to the British seaside town of Margate to study advanced Reiki. After I took time to align with Spirit, it became clear to me that because my boyfriend and I had different core values and life dreams, we needed to break up. Within a month of ending this relationship, my nosebleeds stopped. My daily lethargy turned into excitement for life. I lost my excess body weight. Since then, I'm happy to report, I've never had another nosebleed.

The way I fell into misalignment was a very subtle process. I had a niggling feeling that I was making poor choices, but I ignored this sign. I kept suppressing my needs and putting the needs of my boyfriend first. Looking back on it now, I can see the exact point when I rejected my spiritual being. I was feeling scared and out of control in the relationship with my boyfriend as we burned through my money. I was supporting us both. I can remember pleading with him one day to work with me to change the way we were living. He promised he'd do something different. My intuition told me I needed to walk away for this to occur, but I didn't listen to the inner voice of my spirit, because I felt unlovable and was scared of being alone.

Common Signs of Misalignment

Anytime you're misaligned, you'll feel unhappy, even if you have an outwardly happy and successful life.

Early in my career, one of my dreams was to work in television production. I achieved that goal when I was hired by MTV. A significant memory I have of this particular achievement was feeling proud pulling into the corporate parking lot in my silver BMW, walking up to the security guard, and showing my ID card for the first time. *I made it,* I thought to myself as I entered the brick building.

An event that occurred in the very same parking lot a year later was equally significant. One evening after a long day of work, I walked out and found the lot almost empty. I felt empty too. I couldn't understand why I was dissatisfied with my life. My intuition told me to listen to my heart. I didn't yet realize that another spiritual awakening that would deepen my awareness of what I needed in my life was coming. At the time, I was only expressing *part* of my true spiritual nature through my career in television, which is why I often had an uneasy feeling in the pit of my stomach. That feeling was a sign that I was misaligned with Spirit. When I tapped into that feeling, I became aware that my job was the cause of it. I didn't love my work anymore and felt compelled to pursue a spiritual career, but I didn't know how, and this caused anxiety and fear.

Your feelings are like transmitters giving you messages through your body. To interpret these messages, seek to build a relationship with your internal guidance system and you will begin to understand the signals your body is communicating. At first you will need to practice faith when you follow your instincts. Once you have experienced several successes, your confidence will increase. I corrected that misalignment by leaving my TV job and becoming a spiritual coach.

Recognizing your misalignment with Spirit is the first step in moving toward a big miracle breakthrough. The most common signs of misalignment are:

Unexpressed expectations. Not communicating what you want and need in your relationships with loved ones and at work can create tension in your body that leads to headaches, lethargy, and recurring throat problems, including tonsillitis. Their strongest points of manifestation are above the belly, in your solar plexus, and in your throat, which houses a major energy center related to communication. You may find yourself calm and in control one moment and having an outburst the next. To relieve this tension, ask yourself, "What do I feel? What do I want?" Then, when your emotions are calm and you feel certain, follow through with the suggested action you receive from your intuition.

Resentment. Resentment is dangerous when ignored, because it can spread quickly. When internalized, it will feel as though an intensely uncomfortable energy is rushing through your veins. Unaddressed over the long term, these unprocessed emotions can make you feel physically sick and turn into more serious illnesses. When you feel upset, release the energy of trapped emotions—especially strong ones like resentment—by journaling about them. Do this before speaking to someone you resent. As you gain perspective about the situation, you'll see that the person you're mad at isn't stopping you from getting on with your life. Most of the time, you don't need to tell anyone how you feel directly. As you pointedly focus on what you can change in *your* outlook and actions, resentment loses its grip.

Try asking yourself, "Why am I feeling resentful? What can I do to release my resentment?" Instead of making ultimatums that can cause great pain to you and others, look for the root causes of your resentment beyond the people involved. If you're willing and patient, great miracles can happen in relationships that have been fraught with tension and frustration.

Fear of rejection. Fear of rejection can paralyze you and stop you from taking the actions that your soul wants you to take. Over time, this could compromise the accomplishment of your life purpose. You might not reach out to the people you'd like to be around if you're afraid. You might see yourself as less worthy than someone you admire. Have you ever met and had a great connection with someone, only to find out later on that that person was very successful, perhaps famous in his or her field? Upon discovery of the fame, did you feel yourself shrink a little? That's fear of rejection.

Most of the time, when others say no to our requests, their choices are based upon their beliefs and needs, rather than something unlikeable about us. Yet it's common to fear rejection. When it's time to act and you feel afraid, ask yourself, "If I could not be rejected, what would I do?" Observe your feelings and thoughts to break the cycle that leads to the fear of rejection in the first place. Then do your best to improve your character and a day will arrive when you'll be certain that when you receive a rejection, it is Spirit's way of protecting you.

Procrastination. A sign that you're procrastinating is making excuses for your inaction. There's a constant feeling of weight upon your shoulders, and your head is overflowing with thoughts of not having enough time, resources, or money. You might say, "I'm waiting for someone else to . . . , so there's nothing I can do." So you must ask, "Is that true?" When you've subconsciously decided that what you want won't happen no matter how hard you try, it means that at your core there are feelings of low self-esteem. By procrastinating, you are verifying these feelings by making things more difficult for yourself and setting yourself up for rejection. To counter procrastination, ask yourself, "If success were guaranteed, what action would I take next?" Once you know the answer, go do it!

Fear of failure. Your mind creates a story featuring failure that isn't true and hasn't happened, yet it seems palpable to you. This story may wake you up in the middle of the night. In the day, it may cause you to sabotage yourself. When you fear failure, your imagination works counter to fulfilling your heart's desires. A part of you becomes attached to the idea of failure. The idea of meditating or using other spiritual tools may seem pointless, because you don't believe these efforts can work. If you're afraid of failure, you are likely to decide not to take an action, because you rationalize that this would be the safer thing to do. The irony is that your fear will create your failure.

To overcome fear of failure, ask yourself, "Why do I care so much what others think?" Remember, worse than failure is regret at the end of your life for not having taken action in an attempt to live your dreams.

Deprivation. If you were repeatedly criticized and told not to do certain things in your childhood or were punished for your behavior, there's a strong likelihood you developed low self-esteem. Some think material items are the solution to this pain. Others reinforce their sense of worthlessness by deliberately rejecting the things they want and, more important, need. If you are depriving yourself, ask yourself, "What am I trying to prove?"

Remember, you are worthy of excellent self-care. Being told it was wrong to want the things you want may have led to an unhealthy longing that now results in impulsive actions or addictive behavior (in other words, doing things you know aren't good for you). Ask yourself, "What is a small gift I can give myself today?"

Envy. You see a friend with a lifestyle you want, and it triggers you emotionally. Perhaps she has a husband who buys her beautiful jewelry or perhaps she doesn't have to work and can afford to go for long social lunches and spa treatments several days a week. You may think, *Why her and not me?* You don't want to feel this way toward a friend; you would rather feel happy for her. And on some level you are, but there's still a residual feeling that you are unworthy of the life your friend has. If so, ask yourself, "If Spirit were my provider and all my needs were met today, could I release my feelings of lack?"

Greed. The energy of greed feels like hunger. You are hurting, and because of this want more. You may even feel entitled to more, as though you're being deprived. This type of hunger is connected to the self-interests of the unevolved ego, which keep you from seeing the bigger picture of your life and your purpose. In acting upon your greed, you stifle your compassion and generosity and become separated from other people. Rather than embracing your life lessons, you focus on short-term gain. Taking consistent daily actions that include self-care and income generation toward your big miracle breakthrough can move you beyond any hidden feelings of deprivation. They are a good remedy for greed, which can easily distract you from taking concrete steps to break through any barriers you're facing. Ask yourself, "If all my needs were met today, how would I help others?" By helping someone else, you can regain your power.

It's possible to get back into spiritual alignment quickly. However, the longer you've been out of alignment, the more time it may take you to restore it. Every past action you've taken has led to your current life circumstances. Of special importance is paying attention to your unhealthy characteristics and establishing new, healthier habits to replace them. Do your best to embody patience and expect miracles without being attached to a time line.

Each time you hear an internal critical voice saying, *Why isn't my big miracle breakthrough happening faster? What if the things I want don't ever materialize?* take a deep breath. As you exhale, bring your focus back to the idea of being in alignment.

Set a Spiritual Intention

The first step toward getting in spiritual alignment is setting a spiritual intention. Setting a spiritual intention means you're serious about creating your big miracle breakthrough. You don't expect it to happen by itself. You're aware that action steps are required on your part to set it in motion and bring it to fruition. With a clear intention, you have enough energy and conviction to take bold actions. Setting an intention is the first of a three-part process that also includes making a request of Spirit and following that with a question for Spirit:

Set an intention. Think about what you truly want for your relationships, career, finances, or health.

Make a request. A request sets your intention in motion. You are putting energy toward what you desire.

Ask a question. The answer you receive gives you information about the best way to manifest your intention, and clarity for your next best step.

When you set a sincere intention, Spirit will always support you in reaching your goal. No intention is unreasonable or selfish. Do not deprive yourself of wanting anything you genuinely desire, for that would be a denial or suppression of your spiritual nature. People set intentions for all sorts of things: a soul mate, marriage, financial freedom, their own health, the health of their loved ones, their dream career path, a job promotion, a circle of wonderful friends, a beautiful home, traveling, adventure, and fun. You truly can have what you want. What do you want?

If you are feeling blocked in your connection to Spirit, you may think that Spirit cannot hear you or is ignoring you, but this is not so. Spirit will find a way to communicate with you and give you guidance and support, especially when your intentions are clear.

Set Your Intentions in a Miracle Journal

Setting an intention sends a message to Spirit that you have a strong desire for what you want. You understand that it is up to you to choose and create the life you want with Spirit's guidance. There's great power in writing down your intentions for your life. I recommend that you get a journal in any form you're comfortable with (notebook, laptop, etc.), entitle it your "Miracle Journal," and use it to set intentions and respond to other exercises in this book.

Writing down intentions in your Miracle Journal is especially beneficial right before you go to sleep, because this is the last instruction you are giving your mind for the day. While sleeping, your mind won't be distracted by other activities, like making phone calls, sending e-mails, or crossing items off a to-do list. When you write down an intention, you are a step closer to making it real.

Write your intention in the form of a request and a question, because as you put it onto the page, you move it from an abstract thought to a tangible idea, thereby gaining clarity on your perspective. For example:

- "I want to change my career path. What action is my next best step?"
- "I want a healthy, loving relationship. Should I stay with _____ [name]?"
- "I want optimum health and to weigh 140 pounds. What is holding me back from achieving that?"

Do not phrase the question part in the following way, because then you would be making the decision that you do not have the ability to improve your circumstances:

- "Will I change my career path?"
- "Will I stay in my relationship?"
- "Will I lose weight?"

You get to choose the life you desire. The point of stating your desire and following it with a question is to find information that will help you make the best choice. No matter what is troubling you or why you want guidance, think about the concern for at least a minute. Then, turn out the light and go to sleep. If you think about it and then move on to doing something else, the process won't be as effective.

When you are asleep, your mind is in a receptive state and operating on a different level; your subconscious mind is open. It is easier for Spirit to access your mind when you're in a sleep state. If you're feeling very blocked and this is the first time you're asking for guidance, you may need to repeat this process for several days to get an answer.

It's typical to have vivid dreams after asking Spirit a question or setting an intention. These dreams may be quite abstract. If this is the case for you, focus on the overall primary emotion of your dream when you're interpreting it. When you awaken, assess if the primary emotion in your dream was fear, anxiety, frustration, peace, or gratitude. As you bring the focus back to your emotional landscape, you will be able to make an empowered choice because your dreams can reveal your underlying feelings. Pay attention to any details that stand out from your dream. They are clues to your next best action step. For example, did you see anyone you knew from your life in the dream? If you did, how do you feel about that person? Were you doing an activity that you liked or disliked? Recall as many details as you can and notice your overall feeling.

Another thing that could happen is that you won't remember any of your dreams from the previous night. This means a deeper level of healing is occurring—healing on an unconscious level. Make sure to ask the same question again the next night, and the next, until you get your answer. Whether you do or don't remember your dreams, this process will help you move into greater alignment.

Immediately upon waking, look at the question you wrote down and write an answer to it. If your mind says, "I don't have an answer," write whatever you're thinking in a stream of consciousness. This action will move you toward clarity. The action of writing an answer will eventually override the part of your mind that is unclear. It's as if the wind is blowing the clouds away. In time, Spirit will reveal an answer. The more frequently you focus on connecting with Spirit before bed, the easier it will become.

Establish a habit of writing your intentions and insights in your dedicated Miracle Journal every day, as this will strengthen your connection to Spirit and heighten your ability to receive guidance. Then you'll gain enough confidence to have a breakthrough.

Spirit Has a Message for You

After you've set an intention and made your request to Spirit, do your best to keep your heart open while you wait for a response. Eventually you'll receive a clear message. You may need to ask Spirit your questions multiple times, not because Spirit isn't responding, but because your own fear and resistance may be getting in the way of seeing the signs. When we feel fear, we disconnect from Spirit. If you're feeling afraid, ask for your fears to be released.

Be on the alert for signs from Spirit, so that you can see when new doorways are opening for you, walk through them, and experience your heartfelt desires. A sign may come as a flash of insight or as a strong feeling or sensation. Messages can also come to you through events in nature, such as lightning strikes or the behavior of animals, or from what people say and do. Signs can arrive spontaneously, or they can come in response to our requests.

If you don't connect with Spirit on a regular basis, you could miss very subtle messages from Spirit. You'll have to pay careful attention. As you focus on connecting with Spirit more regularly, your sensitivity and awareness will increase enough for you to more easily notice subtle signs. Practice *looking, feeling,* and *listening* for signs from Spirit.

Look

Once you've made your request, look for signs. At the time of my nosebleeds, my body gave me another strong message. I got the worst allergies I've ever had in my life. I had never experienced anything like it before. My eyes had a terrible reaction to pollen in the air. They were scratchy and swollen—it felt as if sand had been poured into them—and I went for many days barely able to see. At times it was debilitating, and I was scared that I would go blind. Spirit was giving me clear signals through my body that I was not seeing what I needed to see. After I recognized Spirit's message, I never had allergies like that again.

Any type of illness is an indicator that you are misaligned and need to pay very careful attention. Ask yourself:

- "Who was I around before I got sick?"
- "Where was I before I got sick?"
- "What happened that I felt myself move out of alignment?"

Feel

Your body is like a sponge and absorbs energy from other people and your surroundings. If you don't feel good in the presence of certain people and find you don't want to be around them, trust what you're feeling. Your gut is giving you messages.

These messages are normal; it's just that you hadn't recognized them as messages before. Often people get so uncomfortable when they receive messages from Spirit through their body that they turn to food, alcohol, or drugs to numb the sensations, as they can be overwhelming.

If you feel a tugging sensation in your stomach, it means that you need to set boundaries in a relationship; perhaps you're giving too much, to your own detriment. When your energy gets balanced again, the tugging sensation will stop.

If you have a heavy feeling in the pit of your stomach, it means you've disconnected from Spirit. This feeling is commonplace when you isolate yourself or have gone down a wrong path in your relationships, career, or health. It means you're in deep misalignment and need to make some big changes. A change you need to make to get back into alignment could be letting go of a relationship, changing your job or industry, or ending a bad habit.

The feeling of butterflies in your stomach is a sign that you're ungrounded and getting swept up in the moment. It isn't a good idea to make a decision when you feel that way, as it'll likely have an undesirable outcome. Take a step back. If you're meant to do something or take advantage of an opportunity—starting a new relationship or job or purchasing a house, for example—you can trust that it will be there for you when you're ready later on or else something better will come along.

My client Angela[1] and I were scheduled for one of our weekly coaching calls. As soon as she began speaking, I felt she sounded rushed and anxious. She wasn't happy in her home and wanted to move. She told me she'd found a new place to live, but the rent was $700 more per month than what she was currently paying. She didn't want the stress of paying a higher rent, as she had made many financial commitments in order to grow her business. However, her current living environment no longer felt good. I was concerned that she was operating from an ungrounded space and knew she needed to be centered before making any big decisions.

I guided Angela through an alignment meditation and then asked her, "What do you want?" Her first answer was, "More clients to pay for the better home." Hearing her say this, I sensed that she was actually seeking a sanctuary where she would feel safe, peaceful, and creative. "I still think it's a good idea for you to move, but why don't you wait for three months," I suggested. "After listening to you, my sense is that getting the new place for more money would be stressful right now." She agreed.

Five minutes after our call ended, Angela texted me that the potential landlord had dropped the rent by $1,000 when she told him she wanted to think about it. Not only was she getting an opportunity for a better home; the rent was $300 less than what she was currently paying. As you can imagine, she was ecstatic.

You'll know you're aligned when you *feel* centered, calm, relaxed, and alert. When you're looking to make a decision, Spirit's way of pointing you in the right direction is to make you feel good. People often make decisions in response to turbulent emotions, which is always a bad idea. Sometimes you have to make decisions when you don't feel good, but if you've been taking care of your energy by focusing on being in alignment, things will work out in the end.

Listen

Empty your mind of negative and worrisome thoughts on a daily basis, and you'll be able to hear Spirit clearly. It's like hearing a wise and loving parent speak with authority and care as your own voice inside your head.

The voice of Spirit can be very direct. It can guide you to perform a specific beneficial action. At the time when I was depressed about my nosebleeds and wrote my request to Spirit in my journal, I didn't believe I'd get an answer. I vented my feelings and concerns in my journal and had barely any faith, but Spirit somehow got through to me! Spirit told me go make a flyer offering healing sessions. I had such a strong intuition that I needed to do this. Although I thought it was a ridiculous idea, I did it anyway, just because the voice I heard came across so confident and strong.

In 2014, something similar happened. I was driving home on the 405 freeway in Los Angeles, when I heard a voice in my head very clearly say, "Slow down." I've learned to trust what Spirit tells me, so I immediately dropped my speed to 30 miles per hour. It made no sense, but seconds later the chassis on a truck in front of me and to my left detached and flew across my lane before slamming into the barrier. It missed my car by inches. I was able to brake in time because I had reduced my speed, and the car behind me, which had matched my speed, was able to brake too. It was a miracle that I didn't get into an accident.

Many people tell stories of miraculous near misses or of surviving dangerous situations because they heeded a warning Spirit had given them. If you get a firm message, listen to it, and act upon it. I'll admit there have been many times in my spiritual growth when I ignored my inner guiding voice, and it has cost me every time.

Of course, there doesn't have to be an emergency for you to make a request of Spirit. Spirit wants to help with all your goals, even the small ones, such as finding a parking spot or bumping into someone you've always wanted to meet. Spirit is in service to all your goals, because often many small actions can lead to a big miracle break-through. As you focus on your connection with Spirit and practice embodying all aspects of your soul, a spiritual awakening will occur that will give you the momentum to break through any block you're experiencing and have all your desires fulfilled.

Spirit can also help you gain immediate clarity about confusing relationships and situations, both those in the present and those from the past. Once you feel clarity, you may wish you'd known what to do sooner; the truth is that you weren't ready to listen.

Spiritual Awakening

Spiritual awakening is occurring for you when you see your relationships, circumstances, and environment with new awareness. When you're aligned with Spirit, even if you don't yet have concrete evidence that you're on track, everything feels right. It doesn't matter what others around you think of your choices, because when you have a distinct feeling that all is well it means *all is well*.

When you have a spiritual awakening, stress, fear, and pain are reframed, because you have a new understanding about your life challenges. You see that there are life lessons in and a purpose to your difficulties, and this prepares you for alignment with Spirit and a heart filled with love. Suddenly, everything makes sense to you. Things that were upsetting you in your relationships release their grip on you. Any heavy energy around your circumstances dissipates, and it feels as though a weight has been lifted from you. You shift from being fearful to being proactive in improving yourself. You no longer make decisions based on other people's fear. For example, if a friend is fearful about the economy, you remain positive and upbeat. Even if your job or earnings appear to be at risk, you nonetheless can sense that good is just around the corner.

When you start practicing being in spiritual alignment, it can cause a spiritual awakening. Everywhere you look you see another opportunity for spiritual growth. If you lose money or have unexpected bills, you don't fall into resentment; you trust that you'll be able to fulfill your financial responsibilities and have a willingness to do so. Your fears related to money subside. You also realize that a health challenge is Spirit's way of directing you to better self-care. You see that your body is a gift, and you have a new awareness of how to take better care of it. You are also aware that in doing so you can be of greater service to others.

A spiritual awakening can be as sudden as switching a light on in a pitch-black room or more gradual, like the way your eyes adjust to darkness until you can navigate your surroundings. Essentially, during a spiritual awakening you become fully conscious of your thoughts, feelings, and the impact of your actions. You become humble and more willing to learn, even though you may now be more successful and educated than you were previously. The more you know, the more you want to listen and learn.

When you make a request to Spirit for a spiritual awakening, you're telling Spirit that you're clear in your intention and ready to act upon it in your relationships, work, finances, and health. As this awakening happens, it can be glaringly evident where changes need to be made on your part. For example, you may recognize how a codependent friendship is holding you back from getting a better job or see that overworking is affecting your health, because it's preventing you from getting enough exercise and rest. Once you are spiritually awake, there's no going back to sleep or sticking your head in the sand like an ostrich.

Some people do not request a spiritual awakening, but wake up anyway. These people are typically older souls who have a deep spiritual awareness but have feared putting it into action in their life because they are very sensitive souls. These souls may turn to alcohol or drugs to suppress their sensitivity. Perhaps you know some who have promising talent yet sabotage their lives. This may be the reason why they behave as they do. Love them to the best of your ability, and you may be the catalyst who sparks their desire for a big miracle breakthrough.

A spiritual awakening opens you up to more spiritual guidance and to further awakenings, though large intervals of time may elapse between them. A year or more could pass before you have another awakening experience. Your soul needs to integrate your new level of awareness, and this takes time. Some people undergo an intense series of spiritual awakening experiences over a period of several months. This phenomenon, which was given its name by the sixteenth-century Spanish poet and Roman Catholic mystic St. John of the Cross, is known as the "dark night of the soul." You realize what you are doing isn't working in your life anymore. Something has to change. This can be a very painful time, as your feelings of hurt, shame, regret, and self-condemnation bubble up to the surface.

A dark night of the soul often happens when we've made a request for alignment in love. During the year before I met my husband, Nick, I underwent several periods of intense healing and realignment. The Christmas before I met him, I felt a never-ending emotional pain and longing in the pit of my stomach, and my heart felt shattered. I sobbed uncontrollably for hours until I was exhausted and couldn't cry anymore. At the time I did not understand that my heart's capacity was expanding to prepare me for a greater love. My soul was releasing the parts of me that felt unlovable. Space needed to be cleared within my heart and soul to align with him on a soul level. As I was undergoing this personal transformation, Nick went to church and prayed about his desire to get married. I made a similar request around the same time. We met within weeks of his request to Spirit. Do not underestimate the power of making a request for love to come into your life.

Spiritual Growth

Spiritual growth results in your putting your new awareness and knowledge into action in your life. This leads to a series of mini breakthroughs. Sometimes those breakthroughs can feel intense; you may feel as though you're being stretched to the breaking point. Despite the intensity, that pain serves a good purpose. It will help you become more resilient and compassionate and more patient, loving, and forgiving.

Get used to being uncomfortable periodically. If you choose a spiritual way of living, you'll always be faced with new lessons and challenges. The spiritual path isn't the easiest path through life, but it's definitely the most rewarding. As you focus on your spiritual growth and aligning completely with Spirit, you'll continue to leave your old ways of being behind, so you'll also need to get comfortable with letting go and adapting. This process is ongoing, as there are always new levels of consciousness to aspire to.

A beautiful facet of the spiritual path is that as you grow in one area of your life, you'll grow in all areas of your life. For example, as your health improves, your bank balance might too—or relationships in your family may improve. As the adage says, a rising tide lifts all boats. In this case, the rising tide is your rising consciousness.

It is important not to compare yourself to others, as everyone is at a different level of spiritual consciousness. Focus on your own personal-growth goals. As you do, Spirit will continue to give you feedback, which will help you decipher your feelings. Whether you feel good or bad, your feelings can give you information about how best to proceed. Where would you like to focus? What area of your life would you like to align first: your health, relationships, career, or finances?

Declare Your Big Miracle Breakthrough

By now you should have a clear intention of the big miracle breakthrough you desire, because you recognize the signs of alignment or misalignment. When you choose the big miracle breakthrough you desire from an aligned, heart-centered state, you increase your belief that what you want truly is possible. Make sure to create your intention before moving on to Rule 2, Be a Spiritual Vehicle. Be specific and at the same time know that your intention can be adapted at any time, if what you desire changes and you want something more or different. Once you feel certain of what you want, who could you tell about the big miracle breakthrough you desire? Find someone you trust to share it with, and it will help you turn the energy of your desire into a tangible reality. As you share your intention aloud with another person or even with a group of supportive people, your vision of the breakthrough will come into focus. There's nothing to be ashamed of or embarrassed about. You are free. If you've been feeling ashamed or embarrassed, speaking your desires out loud could help lessen those feelings' grip on you.

No one is stopping you from moving toward your aspirations and the life of your dreams. Your heart's desire is within reach as soon as you can imagine it. You can trust that Spirit will present you with a road map. Center, ground, and connect, and then ask for guidance, clear obstacles within your mind, and do your best to be sensitive to your feelings. Keep checking in. Keep the lines of communication with Spirit open.

This constant alignment process is the foundation of every other principle in the book. When in doubt, always start here. It puts you on the map. None of the other spiritual rules in *Big Miracles* will work for you if you fail to adhere to Rule 1, Align with Spirit.

The Center, Ground, and Connect Meditation

Do this Center, Ground, and Connect Meditation in the morning before checking your e-mail or social networks, eating breakfast, or getting the kids off to school. Do it anytime you feel confused about what to do next in a relationship, with your finances, or in any other area of your life. It will help you set your priorities. It is wise to center, ground, and connect with Spirit before you have a job interview or a first date—or any date for that matter—or in preparation for a business meeting or a family gathering, especially if you have a challenging family dynamic. Use it if you're going through emotional turbulence in a romantic relationship. The purpose of the Center, Ground, and Connect Meditation is to align with Spirit. Alignment with Spirit is the foundation of a big miracle breakthrough. At intervals throughout this book, you'll be encouraged to practice this meditation in connection with other exercises.

What you need: If you like, you can play some music in the background while you do this meditation. I love to listen to "The Divine Name: I Am" by Jonathan Goldman, from his album *Healing Sounds: Frequencies II.* Also keep your journal at hand so that you can record your insights as they come in.

There are either three or four steps in this meditation. In brief, these are:

Step 1: Center. Centering is done to align your head with your heart. When you're centered, you experience clarity. You are receptive and open to miracles and surprises. You sense the truth.

Step 2: Ground. When you're grounded, you have a stable foundation from which to connect to Spirit. Doubt is eliminated and replaced with confidence. You are present in your body. Grounding is done to remove stress, tiredness, fear, and anxiety.

Step 3: Connect. Connecting moves you beyond the limitations of the mind. Once you have a solid connection to Spirit, your intuition passes you clues about what's best for you to do next.

Step 4 (optional): Making a request of Spirit. When you ask for insights or support, you will receive guidance on making your dreams come true.

Once you learn this exercise, you'll be able to do it very quickly—in a matter of minutes on some occasions—but for now let's go through the exercise slowly, so I can explain how each step feels and what exactly you're focusing on. Deep inner work such as this must always be done as mindfully as possible, with your full attention.

Step 1: Center

Close your eyes, focus inward, and bring your awareness to your heart. Take three deep breaths to help your energy settle within your body. You are returning to a place of clarity, peace, and knowledge of your life purpose, which your soul has always known. With each breath you are returning to spiritual alignment. Focus on sensing your spiritual energy and true spiritual nature. This is the wisest part of you, the part of you that is eternal.

Take another deep breath and imagine sitting inside a circle of golden light that's roughly three feet in diameter. This is your spiritual home, your circle of power and a place of healing. Think now about what has been causing you concern, draining your energy, or distracting you from the things you want to do. Whatever it is, become aware that there's a heavy cord of energy attaching you to the person, place, or thing that is bothering you. This is an indicator that your relationship to that person, place, or thing is misaligned, because you're expecting that person, place, or thing to change to suit your needs, but the person may not be willing to do so or it may not be possible for that place or thing.

To find the solution, turn your focus inward. Pull the cord of energy back inside your golden circle of light. As the cord returns inside your golden circle of light, visualize it turning from a heavy rope to a golden ray of light.

Now, take a deep breath and allow yourself to feel the full spectrum of your feelings regarding the circumstances that are bothering you. Let this energy move through you without either attaching to it or trying to suppress it. This is how you stay centered in any situation. In this step, you are recharging and revitalizing your energy field. When you find your center, you'll be receptive to new spiritual guidance.

Step 2: Ground

Take a moment to review when an interaction with someone bothered you, or you felt disappointment regarding an outcome. This could have been five minutes or five years ago. The point is when you think about it, you feel some sort of emotional pain regarding the situation. This could include a misunderstanding with a friend, a relationship breakup, not getting a job promotion, or anything that takes up your mental space and is a distraction for you. As you do this review, you will be clearing your energy, which will ground you in your body, increasing your ability to focus. Whenever you feel uncomfortable emotions or physical pain, your spiritual essence hovers above your physical body creating feelings of anxiety, insecurity, and fear. The act of grounding brings your soul fully into your body and leads to peace, calm, and a sense that everything will be all right, even if it still holds remnants of pain or a sense of uncertainty.

Take a deep breath, and as you exhale release your expectations about the outcome you desire for yourself, whether it be a relationship, career, financial or health goal and the expectations you've put upon others to support you in getting what you want.

Bring your awareness to the base of your spine and sense the power of the vital life force that's present here. Notice if it spirals, pulsates, or does both. Imagine your life force as a powerful red flame connecting to the earth and representing your intention to ground your creative power and your ability to manifest your heartfelt desires.

As you sense heat building in the base of your spine, visualize it dissolving any unresolved feelings you may have about your life and purpose.

Remind yourself that you are safe and all is well. There's no need to rush; you have the time you need to fulfill your life purpose. You are grounded in your body.

Step 3: Connect

Having centered and grounded your energy, you are ready to connect to Spirit. Bring your awareness to the area above your head and sense a powerful waterfall of healing light pouring down into your body, energizing you and filling every cell of your body with love, wisdom, and strength. You may feel your body sway gently as it absorbs waves of spiritual energy.

As you are being showered with golden light, you may feel the loving presence of Spirit surround you. Remind yourself that you are a spiritual being living in a physical body. Your body is a sanctuary. You are connected to Spirit.

Bring your awareness back to your heart, where your focus was when you began this process. Notice the difference taking a few minutes to center, ground, and connect has made in how you feel. You'll strengthen your connection to Spirit and increase the potential for miracles each time you move through the steps of this meditation.

Step 4 (optional): Making a Request of Spirit

You can ask for support and guidance in a relationship, your career, your finances, your health, or in any other area of your life where you'd like guidance. Once you feel aligned, here's how to make a request to Spirit. You can speak it aloud or imagine saying it inside your head:

Dear Spirit,
I would like to have a big miracle breakthrough in my
_____ [finances, relationship, health, etc.]. Please
remove any blocks to my _____ [abundance,
love, joy, etc.]. I am ready to release my _____
[debts, doubts, poor habits, etc.].
Thank you,

_____

[your name]

Completion of the Meditation

Take three deep breaths and slowly open your eyes. It's a good idea to write down any insights you've gleaned from your new state of alignment while they're fresh in your mind. The purpose of centering, grounding, and connecting isn't only to prepare for guidance from Spirit; it's also to gain a new level of understanding about your environment, relationships, and past and present circumstances. By practicing this meditation, you'll develop a sense of peace, calm, and deep knowing that Spirit is taking care of you and that everything you need will be provided for you and your loved ones, even if you don't yet have the physical evidence.

2

RULE 2: **Be a Spiritual Vehicle**

If Spirit is my driving force,
what must I surrender?

When you are acting as a spiritual vehicle, you gain a deeper level of insight about your life, your intentions become clear, and their achievement is believable and doable. This gives you momentum. Being a spiritual vehicle in everything you do allows you to move forward with certainty and integrity toward the outcome you seek, whether that is meeting the love of your life and getting married, bringing greater harmony to an existing relationship, earning a million dollars in annual salary, or paying down an outstanding credit-card balance. Being a spiritual vehicle accelerates your progress toward big miracles, because doing so gives you such a strong sense of purpose that you can move through any obstacles you encounter on your path with ease and grace.

Choosing a spiritual path means choosing a path of continuous personal growth and actively seeking your spiritual transformation. The main purpose of the spiritual path is to expand your capacity to both give and receive love. No matter what intentions you hold at present, choosing to be a spiritual vehicle will help you head in the right direction in all areas of life. Perhaps you're currently hoping to enter a new relationship. Perhaps your dream is staying in an existing one and deepening your commitment to your partner. Or perhaps you're working up your courage to leave the relationship you're in and start a new chapter in your life as a single. No matter which direction you intend to move, you can be a spiritual vehicle for everyone whose life you touch. Relationships can intensify our spiritual lessons. Every relationship is an opportunity to expand your horizons, connect with your higher self, and express compassion for yourself and others. The same rule applies in your workplace. No matter which direction you're aiming, you can choose to be a spiritual vehicle.

The great thing about this choice is that, when you are acting as a spiritual vehicle, you are putting your newfound spiritual alignment into action. If one avenue you try to go down is closed to you, Spirit quickly guides you in a new, more navigable direction. As a spiritual vehicle, you are better attuned to people and your surroundings. You are better able to manage interactions with difficult individuals and recognize where you need to adapt and be flexible. You are empowered to be more fluid and conscientious and to forgive misunderstandings. You recognize that there's more than one way to find a solution. Because Spirit is working through you, you're able to be proactive in creating win-win situations everywhere you go.

First, Free Your Mind

To receive help from Spirit, you need to become a clear conduit for spiritual energy. You must work diligently to remove anything in your mind, heart, or body that could prevent you from taking steps to achieve a breakthrough. Once those impediments are gone, you'll be able to clearly act upon your intuition and hear guidance from Spirit in everything you do, from the choice of food you put in your body and where you shop to the people you surround yourself with on a daily basis and how you behave in your professional life.

A good first step in removing blocks is freeing your mind from the grip of fear. Whenever you have a specific intention in mind, you must be willing to surrender to the path that leads to the desired outcome, whether it is related to your health, relationships, career, or finances. You can be sure that fear-based thoughts and feelings will arise anytime you set a goal, because when you do something new, doubt that you can achieve it usually arises. It takes courage and consistency to follow the path where it leads.

Although people may profess they want freedom from fear, pain, anger, and limited thinking, when it comes time to take action to go after what they want or to demonstrate that they can be the people they claim to want to be, fear overtakes them. Fear of taking action kicks in for many reasons, one of which is that change—even the positive changes we desire—brings us into contact with the unknown. Most commonly, people fear that they aren't good enough, smart enough, attractive enough, or lovable enough to have what they want. These types of fears often lead people to give up on their dreams without ever giving the dreams a fair shot. They think, *Why bother?* It is imperative not to let fear sabotage your good intentions.

Eventually, the dreams of people ruled by fear burn out and become like the embers of a dying fire. Those people's lives continue, of course, but seem more mundane and burdensome than they did when they were still working toward goals they cared about deeply. It's better to try and fail than to give up preemptively. Those who let fear, anger, and self-criticism stop them from realizing their goals usually have regrets and feel disappointed for the rest of their lives, whereas those who try their best and fail usually can move forward without feeling ashamed or cheated.

Fear has a cousin: resentment. When you see someone else fulfilling a dream similar to yours, feelings of resentment may arise if you're not being the spiritual vehicle you could be. If you're feeling blocked or stuck, you may catch yourself thinking, *Why her and not me?* or *He's not so great.* This kind of thinking directs your attention to the wrong place: away from you. Tearing others down, even just mentally, drains your creative energy. Let's say that a single woman sees her closest friends getting married one by one around her and begins feeling left behind. When she's around them, her self-esteem drops, and she begins to resent them for the negative emotions she feels. Her resentment doesn't harm them as much as her, because she soon stops going out, which lessens her odds of meeting someone special.

A couple of years after I gave birth to my son, an old friend from London admitted to me that she had been envious of me and resentful of my happiness because she'd had two miscarriages. Her anger had led her to avoid me. When we reconnected, my friend explained that my presence had been a reminder of her own struggle with fertility. She also said that she hadn't liked the woman she'd become and had taken time away to realign herself spiritually.

An interesting thing happened to my old friend once she recognized she wasn't aligning her behavior and choices with her spiritual beliefs. After doing her inner work, she realized she wasn't with the right man. She separated from her husband and spent some time alone. Then she met someone else with whom she really clicked and ended up having her dream life with him and two children they adopted. She no longer resents the happiness of other couples and parents, because she's too busy attending to her own marriage and family.

Although it isn't pleasant to envy another person's happiness, success, or advantages, if you do find yourself feeling envious, it is a sure sign that you have a heartfelt desire that needs your attention. Envy doesn't mean you're a bad person, just that you have inner work to do. You are projecting fear in the form of resentment on another person, because you're not willing to admit how angry you are with yourself for failing to take responsibility for your dreams.

To free yourself of negative thoughts and feelings, you must be honest with yourself about them. You must search high and low, inside and out, for the sources of the resentment or envy you feel, so you can bring your focus back where it belongs: to your own behavior and intentions. Resentment poisons the soul and disrupts spiritual connection. Free your mind by forgiving yourself and others, and solutions will appear.

Cultivate patience. Our mind can be like a messy trunk filled with a jumble of tools, spare tires, oil-soaked rags, and garbage. For big miracles to occur, you must first clarify and organize what's in your "trunk," so you can see what preconceived notions you want to get rid of so they can be replaced by those that fill your heart with peace and gratitude. This can take time, but once you've done this, your feelings will stabilize and you'll calmly discover that you have more room to open up to Spirit.

As a spiritual vehicle, your mental "tires" will bounce over bumps in the road of your relationships, career, finances, and health. As you pick up momentum, your awareness will shift, so that you can plainly see how *you* are the main thing holding yourself back. You'll also understand what is and isn't working in your life, and why. You'll have so much clarity about who you must become to have what you want, in fact, that even if someone important to you, such as a spouse, parent, business partner, or friend, disapproves of your choices, the disapproval won't destabilize you—at least not for long.

But don't expect the worst. Expect the best. You'll find that most of the people in your life will be genuinely pleased for you. They want you to have everything your heart desires. Perhaps the thing I love most about being a spiritual vehicle is that it brings a new level of connection and trust into our relationships and adds sweetness to our lives.

Set Your Intention to Be a Spiritual Vehicle

My client Jessica, a graphic designer at a corporation, had a recurring desire to become a yoga teacher. She kept dismissing the idea because she was a single mom and couldn't imagine how she'd pay her bills during the training period if she quit her current job. Her mind presented her doubt after doubt about money and scheduling to dissuade her, yet she continued to hear the calling of her heart. During a discussion of her options, I suggested she research yoga teacher-training programs. Investigation feeds the mind and gives Spirit a chance to speak, so it's always a good place to start when you discover something new that you want to try.

Through research, Jessica got clear about the specific type of yoga she wanted to study. In comparing the price of courses at different studios, she was excited to discover that some offered payment plans. She also learned that she could take the requisite classes in the evenings and on weekends. She decided that she needed a course with both a payment plan and flexible dates, because she might need to make up classes she missed due to her work schedule and childcare responsibilities. She phoned the studio that met most of her requirements and learned that the faculty members there were willing to be flexible in response to her personal situation.

On our weekly call, Jessica made a declaration that she would go ahead and register for the certification program if Spirit would give her a sign of affirmation. She then phoned me the very next day to tell me that when she was getting into an elevator, she saw a receipt lying on the floor. Written in black Sharpie ink at the top of the paper was the word "*Yogi.*"

"Do you think it's a sign from Spirit that I'm meant to go ahead with the training?" Jessica asked me.

"What do you think?" I asked in return.

"Yes, it's a sign. But I want to make sure I can follow through," she said.

"Make the commitment, and I'm sure it *will* work out. You could rationalize that it was a coincidence that a piece of paper with the word 'Yogi' happened to be on the floor when you rode the elevator. You could say that it didn't mean anything. But if that were the case, why would you get so excited about seeing the word '*Yogi*' there—particularly when teaching yoga is something you want so much?" I said. I could feel Jessica's excitement mixed with fear. "New doors will open for you. You'll see," I added. "In your heart, you know Spirit is communicating with you."

Later that day, Jessica followed the voice of her inner guidance and made the commitment to train as a yoga teacher. In overriding her fear, she allowed herself to become a spiritual vehicle, and she felt ecstatic about her decision! Taking that step put her on the path.

What's the lesson here? It's time to reach toward the outcomes you desire in your heart. If there is something you are serious about doing, make a sincere request to be a spiritual vehicle in this endeavor. Then look for signs of confirmation. You can trust that Spirit will support you and show you the right actions to take. And remember, you don't have to know how the journey ends at the beginning as long as you trust that there's a reason Spirit wants you to take a road trip. It may be that you'll meet someone you are destined to meet, learn something you need to learn, or be a teacher to someone. In Jessica's case, after a gradual two-year transition, she did become a yoga teacher. There had been nothing to fear, as she was easily able to find work and take care of her children following her transition out of corporate life.

Before you set an intention, you must empty yourself of any emotions, thoughts, or mental habits that don't allow you to be entirely open to Spirit. Doing so will enable you to connect to and receive the guidance you're seeking from your intuition and to perceive spiritual signs in your environment, such as the written message Jessica saw in the elevator. In truth, staying open to receiving guidance is an ongoing process. Clearing must constantly be going on if we are to lead intentional lives.

You can't have a breakthrough without making changes. The bigger a breakthrough you desire, the more beliefs, habits, fears, resentments, and old junk from the "trunk" you'll have to let go of. Until you get comfortable with making change, it may feel hard and perhaps somewhat painful to embrace the process of letting go. As you make progress toward your goals, however, you'll find joy replacing your pain, because you'll have experienced many small miracles that brought you closer to achieving your heartfelt intention.

Do not rush to set intentions before reflecting on them. Make sure you understand *why* you want what you want. It's important to feel happy while you are working toward your results, rather than doing things in trade for future happiness. Doing things that leave you feeling empty just because you think they must be done is not how Spirit operates. Spirit leads through love.

If you're thinking, *When I get the house, car, recognition, dream vacation, six-figure income, relationship, or . . . , that's when I'll be happy, peaceful, relieved, and so on,* you need to know that it doesn't work that way. In order to achieve what you want in the future, you have to focus on being a spiritual vehicle in the present.

Once you're a spiritual vehicle moving with intention—meaning that you're intuitively connected to Spirit and following through on expressing a purpose that your soul loves—that's when you'll feel the full effects of a big miracle breakthrough in your life.

How to Become a Spiritual Vehicle

The following guidelines will help you stay on track toward your big miracles.

Clear your energy daily. When you don't do the things you intend to do and you can't understand why you aren't doing them (for example, eating healthy, getting enough sleep, taking care of your clients, or focusing on generating income to support yourself), it means you're filled with energy that's blocking your connection to Spirit. It's imperative to clear that energy. If you keep resisting doing what you know needs to be done, you'll begin to feel exhausted. The best way to clear your energy is to do something that feels relaxing, fun, or nurturing:

- Sleep. You may feel terribly guilty for taking a nap in the middle of the day, but it will give your mind time to rest and empty itself. Once you are recharged, you will be more receptive to Spirit.
- Exercise. Take a gentle walk or do a yoga class that challenges your body and refocuses your mind on what is going well in your life. As you move physically, you will clear your energy field and gain a clearer perspective.
- Listen to an inspiring talk. Exposure to uplifting ideas can raise your energy level and increase your receptivity to your intuition, revealing pearls of wisdom. Journal about your insights afterward.
- Meditate. Pick a style of meditation practice that resonates with you: silent or guided, whichever your soul wants.
- Listen to music, dance, or sing. Both sound and movement help us to release unproductive thoughts.

Be honest about what isn't working in your life. What isn't working in your career? What isn't working in your job? If you don't have a job, what isn't working about your efforts to find employment? What isn't working about your cash flow and bank balance? Look deeper to identify why things aren't as you would like them to be.

And what isn't working in your health? What isn't working in your diet? What isn't working in your daily routine? What isn't working in your home? If you are married or in a relationship, what isn't working there? Is there anything else that isn't working in your life?

It can be scary to look closely at the state of your marriage, health, career, and bank balance if you think you won't know how to change or where to start. Perhaps you feel you don't have enough time or some other resource. Look closely anyway! Denial will keep you stuck and inhibit your progress. Taking a look is a precursor to taking action. Sometimes just seeing what needs to be done is sufficient to unblock the flow of energy.

Go back to Rule 1, Align with Spirit, and remind yourself that everything you need to live a happy and prosperous life is accessible to you now. Review your intentions.

If you feel unhappy, pinpoint the source of your dissatisfaction. Ask yourself, "Why do I feel unhappy?" At first, this question may seem overwhelming, so you may find yourself answering, "I don't know." When we choose not to know, what we're really saying is, "I don't have the energy to make a change in my life. If I try, I think I will fail" or "I'm ashamed of wanting what I actually want." When we say, "I don't know," we're avoiding taking responsibility for our lives and desires. Dig deeply for your reasons.

If you continue to experience confusion or draw a blank, you can always reframe the question. Write your answers in a stream of consciousness in your journal. Try asking:

- "If there is a reason (or reasons) why I am unhappy, what are the first thoughts that come to mind?"
- "Is the reason something I did or said?"
- "Is the reason something that someone else did or said?"

Don't think too hard about your answers. Let your intuition guide you organically to your truth. You may be surprised when memories of people and events from your past surface. *Why am I remembering this now?* you may wonder. A better question would be: "How does this memory make me feel?" Memories are thoughts connected to strong feelings. All these memories have been sitting in your energy field. Because you haven't felt your feelings, they have affected your ability to move toward your achieving your intentions.

Your body can also provide insight as to the sources of your dissatisfaction. Is there a place in your body where you feel discomfort most acutely? Once you've identified a specific body part, write in your Miracle Journal about what that part is trying to tell you.

Here are a few examples of symptoms and what they may mean:

- A tugging feeling in your stomach can mean you are having an issue in a relationship.
- A persistent migraine can signify that you are procrastinating.
- A loss of sex drive can indicate you carry resentments in an intimate relationship.
- A lack of energy could mean you have overextended yourself and need to put boundaries in place at work or with family.
- A rash could be brought on by feeling nervous and unsafe in a relationship.
- A back pain could represent the worry that you cannot provide for yourself or loved ones adequately.

Be willing to follow through on the spiritual guidance you receive. You prayed for the answers and then they appeared, so practice trusting the information. Trust builds on the signs you are looking for, so be vigilant for evidence. My client Rachel left her corporate banking job to work independently as an executive coach after she had her first child. She had doubt she could make enough money doing this work she loved and when she considered quitting her dream, the next day she received a phone call from a woman who found her online and hired her.

Take responsibility for your life. If you want to have better relationships with your parents, siblings, or spouse, be the one to reach out and open the lines of communication. Practice listening for the others' feelings and needs. What story do you tell yourself that blocks your ability to have a loving relationship? Every time you blame someone else for your circumstances, you disempower yourself. If you want to make more money, stop making excuses for your circumstances. What story do you tell yourself about your job and finances? Every time you claim you don't have the necessary resources, you keep yourself stuck.

Every story you tell about being a victim is related to an energy block. Blocks can be related to any aspect of your life, including your love life, health, social connections, and finances. To shift an energy block related to money, write down how much money you want to make. What's the minimum balance you want to see in your checking account? What's your motivation for making that amount of money? To shift an energy block related to your health, write down how you want to feel. What level of fitness do you want to achieve? How do you want to look?

Study your answers carefully. To succeed, your answers must be aligned with Spirit—meaning you must be aiming for a certain financial result or a certain body weight for a reason that is true to your authentic self, not a reason you think is right or will be acceptable to somebody else. When you admit the truth to yourself, illusions you've been maintaining in your life will start to be revealed. You'll soon recognize that the energy it takes to keep a façade in place is exhausting. With this recognition, you will find yourself shifting away from avoidance and toward wanting to embrace your responsibilities.

Activities required to fulfill your goals that seemed difficult, mundane, and burdensome to complete will take on a glow of satisfaction when you see how you're in charge of your results. As long as you're thinking thoughts like, *He has to change first,* you won't be able to get what you want from your interactions with anyone. When you take responsibility for your life, you'll be more accepting of people as they are, which will improve your relationships.

Clean up your relationships. If you want true intimacy and love in a close relationship, you must be gracious in *all* your relationships. Look closely at what you say and do to others. Do your best to avoid judgments and unkind remarks. Apologize for offenses if they occur.

Also look closely at what you say and do to *yourself.* Listen carefully for the voice of your inner critic. Pay attention to when you judge yourself or anticipate rejection. If you can recognize your negative self-talk, you'll have the ability to change it. Always be kind to yourself. As you act gentler and more encouraging, fear of rejection will subside. There will no longer be a feeling of inadequacy or pressure attached to your performance.

Self-acceptance leads to acceptance of others. As you become self-accepting, you'll find any desire to change others or shape the way they do things or think losing importance. You'll stop worrying about their perceptions of you. As you relax in your body, the possibility of having heavy conversations or intense confrontations is less likely, because your outlook and approach are neutral and your energy is receptive. Others will feel relaxed in your presence.

Seek the good you want in yourself. What do you appreciate about your closest friends and loved ones? Cultivate these traits in yourself. If something is bothering you in a particular relationship, evaluate your expectations. Be honest about what you want. Once you recognize your needs, see if you can find ways to fulfill them for yourself. Share your happiness.

If you decide there is no value to maintaining a relationship with someone who has been a major part of your life, ask, "What do I fear will happen if I let go?" Most of the time, what we fear doesn't happen. But if what you fear does occur, it's confirmation that you weren't in alignment with the other person and were destined to go in different directions. Once your ongoing relationships are clean, you'll be a better conduit for Spirit.

Focus on what is working in your life today. Miranda came from a poor family and grew up in an area that didn't have good schools; there was no expectation that she would pursue higher education. As an adult, she resented her past and desperately wanted her daughter to have the college education that hadn't been available to her. After her husband left her, she found strength and community in a local church and got involved with a charity. Through volunteer work she met kids who had no parents or had been in violent homes. Caring for them helped her gain a different perspective on her own childhood and let go of her past difficulties.

Miranda began to focus on the love she'd received from her parents and on her great relationship with her daughter. She reframed her past circumstances and feelings of inadequacy by applying for several jobs that required a college education even though she didn't have one. One of the companies she interviewed with saw potential in her and hired her despite her credentials because of her positive attitude. They felt she could be trained in the skills required. She worked tirelessly and never complained. She was grateful for the new job.

Miranda used a large portion of what she earned to provide her daughter with educational resources. Her big miracle breakthrough was the day her daughter was accepted to and granted a scholarship by an Ivy League college.

Miracles Require Sacrifices

We must be prepared to make sacrifices in order to be spiritual vehicles. The sacrifices Spirit asks us to make lead to greater fulfillment and can make our lives better than we've even imagined. But we may not be able to see why we must make the necessary sacrifice until we do.

Spirit sees our lives from a higher perspective than we do, so it can take a leap of faith to let Spirit lead us. When we realize that furthering a dream will require us to make a sacrifice, we often resist doing what is needed, because we fear we're going to lose something. We may experience guilt or anxiety. Trading certainty for uncertainty seems too dear. This resistance is a product of the ego, which wants to control our progress and insists that we know more than Spirit does about what's best for us. It comes from failing to trust that Spirit is there to support us.

We must change ourselves in order to achieve success. We literally cannot have it by staying the same. Therefore if a change is what must come, you can be sure that a sacrifice of some kind will be involved. If you want to be a spiritual vehicle, a good question to ask yourself is: "What is my next best action, even if it feels painful?" Listen for the voice of your higher self, which sounds different from the voice of the ego. Your higher self understands that sacrifice is necessary for your spiritual growth and can reassure you, whereas your ego will be critical and doubtful.

When you're in a situation where a tough decision is required and your intuition urges you do to something that feels scary, it likely means you're being called to make a sacrifice. To follow through with the least pain, surrender to what is being asked of you. Ground yourself in your role as a spiritual vehicle. Sacrifice can be tougher when it involves our loved ones or other interested parties, but you can trust that Spirit has a handle on everyone's best interests. Remember, they are also being called to grow spiritually in their lives in response to different circumstances.

A few years ago, I had a strong intuition that I should attend two live events, one in the Midwest, the other on the East Coast. Attending meant taking two separate business trips and spending two weeks away from my husband and young son. I felt torn and guilt ridden by my decision to follow my intuition and go, but I went nonetheless, because I trusted that Spirit had a purpose for me to be at those events—one that would make sacrificing time with my family worthwhile.

On the last day of the first event, I met a woman whose son had survived being severely shaken by a babysitter when he was just thirteen weeks old. The doctors had told Kimberly McCord that her brain-damaged son wouldn't live past the age of four, but when we met, her son, Carson, was already twenty. After we met there, Kimberly decided to do an intuitive reading with me via telephone. The second of my trips, already scheduled for the next month, would bring me to Pennsylvania, near their home. I'd be able to meet Carson in person.

Having tuned in to her life with Carson through the reading, I loved having the opportunity to see mother and son together. I was able to give Kimberly confirmation of the amazing job she was doing taking care of her son, who is an angel here to educate people about child abuse, as is she. They are powerful spiritual vehicles, helping the rest of us to wake up to our spiritual natures and be kinder and more compassionate through their example. I was able to sense some important ways his caregivers could help Carson ground and clear his energy using a spray made of pure essential oils, and a black tourmaline crystal. When Kimberly shared these tools with Carson's caregivers, she said their hearts were touched by being able to interact with Carson in new ways. It deepened their appreciation of life and human connection.

The most important thing I gained personally by making the sacrifice of those two trips was that when I returned home to my family, I had a much greater appreciation for them too. In retrospect, I understood exactly why I was meant to take those trips. I now understand that when Spirit calls me to travel, even if it requires a personal sacrifice, it's for a very good reason.

Keep Your Heart Open

If you want to become a vehicle for Spirit, you must first come to a personal understanding of what being a spiritual vehicle is for you. Once you do, only then will you experience the kind of breakthroughs that can accelerate your journey to the fulfillment of your intentions. This means you need to tune in to your heart to decide how you want to express and define yourself.

Spirit has the power to move quickly and inspire you when your awareness increases, so it's imperative to be super mindful and remain conscious of your actions. The momentum can feel overwhelming. You may have had a vision you wanted to realize for years, but even so, once you set your plans in motion, you could suddenly find yourself wanting to slam on the brakes.

Have you ever heard the expression, "Be careful what you wish for"? That is the sensation we often get when our goals are suddenly within our reach. It shifts the ground under our feet, and that means we either have to adapt or we'll be destabilized—or even get knocked down. At the critical point when you see that a milestone in your life, such as a promotion or a marriage, is achievable, if you don't surrender to the guidance of Spirit, there's a high probability that you will sabotage your dream. This can show up as your resistance to doing what needs to get done or saying the wrong thing. Ego or insecurity may creep into the driver's seat of your spiritual vehicle.

If you give in to fear and emotional blocks, when happiness arrives, it will be short-lived if you have lost your connection to Spirit. Without that connection, you cannot hope to understand the reason for making your journey.

As spiritual vehicles, we must operate from a higher state of being. You become a spiritual vehicle by reaching for a higher consciousness and opening to receive the energy of your soul. When your soul energy is integrated into your body, you become a spiritual vehicle, and your soul will steer you to the outcome you desire in any given situation.

Sometimes we must allow ourselves to be vehicles for Spirit to accomplish objectives we never would have chosen for ourselves ahead of time, such as caring for a parent with dementia, taking a second job to put a child through college, or becoming a champion for a cause that we ourselves have been touched by. Spirit always provides context for us to be of service to the world.

For your soul to drive your life, your spiritual essence must download into your physical body. If you are ready for this to happen, you'll feel a sense of excitement and anticipation when you think about everything you can do by allowing your soul to steer your destiny.

It feels like a light switching on in your body when your soul comes in. You have a certainty that is inexplicable. Even if there are big challenges to break through, you're able to see exactly where you're headed. You may even clearly see yourself living in a particular part of the world, succeeding in a particular profession, winning awards in a certain niche of expertise, earning a specific amount of money, or becoming a parent. If you experience this feeling of certainty, it means the outcome you desire is part of your destiny. It is meant to be. All you have to do is show up, listen to your intuition, and act upon the guidance you receive.

Even if you don't feel certain that you are ready to be a spiritual vehicle, if you have the desire to be one, it means you're ready. You are simply experiencing remnants of fear that you must be willing to surrender.

Here is a guided meditation exercise to show you how to be a spiritual vehicle and a map showing how to get from where you are now to your big miracles.

Taking a "Road Trip"
in Your Spiritual Vehicle

You may sit or recline to do this brief exercise.

Begin by closing your eyes and bringing your awareness to your heart. Take one of your hands and place it over your heart to help you focus inward. Then take three deep breaths into your body. Once you are connected with your heart, put your hand back on your lap or by your side. Bring your focus to the top of your head and imagine yourself opening up to your soul. Sense a glowing golden light pouring into your body. You are filling up with vital energy. Your body is more than a body. It is a matrix of energy, which, in its entirety, makes you a spiritual being in a dynamic state of flow.

Bring your focus to your mind's eye, a place of inner vision that gives you the ability to see your soul's desires. Imagine your dynamic energy-self standing on the path of your destiny. Review the big miracles you desire at this time by asking:

- *"What are the specific outcomes I desire in love?"*

- *"What are the specific outcomes I desire in health?"*

- *"What are the specific outcomes I desire in wealth?"*

- *"What are the specific outcomes I desire in family?"*

- *"What are the specific outcomes I desire in business?"*

- *"What are the specific outcomes I desire in travel?"*

- *"What are the specific outcomes I desire in education?"*

- *"What are the specific outcomes I desire in my lifestyle?"*

Take your time. View these categories one by one. It is likely that there will be many ways the outcomes you see will overlap. Allow yourself to feel the specific outcomes you identify in your body, using your imagination. Activate the emotion associated with each circumstance that represents your idea of the perfect outcome.

Next, imagine yourself floating above your physical body and looking down at yourself. See your body on a map and your desired outcomes as destinations that are situated in various places on the map. From these, pick the one outcome you desire that feels most important to you right now. Sense the distance between where your body is and the place you want to be.

When you can see these two points and the distance between them clearly, ask yourself, "What needs to happen for me to get from point A to point B?" Let the answer come to you through your intuition. Feel your connection to Spirit deepening.

Now let the creative energy of your soul move fully back into your physical body. Notice how you feel revitalized and have more awareness. You are fine-tuning your spiritual vehicle through this exercise. When you are done, your spiritual vehicle will be fully aligned with Spirit.

Bring your awareness back to your heart. When you open

your eyes, you will know what needs to be done next and in the future to create your big miracles.

Trust the experience you had. If you begin to doubt or wonder how it is possible to accomplish the goal you've chosen for yourself, this will disconnect you from Spirit until you address your doubts. Repeat this process as many times as necessary over the days, weeks, and months ahead, until you feel confident in your ability to fulfill your desires. Focus on making small adjustments in your perception every day to remain aligned.

This is a very powerful exercise. Keep opening your mind and heart to the wish that you will experience your big miracles. It will happen!

Be Prepared for the Quickening

After you begin moving toward your heart's desire, your energy quickens. Everything in your life seems to be happening faster. Any heavy or defeated feelings you've had are replaced with excitement for what's to come. Time once dragged, but now it's as if there are no longer enough hours in the day to get everything done that you want to do. If time is flying for you, you are likely in the quickening mode. You made a wish for big miracles, and now you are accelerating toward them.

Imagine that the big miracles you want are to double your income, live in a beach community, and be happily married. This is your destination. Before the quickening mode begins, you may feel as though you are stationary, going around in circles, or lost. Then you gain clarity about your direction. Your soul reveals how to get from point A to point B, and it's as if your destination has been input into your personal GPS system. Your course is clear to you.

A couple of phenomena are likely to occur when the quickening begins. The first has to do with *faith*. If you don't trust your abilities, you'll keep putting your foot on the brake or cancelling the settings you've put in. Your ego may feel as though things are moving too fast and telling you, "Slow down. Something is going to go wrong." It wants to disrupt your flow. You know that you have to bolster your belief in yourself by aligning with Spirit if you are falling into a start-stop pattern.

There is great power in continuing to do what you must do even when you don't have any overt evidence that you'll succeed in reaching your destination, because it means you have embraced faith. Faith is a requirement when you're planning for a breakthrough.

When your ego steps forward, even if you know what needs to be done, you may agonize over making the decision. You may ask, "If I let go, will I be empty, scared, or lonely? How will I deal with the consequences of my decision?"

This is when you will need to deliberately ask the following two questions:

- "What am I trying to protect that is preventing me from changing?"
- "Where am I being inauthentic?"

At first, it may seem impossible to arrive at clear answers, but I assure you they will come if you keep asking. Perhaps you've been thinking that you've got to earn a lot of money before you can become a humanitarian or that you must be in perfect shape before you can meet your soul mate. Maybe you've been in denial that you'll need to boost your income significantly to afford your dream lifestyle. Remember, it's important to be honest *with yourself* about what is and isn't working in your life. With awareness, you'll feel the baggage that slows you down releasing. No matter what's revealed to you, you must keep moving forward on your path.

Sometimes letting go is an active process. Other times it's passive. If you've been living beyond your means and your desired outcome is to be debt free, you may be called to take actions to reduce your expenses, such as moving to an apartment with a lower rent, eating in, making more sales calls, or creating a spending plan. Do you see how this works? By taking these actions, you'll be letting go of your current home, of dining in restaurants, of leisure, and of shopping. In addition, you'll be releasing fears of how others see you or how you see yourself in relationship to success and other markers of material status.

Passive letting go, by comparison, has to do with our thoughts and emotions. This kind of letting go is necessary if you have been in a toxic relationship and are searching for true love. It may mean resting, allowing clarity to come about the truth of the relationship, so you can heal. When you are passively letting go, you create space to be receptive to signs indicating the next guided action you can take. At that point it may be appropriate to take action steps again.

As you look at your life today, what are three things you could do that are active or passive forms of letting go?

The second phenomenon that you can expect when the quickening begins in your life is that your soul will present you with *information* about everything you need to *clear* to remain in flow. Anything that does not align with the big miracles you desire will start rising to the surface of your mind for clearing. The bigger the miracles you desire, the more clearing will be required. Often life circumstances that were never an issue before will move to center stage in your mind. These things, including the state of your job, home, and relationships, will become intolerable to you, and you'll feel urges to change direction.

My best advice is to surrender to the clearing process. The quickening happens when your energy begins to clear, but you have to be diligent and continue to clear your energy field on a daily basis or else you may not be taking full advantage of the quickening process.

There's a point during the quickening that's like the moment when a plane that has been accelerating on a runway suddenly lifts off and ascends. To get there, you must keep asking yourself, "If Spirit is my driving force, what must I surrender?"

If you work in conjunction with the spiritual realm as you live your life in the world, the miracles you're hoping for will eventually arrive. It's only a matter of time. Every time you surrender a fear, an unproductive habit, or a limiting characteristic, another piece of your soul returns to you and brings you a step closer to wholeness. Just let these blocks in your energy field fall away. The more blocks you clear, the happier you'll be.

Understanding and Releasing Limiting Characteristics

Surrounding your body is an energy field that, in its optimal, spiritually aligned state, is dynamic—your energy flows freely through the field. When you're out of alignment, the field contains stagnant pockets of energy—places where your energy gets stuck. A combination of dynamic and stagnant energy permeates your entire being. When a thought combined with a feeling grows in intensity, it becomes a characteristic. Each characteristic finds a place in your mind, body, or spirit with which it most resonates. For example, if you carry resentment toward a friend, the energy is more likely to accumulate around your head; if you worry about what could go wrong in a new romantic relationship, you may often feel butterflies in your stomach. As you achieve greater spiritual alignment, your energy circulates more fluidly and stagnant characteristics will be revealed to you. They'll seem disharmonious.

Below, you'll find a list of limiting characteristics that can block your ability to achieve a big miracle breakthrough. Some of these characteristics will be strongly present within you, while others will be barely there. You may find that some are congregated in a particular part of your body or energy field. Look at the list below, and for each trait ask yourself:

- *"Is this characteristic present within me?"*

- *"If the characteristic is present, where is it located (mind, body, or spirit)?"*

- *"On a scale of 1 to 10 (with 1 indicating a weak presence and 10 indicating a strong one), how present is this characteristic in me?"*

- *"If there was an event in my past in which I demonstrated this characteristic, what memory would bring it to my awareness?*

- *"What can I learn from this characteristic?"*

- *"If I were to replace this characteristic with a positive attribute to support my ability to have big miracles, what would that attribute be?"*

Also ask the question listed beside each limiting characteristic below. Each question has been designed to heighten your awareness, so it will be easier to let go. Keep coming back to the questions until you feel clear and peaceful.

As you answer the questions, you'll gain momentum. You'll

have a deeper understanding of yourself and others. You'll also feel happier and more grateful for everything that's happening in your life, because you'll recognize that there is a purpose to its existence. You may even find that some of the things you've wanted for a while no longer seem important to you.

LIMITING CHARACTERISTICS

Longing: What or whom do I long for?

Regret: What do I most regret?

Fantasy: What is my ultimate fantasy?

Idealism: Do I have any unrealistic expectations?

Attachment: Who am I holding on to who doesn't reciprocate?

Pain: What is hurting me?

Guilt: What can't I forgive myself for?

Fear: What scares me daily?

Jealousy: Who triggers me?

Rushing: Why do I rush?

Ego: What will I do if I don't get my way?

Vanity: When I look in the mirror, how do I feel?

Insecurity: What is the worst thing that could happen to me?

Control: What or whom do I want power over?

Denial: What aren't I admitting to?

Blame: Who am I holding responsible for what isn't working in my life?

Criticism: Whom do I judge?

Anxiety: What keeps me awake at night?

Complaining: Why do I gossip?

Greed: What do I have too much of?

Negativity: Who or what is a downer in my life?

Lying: What will happen if I tell the truth?

Manipulation: How do I get my way?

Aggression: Whom do I want to confront?

Cravings: What are my secret desires?

Obsession: Who can't I get out of my mind?

Selfishness: Whose needs aren't I considering?

Impatience: Who betrayed me in the past?

Anger: Who isn't listening to me?

Resentment: Who hurt my feelings?

Isolation: Why am I trying to protect myself?

3

RULE 3: **Commit to Your Breakthrough**

What am I waiting for and
why am I waiting?

Many actions precede a big miracle breakthrough, so you must be committed for the duration needed to reach the goal you're working toward, whether that goal is weight loss, running a marathon, making a career shift or seeking advancement, going back to school for a higher degree, getting a painting accepted in an art show, establishing a new relationship, expanding your social circle, or saving money for your dream vacation or retirement. When you make a commitment to follow through to completion on your goal, you activate inner powers. You can know the commitment you made is real, because it brings you feelings of safety, peace, and resolution.

When you keep your word to follow through, you build confidence in your ability, courage that breakthroughs are possible, and conviction that they will happen. It's a demonstration of faith in action that is magnetic. People will like being around you, because they're both impressed and inspired by your determination and because you're radiating positive energy. You may see improvements in the quality of your friendships and business associations. Knowing you're able to get things done, people will approach you with all kinds of opportunities and include you in their plans and adventures. In business, they'll even pay you more for your services.

You cannot rely on others to do what needs to be done if you expect outstanding results. You must also be so emotionally invested in the success you desire that you're willing to put in the hard work whether or not anyone else does. It's not that you cannot or should not trust others; it's that you need to develop self-reliance. Too many people make excuses for inaction. Don't be one of them. You don't need to wait for permission or for better conditions to arise before you take a necessary next step.

Have you ever had a friend who kept suggesting you get together, and then she never called? Did you call her, or did you simply give up on the friendship? If you want to have a great social life, be proactive and set something up. It could be a Sunday picnic in the summer or a casual potluck dinner. Reach out to some people you know. Text, e-mail, or phone them. Tell them to bring their friends. Then, whoever shows up shows up. Not only will you have a great time; you may forge new friendships with the friends of friends who come to the gathering. If nobody shows up or only a few people do, you can still have fun eating in the sunshine.

If you've taken all the actions you can and done your best toward achieving a goal, but you don't get the outcome you were hoping for, there's a clear indication that you need to take additional actions or adapt your approach. When this happens to people who are committed, they understand that Spirit is nudging them to move in another direction that is more aligned with the conditions in their environment.

You have to be committed for your own reasons, not someone else's. Otherwise you'll probably stop doing what you said you'd do when you're faced with even the tiniest of obstacles or if fear crops up. Will you still go to the gym if your husband sleeps in? Or if your favorite trainer quits? Regarding any goal or commitment, always check your motivations. Ask, "Why did I agree to do this? Do I still really want this?" If the answer is yes, remember that going the extra distance to follow through on a commitment is what will lead to a breakthrough. If the answer is no, then you need to change your commitment, so that you're going after something you really do desire.

If you're dishonest about your feelings about a particular goal, you won't have the willpower necessary to keep your word to yourself—much less to anyone else. Making a commitment from a sense of guilt or obligation will backfire on you. It gives you a false sense of control, yet the irony is that you're depriving yourself of the things that would make you feel happiest. Remember always to make commitments from your heart.

To fulfill a commitment, you need to set yourself up for success. This means you need to create a supportive environment around yourself and eliminate any sense of deprivation involved in working toward the goal by taking great care of yourself while you're implementing the steps of your breakthrough strategy. For example, if your goal is earning a graduate degree and you only study and never take breaks, you could begin to feel deprived of sleep and human contact. Lack of sleep clouds the mind and makes studying difficult. Lack of human contact makes us lonely, even resentful. Fulfilling your physical and emotional needs should be part of any reasonable success strategy. Start putting yourself first to recharge your energy.

It's important to be honest with yourself. If your intentions are in the right place, but you are failing to follow through, ask yourself the following questions:

- "What do I really need in order to stay committed?"
- "What excuses am I giving for not living up to my commitment?"
- "Do I have enough support and accountability for my choices?"
- "Am I sabotaging my efforts because I feel deprived? If so, of what?"

If you keep breaking a promise to yourself, you'll stop believing in yourself, and this may cause you to stay stuck where you are. Whenever you repeatedly say you'll do something and don't do it, you erode a little more of your faith in your capacity to do what needs to be done. Eventually you can no longer trust yourself. Then you quit and make the excuse that the thing you want is unattainable because of your circumstances. That's when life becomes small. It's the opposite of a big miracle. When an opportunity is presented to you, if you've given up on yourself, you're not going to go for it. Because you haven't demonstrated commitment in this area before, you won't believe in yourself.

Honoring a commitment feels amazing and is a confidence builder. Sandra attended one of my workshops and reached out to me for life coaching. Her husband had just had a heart attack, which she said was her wake-up call to lose forty pounds. In addition to that, she had a longer list of things she wanted to change, including switching her career from banking to chiropractic. That was her dream career. When we met to discuss her next steps, she said, "I can't go on living like this."

"Are you committed to doing what's necessary to create the life you want?" I asked.

"Yes, one hundred percent," she said.

She was supposed to start coaching with me right away, but at the last minute decided to postpone for three months. The three months passed. When I checked in with her by phone, she sounded upset. She told me she'd gained another twenty pounds and still hadn't sent an application to the chiropractic college she was interested in attending. We made a new start date, but again she cancelled, giving me another plausible excuse.

From my perspective, although I'd heard her say she was completely committed to a breakthrough, her actions didn't reflect this. She hadn't let me down, though. Her issue wasn't about me or my services. She'd broken her commitments to herself.

When in the past have you made commitments and broken them? What was your excuse? Pin it down. Thought precedes action. Your excuses are the clues to where you're stuck. For example, if you keep making the excuse that you're late because you're so busy, you could be overscheduling because of the fear of missing out on an opportunity or feeling anxious about slowing down enough to review your lifestyle. Or you say you want to be in a loving relationship, but stay in every night because of an underlying fear of rejection. Maybe you want to pursue a new career path but don't believe you have the ability to succeed, so you talk about it rather than take the first required step.

Characteristics That Hinder Commitment

The three most common things that get in the way of commitment are fear, low self-esteem, and doubt. Let's take a look at these issues one by one.

Fear

You must be vigilant about both your conscious thoughts and your daydreams. Be alert for times when you begin to imagine an outcome that you don't want, so that you can halt, then challenge that negative imagery in your mind. Instead of thinking about the things that could go wrong, how your plans won't work out, or how you'll be disappointed, ask yourself:

- "What are the facts related to my circumstances?"
- "Based on those facts, why do I choose fear instead of success?"
- "Instead of what I fear happening, what do I want to happen?"

Low Self-Esteem

If you have a negative self-image, you'll psychologically and emotionally quit trying to get the things you want before you even begin taking action in reality. The way quitting internally typically manifests itself in someone's life is in a pattern of making excuses. The next time you catch yourself offering up a reason that something isn't possible, stop and ask yourself:

- "Has someone else ever managed to do this?"
- "Why do I assume I can't do it?"
- "Is there anything in my past that is evidence I could do this?"

Doubt

It would be great to be given a guarantee of success before we go after something we want, but most of the time that doesn't happen when we start something new. Having a breakthrough demands that we step into personally uncharted territory. You may need to invest time, money, and energy to achieve the results you want. Going beyond your comfort zone often requires emotional vulnerability. For example, it takes courage to ask someone out on a date if you're not certain you'll get an affirmative answer. There are many situations in life where you have to be willing to accept the possibility of rejection. If you're uncomfortable not having confirmation ahead of time, it could mean you lean toward uncertainty. Get honest about your doubtful feelings. Ask yourself:

- "If I knew I could not fail and would not be rejected, would I go ahead?"
- "If I gave up on my dream, how would I truly feel?"

Accountability

The first commitment you made in this book was to align with Spirit. How are you doing with that promise so far? When you set an intention to be a spiritual vehicle, you made a deliberate commitment to be answerable to your heart and soul. A commitment is accompanied by mental resolution. The certainty of it feels good, and it relieves any tension that you're feeling from having divided impulses. Accountability is the key to fulfilling your commitments.

When you break a commitment, don't begin self-recrimination and mentally beat yourself up; correct your approach. Check in with yourself, identify what went wrong, and then make a plan to support yourself better so you'll be able to keep your word. You've likely broken promises before and you probably will again until you get serious about honoring your responsibilities.

Instead of feeling guilty for how you've let people down in the past, make a commitment today to follow through on what you said you'd do. If you think you're going to default on a commitment you made that involves someone else, tell the person that you won't be doing it or that you cannot do it within the agreed-upon time frame just as soon as you know. You can lessen resentment by communicating what's going on. If you habitually say yes to things you don't want to do or that you cannot do in time, it's highly likely you'll sabotage your situation or the relationship.

When it comes to fulfilling your own dreams, it isn't someone else's responsibility to tell you what you need to do or when to do it. You can surround yourself with people who support you—everyone from friends and family to business mentors and coaches—but they can't live your dreams for you. Commitment means staying with things until you're done. Too many people give up before the breakthroughs they want happen.

If you need support, ask for it. Change the variables until you can keep your word.

In personal relationships, if you don't come home on time, people will worry about you. A spouse or significant other may begin to suspect that a betrayal is taking place. If you go on a spending spree when you've promised to save money for a family vacation, your behavior may cause friction. Tension can erupt in arguments and weaken the bonds of your relationship. If you routinely break promises to your children, such as promises about going to their recitals, performances, and sporting events, the disappointment can permanently scar them.

Can you commit to the vision you share with your loved ones? Can you commit to your parents, your children, your partner? If you feel you're been waffling in your commitments to the people in your life, renew them by choosing simple actions you can do right away that demonstrate your commitment.

In the professional world, if you don't do what you say you will, it's very hard to advance your career. Can you commit now to doing what you say in your business and mean it? When you have a deadline, do you stick to it or push back the date? Creating a deadline for yourself, particularly if you're an entrepreneur in charge of your own work schedule, is only effective if you take deadlines seriously. When you choose a date for a deadline, pick something that will test you, but not paralyze you. Check in with yourself and see what feels best.

In your personal life, if you said you'd help a close friend, be clear about what you are and are not willing to do. Don't overcommit and then let a friend down. If a good friend needed help moving and an opportunity to go on a date or to advance your career came along, would you maintain your commitment to your friend as you promised? By having integrity and keeping your word, not only do those around you see you as trustworthy; you also strengthen your personal faith that things will work out.

Spirit responds to our commitments. You can have faith that you'll get what you want in the time you are meant to get it.

Urgency

To create a big miracle, you must have a sense of urgency. Most people sense the urgency of acting quickly in an emergency. My son and I were inside a store when through the window we saw an elderly woman outside have what looked like a seizure and fall over backward. I ran outside as fast as I could, dropped my handbag on the ground, and attended to the woman. Two other people came outside and stood there looking helpless. "Call 911," I told one of the bystanders. "Help support her head," I told the other. There was no time to think or wait, as it was potentially a life-or-death situation. Decisions had to be made quickly.

Imagine what you could achieve if you consistently took decisive action. Without believing that your activities require your immediate attention, you're not likely to follow through on them. For breakthroughs to occur, we must act on a timely basis.

The world is full of opportunity. Knowing how many wonderful opportunities are available to you, why do you not do what needs to be done? Rather than waiting for a dire situation to occur that forces you to act, commit to taking action on behalf of your intentions today. Find a source of motivation to take action after action every day until your goals are reached and your promises fulfilled.

You need a reason that is bigger than the obstacles lying in your path. Imagine the consequences of not getting what your heart desires or of losing what you love the most because you failed to act. You'd be filled with regret, wouldn't you? Urgency matters, because without it you'll probably miss your opportunity to have the best life you could.

If you're fortunate enough to survive to old age, how will you feel if on your deathbed you're thinking, *I could have done this and I should have done that,* while wishing for more time? What if today was your last day? There's a real possibility that it could be.

Think about it for a moment. Allow yourself to feel the emotions associated with this idea in your body. Is there something you'd like to get done today in order to feel that you've lived the day well? Is there something you're doing that you'd like to do differently?

Here's a meditation exercise to help you create a sense of urgency about taking the right actions to have a big miracle breakthrough without having to experience a real-life emergency.

Your Last Day on Earth

To experience the full benefits of this exercise and to feel safe acknowledging the extent of your feelings, it is a good idea to do the Center, Ground, and Connect Meditation (see p. 23) first. If you already feel aligned, it is enough to take a moment to close your eyes, focus inwardly, and bring your awareness to your heart. Choose to be present. Every time your mind wanders, bring yourself back to your present moment. When you feel calm, begin.

As you do the exercise, strong feelings may arise. You're about to look at your true circumstances and what has brought you to this exact moment in your life. Go slowly and allow any emotions you feel to flow through your body and spirit. Remember, there is nothing to fear. You're safe. Spirit is with you. Begin whenever you're ready.

Your Yesterday

Reflect on your day yesterday from start to finish. Ask yourself:

- *"What did I do?"*

- *"How did I feel?"*

- *"What didn't I do that I wish I had?"*

- *"Why didn't I do it?"*

Your Today

Now reflect on your present circumstances. Ask yourself:

- *"What is most important to me right now?"*

- *"What makes me feel happiest?"*

- *"What causes me stress?"*

- *"If I could resolve a big problem, after which everything in my life would be great, what problem would that be?"*

Your Plan of Action

Pretend that today is your last day alive. Ask yourself:

- *"How do I choose to feel today?"*

- *"What will I do today?"*

- *"What is my motivation for doing it?"*

- *"What will happen if I don't do it?"*

- *"How do I feel about that?"*

Put your plan into action. Follow through today!

Stop Wasting Time

If your present-day circumstances are not as you like or seem too painful to bear, you may find yourself wishing the precious hours of your life away. That's no way to live! You don't know how long your life span is. None of us do. You should be relishing your days on earth.

We cannot make up for missed opportunities or wasted time. None of us can buy time. Founder of Apple, Steve Jobs, who died young after battling cancer, once said, "My favorite things in life don't cost any money. It's really clear that the most precious resource we all have is time."[1]

When you wait for things to happen, it may create the illusion in your mind that there is an abundance of time available to you. With this perception comes a lack of gratitude for this finite commodity. Time is precious. This is why you need to spark a sense of urgency within yourself—so that you do not realize too late what a gift your life is.

When you become aware of how you are moving through your life, you will be better able to identify where you're self-sabotaging and creating unwanted circumstances. You can stumble through your days and tread with trepidation, waiting for your life to end, or you can walk proudly and dive into the activities that will bring you the results and breakthroughs you want.

All physical life will eventually come to an end, but from the perspective of the realm of Spirit, life is eternal. What you're seeking you shall find in time.

Most people speak negatively about time. But they're really upset about their lack of fulfillment or productivity or how they're spending their time. They may be bored, unhappy, or overwhelmed. Everybody has the same twenty-four hours in a day to use as intentionally as possible. The key to increasing your productivity and feeling less constrained by the limitations of time is to improve the quality of your relationship with time.

Right Timing vs. Procrastination

In your mind, it may never feel like the right time to pursue your dreams. My friend James, a computer programmer, had always wanted to take a tour of the Galápagos Islands. Every year he said

Your Relationship with Time

Ask yourself the following questions:

- *"In the past have I seen time as my friend or enemy? Why?"*

- *"What do I typically say about time in relation to my life and goals?"* (For example: *"I never have enough time," "Everyone wants my time," "I have no time to relax," "Time is such a drag."*)

- *"What are some activities I am not doing because of time constraints?"* (For example, skipping workouts in the gym because of work deadlines or refusing a friend's invitation to see a movie because you need to clean your house on the weekend.)

- *"If I had more time available to me, do I think I'd have more meaningful relationships? Why do I believe that would be the outcome?"*

- *"If I had more time available to me, do I think I'd make more money? Why do I believe that would be the outcome?"*

- *"What is the thing I most love doing with my time?"*

- *"How much time do I dedicate to the thing I love most in my day?"*

- *"In the past, when and how have I wasted my time?"* (By the way, if you don't regret how you used your time, then you haven't wasted it.)

Review your answers and see where you can reframe the ways you deal with time. When you reframe your view of time as a conduit to your big miracles rather than as an obstacle to your success and joy, you may well find your stress over keeping your commitments dissolving and being replaced with peace.

he'd go, but then his job took precedence over his dream vacation. To outside observers, it may have looked as if he was procrastinating, but in truth his inner guidance told him he needed to sacrifice one goal for the other, because he didn't believe he could achieve both. When he finally went, he said it was worth the wait.

If you're aligned with Spirit and being a spiritual vehicle, then your timing will naturally be right. You'll be in the flow of life, and Spirit will guide you.

Another friend, Jodie, was holding out for Mr. Right. The guy she was dating adored her. But when he proposed to her, she was too scared to commit, so she procrastinated. After two more years of settling for her indecision, the boyfriend ended the relationship. She was devastated when she found out that he'd met someone else and was getting married. She realized that her fear had been an obstacle to the intimacy she craved. Sometimes you have to take the leap and trust that if you follow your heart's desire, everything will work out well.

There is a time to act and a time to wait when realizing your dreams. Failing to act when you should is procrastination. Waiting to act for valid reasons is indeed preferable. Your responsibility is to fine-tune your energy, so you can tell the difference.

If you're wondering if you should act or wait, it's a good time to do the Center, Ground, and Connect Meditation (see p. 23) and then ask yourself:

- "What would be the benefit of waiting to take action?"
- "If I take action now, what would the consequences be?"
- "If I don't reach this goal, what would the consequences be?"
- "What would the benefits of pausing briefly regarding this goal be?"
- "What could the negative outcomes of waiting for a longer period be?"
- "Why do I feel the need to wait so long?"
- "Is there something overwhelming about taking action?"
- "Do I have enough information to move forward with my goal?"
- "Is what is missing to move forward truly a reason to wait?"
- "Is there another action I can take that would move me closer to my goal?"

Procrastination is the result of fear that turns into blocked energy as it accumulates. Time is energy, and it is always moving, even when it seems as though things have come to a standstill in our lives. In an article published in *Scientific American,* Rhett Herman, a physics professor at Radford University in Virginia, confirmed that the earth moves around the center of the sun at 67,000 miles per hour and whirls around the center of our galaxy at 490,000 miles per hour,[2] although we do not feel any movement. The effortless, linear flow of time creates the illusion that we're standing still, yet energy is constantly moving. You can be proactive in moving toward your desires or be moved in a direction that isn't what you want. Time never stands still.

To get into an effortless flow when you feel afraid to take action, it is a good idea to step away from the activity you're pursuing, so that you can return to it later with fresh perspective and renewed energy. Let Spirit carry you to what you desire. That means being willing to take an action, yet not forcing yourself to take action; being passive, but not irresponsible or checked out. It also means not making demands on other people to give you what you want when you want it. You will be able to sense the right timing of every action when you're aligned with Spirit, because you'll feel confident and calm.

Feeling stuck in your life is a sign that your energy is blocked and you need to clear it. As long as it's left unaddressed, you may feel as though pressure or a burden is weighing upon you. The best thing to do when you feel blocked is slow down and try to figure out exactly what is causing your pain. Most pain is related to fear. Once you see what you're afraid could happen, you'll have the ability to break through the fear and continue to act.

When you're in flow, even when you're facing challenges and have a lot on your plate, life feels relatively effortless, because there is little or no resistance.

Resistance

As you take step after step and get closer to your big miracles, you're likely to feel more resistance. These are the times when many people give up on their dreams, because they cannot handle the pressure. They think something is going wrong, and they want to stop the uncomfortable feelings that change brings up. The faster you change, the more radical the transformation feels. It can also feel liberating and exhilarating to be committed and see your momentum grow.

Persistence is a necessity for breaking through resistance as well as external obstacles such as criticism. If you've made a request to Spirit for guidance, acting upon the information you've received will be critical to your success. For example, if Spirit tells you to go out even though it is raining, go out. There may be somebody you're supposed to meet at the supermarket.

Recently, Spirit told me to get on an airplane and fly to Los Angeles to attend a two-day networking event. When I got there, I met a woman who was agonizing over whether to stay with her husband. She already knew the answer, but in sharing her feelings and using me as a sounding board she came to a greater understanding of her impending decision and felt more at peace. Sometimes your persistence in seeking a relationship with Spirit will allow you to be a spiritual vehicle for helping others, which in turn will serve you.

Be persistent in expecting a positive outcome. If your energy is clear and you keep taking right actions, you'll find yourself experiencing synchronistic events that someone less spiritually aware would consider strokes of luck or crazy coincidences. When it clicks that your actions are a force of creation and that the things you imagine can in fact become real, a hunger for proactivity will drive you forward. You'll no longer procrastinate and resist change. You'll take concerted action. You will recognize that there is meaning to each interaction, great or small.

When you feel resistance, it's always an indication that you have energy blocks that need to be cleared. Externally, these blocks typically show up as the rejection of your ideas or dismissal of your presence by others. Internally, these blocks show up in the form of emotions such as feeling hurt, rejected, disappointed, abandoned, betrayed, angry, resentful, frustrated, scared, ashamed, or guilty. You could take this as a sign that there is no point in pursuing your goal any further. But it's just a sign that you need to clear the energy block and realign with Spirit.

In reality, it is more common for people to say no than yes. It's also common for people to initially reject an idea or an unfamiliar experience several times before they say yes. My client Sarah was a novice yoga instructor with big dreams. When only one person turned up to take her first yoga class, she could have quit. Thankfully, she didn't give up. She taught the class to the best of her ability and kept her commitment to teach. She continued to invite people to her classes and today has a large and loyal community of yoga students around her.

Remember, if you experience increased resistance at any time, it very likely means underlying limiting beliefs are rising to the surface of your consciousness and that a big miracle breakthrough is within reach. You may find your energy levels dropping. You may be overcome with tiredness, lethargy, exhaustion, depression, or irritability. No matter what you do, everything feels wrong, and you may start to believe you're moving in the wrong direction or that your goal was a bad idea. You may start to believe that all the people who said no to you or said, "You'll never succeed," were right. You may also find low self-esteem, fear, sadness, and even deep-seated grief coming to the surface. You may rationalize that before you pursued your goal everything was fine. Insecurity may grip you and make you doubt your actions.

All this is just your unevolved ego mind trying to maintain the status quo. Don't let it stop you. For everything negative in your life, there is a positive on the flip side. This is the Law of Polarity. Experiencing resistance means you have to keep taking action—sometimes massive action—until you reach a tipping point that works in your favor.

Resistance can show up in many forms of self-sabotage, including being overly critical of yourself; showing up late to appointments, family gatherings, a friend's birthday party, or work meetings; missing scheduled phone calls with your parents or clients; not paying your bills on time; getting caught up in emotional drama; and putting out one fire after another in your life. As long as you keep making excuses for your lack of action and keep blaming other people for your circumstances, you won't break through.

Your resistance is a gift, because it's showing you where you are stuck. If you embrace your resistance, use it as a messenger, and then take appropriate action despite it, you'll find the things you want to happen occurring faster and leading you to miracles. Each new action you take will get you closer to your new life. You can leave your old life behind.

If the pressure of creating a big miracle feels too great, that's a sign that it's time to connect with Spirit. Symptoms that you're moving too fast may include feeling distracted, doing everything but the most important things you need to do, creating dramas where none exist, making assumptions about what others think or how they're going to respond to you, and generally playing the victim.

Be vigilant about indulging such behaviors. It's easy to feel sorry for yourself or blame someone else, but the person who suffers in the end is you. Instead, go take a nap or listen to a guided meditation, some Reiki music, or the lecture of an inspirational speaker. An hour of time out can work miracles for your attitudes and mood. Pausing gives your mind the ability to relax and shift its perspective to something positive.

To overcome resistance, surround yourself with supportive people who have an optimistic outlook. One of my friends was excited to tell me about dating a new man she really liked. But the next time I spoke to her she sounded depressed. In between our conversations her mother had told her it wouldn't work out because of their religious differences. My friend is Jewish and her boyfriend is Catholic. My friend was ready to break up because she wanted her family to get along with her new beau. "Your mother is always a downer about anything you do," I reminded her. "Why are you surprised she reacted that way to your news?"

If you seek people's approval, especially the approval of loved ones, and they don't give you the encouragement you're hoping for, it can be quite a blow. But you can put this in perspective by remembering that if people respond unenthusiastically, it is most likely because of their own personal reasons, including the fact that they don't have an interest or investment in your goal. If you worry about what others will think and anticipate a negative outcome, you'll never be able to break through your own resistance to improving your life.

The goal you desire and the vision you have are yours for a reason.

Find likeminded people to share ideas with or get a coach to support you in moving through your insecurity.

One way to move beyond your resistance regarding your goals is to ask yourself, "What is the worst thing that can happen in this situation (or relationship, job, and so on)?" It is possible you could fail and be criticized by loved ones or snubbed by people in the industry you want to succeed in. It is possible you could have an empty and meaningless life and end up broke and living alone in your old age. But what is the likelihood of such disasters happening? Imagining a worst-case scenario usually leads to finding solutions to problems posed by your fears.

An excellent way to dislodge internal resistance to your intended goals is by eating nutritious foods, exercising, breathing consciously, meditating, and writing about your thoughts and feelings in your Miracle Journal. These self-nurturing tools can help you to gently dissolve your mental and emotional blocks.

Three Ps That Break Through Resistance

A few years back, I was excited to attend an intimate question-and-answer session at Soho House in West Hollywood, California, with award-winning filmmaker Paul Haggis, who penned *Million Dollar Baby* and *Crash*. He was the first screenwriter to write Best Picture Oscar winners in consecutive years. I was fascinated to learn from him how he created his success. He says, "When Soho House opened in L.A., I burrowed my way into one of its booths in the bar and almost never left. I would show up around 10 A.M. with my computer and have breakfast, lunch, and sometimes an early dinner while writing."[3] On some days it would get to be 4 P.M. and he still hadn't written a thing. Then he'd find his urgency toward the end of the day when he felt the pressure of not having enough time and get writing.[4]

Haggis also told us about his determination to get *Crash* made despite encountering a series of *nos*. All the odds were against him. He first pitched it as a TV show, and all the networks said no. Then he turned it into a movie script, and all the film studios said no. Haggis was unknown, and he was a TV writer. Back then, it was still very hard to cross over from television to movies. Even after he found a production company, preproduction was shut down several times because he didn't have the right A-list talent to get financing.[5] His breakthrough resulted from his not giving up despite the odds and despite his own resistance; his urgency to share a message through storytelling created enough internal drive to achieve his vision. He's a prime example of how you can break through resistance using persistence, patience, and passion.

Persistence. Continue to take action in the face of adversity, and do not give up. If you feel fear in your body, remember that it's only a feeling and cannot hurt you. If you hear a voice in your head saying, "You're making a mistake!" know it's the voice of fear, for the wise, loving guidance of your higher self would never speak to you in this way. Rather, it would gently say something like, "Have you thought about moving in a different direction? Where do you think pursuing this path will lead you? Is this truly what you desire?" The guidance would feel calm and loving, never forceful or critical.

Patience. As you begin to take action, give yourself a chance to see results. If you do not see an immediate outcome, don't jump to the conclusion that something is going wrong. This shuts off your connection to Spirit and your life purpose. If you have a big goal or you have many energy blocks or limiting beliefs to clear, it could take months, even years, to make progress. If you're on the right path, you'll usually receive signs of confirmation. Look for those signs.

Passion. You must be filled with a deep desire for any goal you set; however, you must temper your desire with nonattachment to getting the outcome you want. Be enthusiastic, envision the future you desire, and take action to manifest it, but watch for your hidden expectations about what it means to get what you want. Check in with your intention to make sure it is pure and aligned with what you say. Focus on doing your best, and trust that no matter what happens, there is a valuable lesson to be learned.

Resistance may seem like your enemy, but it's really your friend. Once you break through your barriers, you'll be able to look back and see the blessings of your struggles. Our challenges make us stronger and smarter. If you're experiencing resistance, ask yourself:

- "What am I resisting?"
- "Why am I resisting taking this action?"

Most of the time you'll find that your resistance is related to some form of fear. Anytime it isn't fear and really is a warning from Spirit, you will get a repeatedly uneasy feeling in your stomach when you think about the situation. Things may look positive on the surface, but the inner feeling you have of mistrust or of something being off will be stronger than the external circumstances and relationships. You may also have a deep-seated knowing that something isn't right. You may not be able to rationalize it or have evidence for the sense of impending trouble, but you just know. And that's a clue to take a closer look at what's going on.

Pause briefly if you feel overwhelmed by your circumstances. You may only need an hour or so to get your head back in the right space. It's important to regroup, so you can take action from a position of spiritual alignment. As you increase your commitment, achieving your goals will get easier.

4

RULE 4: **Forgive Mistakes**

*What is the worst thing that could
happen, and the likelihood it will?*

What if your mistakes are miracles waiting to happen?

A mistake is an action that is misaligned with your spirit's desire because of an impulsive decision, a hidden compulsion, or a missing piece of information. The circumstances that seem to indicate things are going wrong in your life are actually signposts guiding you to your heart's desire. When you're connected to Spirit, you'll have the ability to recognize a miracle in disguise. By viewing it as a source of information, you'll be able to give any difficulty a positive outcome. That's in the nature of a big miracle.

Most people expect the worst outcome instead of the best, because it's a conditioned response. That's why the line, "I've got good news and bad news. Which do you want first?" typically causes anxiety. A simple down tone in a person's voice can lead you to assume the worst. If you've been repeatedly hurt in relationships, you'll expect to be hurt again. If you have a history of failed business ventures, you'll likely set yourself up for failure again.

As long as you think that you have no control over your circumstances, you'll continue to make mistakes. However, if you reframe your perception of a mistake as an opportunity to learn and grow, your next breakthrough will be within your grasp. Everyone makes mistakes. One of the keys to making a big miracle breakthrough is figuring out the best action to take following your mistakes and those of others. You must seek the meaning of the mistake to discover the miracle.

The Russian physiologist Ivan Pavlov proved the existence of conditioned responses in a famous experiment in which he rang a bell and then gave dogs food. After several rounds of bell ringing followed by food, the dogs began salivating as soon as the bell was rung.[1] Like those dogs, you're conditioned to respond in a certain way to a variety of triggers. When you look for the reason behind your conditioned behavior, you'll be able to break negative patterns that are keeping success at a distance. Once you develop the ability to recognize a series of actions that lead up to mistakes, you'll be able to anticipate, change the next action you take, and therefore change the outcome. A mistake will no longer have the effect of halting your progress.

The Gift of a Mistake

Among other things, a mistake can help you clarify where you need to create an attitude adjustment. If you retrace the steps that led to the mistake, you'll be able to identify what you specifically did that caused it. You can then apply your new awareness to the next opportunity that is similar to that situation.

If you think, *What's the point? I'm just going to mess up again,* and don't forgive yourself, then you'll never manifest the opportunity you desire. Forgiving yourself is empowering, because it frees you to learn and to try again.

Making mistakes teaches us humility. It opens our eyes to new ways of doing things.

In each mistake you make, if you look carefully, you'll find that there's a way to improve who you are and how you're operating. But you must look with honesty and without judgment. Being objective and also compassionate opens the gateway to forgiveness.

Be Proactive in Reframing Your Mistakes

As long as you see your mistakes as something bad, you'll continue to feel stuck and overwhelmed. Judging your actions as wrong has a negative consequence in your life and for your ability to move forward. Mistakes also come from procrastination and a lack of action to follow through on commitments. The biggest thing that holds people back is a fear of failure, because taking a wrong action could lead to negative consequences in their relationships, career, or finances, preventing them from taking necessary risks.

Fortunately, Spirit does not judge us poorly for our mistakes. Spirit views them as lessons. When you work with Spirit as your guide, you'll learn the lessons necessary to help you become a more whole and happy person. The happier you become, the more lives you'll brighten. With wholeness comes a desire to serve and contribute. As you make more of a contribution, you'll have greater success in your career and finances.

There are many possible roots to the fear of failure. Common roots of fear are feelings of shame, guilt, unworthiness, and abandonment. To free yourself, you first have to identify the specific root holding you locked in fear—even though just the thought of doing this can prompt a fearful response! You can break through the fear by looking to the past for evidence of its reality or nonreality. Rest assured, almost all fear is based on an imagined rather than a real threat.

For several years, I had a fear of flying and avoided it at all costs, even though I wanted to meet people from all walks of life and to make a global impact with my business. I was embarrassed by this fear, which even made me question my ability to help people. Yet I also knew my fear of flying and dying was irrational. After I sought out the hard evidence, the statistics proved to me that it was not a realistic enough concern to continue to let it stop me. In 2006, David Ropeik, a risk communication instructor at Harvard University, found that the odds of dying in a plane crash are one in eleven million.[2]

My fear was causing me to make the mistake of not traveling and missing out on business opportunities that would generate more income. The way I overcame this fear was by increasing my air travel. In one year, I flew fifteen times. I also created a meditation tape that I listened to before going to sleep and on the plane to recondition my fear of flying to excitement about traveling and the opportunity to meet new people. For example, on one flight I sat next to a lovely woman who went on to become a VIP client.

Our mistakes are often where the greatest growth can be made. When we reframe the ideas that lead us to make mistakes, we can alter our behavior more easily and change our destiny. In *The Law of Success*, Napoleon Hill describes how he asked a highly successful man, "What helped you overcome the great obstacles of life?" "The other obstacles," the man replied.[3] Obstacles give us strength, because they help us grow. You must be willing to make mistakes and not be attached to the outcome if you fail. Instead, forgive the mistake and move forward. When faced with an obstacle, do not give up. Instead, use it as an opportunity to make an improvement in yourself and your circumstances. Ask yourself, "What is a new way I can handle this to create the result I want?" This will ultimately lead you to a better outcome than you imagined possible.

To reframe a mistake, you must discover the lesson to be learned from it. You can shift your perspective by answering these questions:

- "What is the mistake I made?"
- "Why do I believe it was a mistake?"
- "What do I think I could have done differently to avoid the mistake?"
- "How can I let go of self-judgment and trust that my ideas are leading me to my desired outcome?"
- "What do I need to stop doing to release fear related to this mistake?"

When you view a mistake as a learning opportunity, it gives you permission to try a new approach and move forward with confidence. Taking an action, even if it's not perfect, is better than taking no action, because with movement you at least give yourself the opportunity to figure out a way to make things work.

When you are tuned in and fully connected to Spirit, even if others tell you that you made a mistake or reject you, their opinions and actions won't matter, because you'll feel that you are on track and in alignment. Your sense of spiritual connection will give you the energy required to keep moving forward without delay on your path. This will ensure that you don't quit before the miracle happens. Remember, when you reframe your view of a mistake as an opportunity for learning, it will no longer have negative power over you. This means that when you do inevitably make a mistake, it will no longer slow you down or stop you.

Don't wait for a miracle to happen. Be proactive. Work with Spirit as your guide and you'll know exactly what to do when you make a mistake in the future—or even better, when you see that you are about to make the same type of mistake you made in the past. In this way, you'll find that you quickly forgive yourself for the past mistakes you've made that used to embarrass you and hold you back. You'll have the ability to take bold actions that will benefit you greatly.

Did You Do Your Best?

From now on, if you do the best you can and still make a mistake, know that good is on its way to you, even though you do not yet see evidence of its manifestation.

A lot of my friends are actors, because I've lived in Los Angles off and on since my twenties. My friend Sophie was devastated when a TV show on which she was a recurring guest star was cancelled. She wondered if she had been a contributing factor in its failure to get picked up for another season.

"Did you do your best?" I asked her.

"Yes, I put my heart and soul into the production. It was going well," she said.

What she did not realize at the time was that Spirit was guiding her toward a costarring role in a Golden Globe Award–nominated TV show. Sometimes you'll think you've made a mistake, and that may give you an urge to give up on your dream. Even when something doesn't go as hoped or planned, it doesn't mean that you've made a mistake.

Another friend of mine was devastated when her husband left her for someone else. She perceived her marriage as a mistake. One failing was that she had not set a clear boundary in place when she found out he was having an affair. She had strong suspicions that he was having an affair, but she could not bring herself to act on her feelings because she felt unlovable. She felt humiliated that she'd placed her trust in this unreliable man; as she looked back over her relationship she saw how she'd compromised her needs for his on a continual basis. Her dreams were pushed aside until they were gone.

After her husband left, my friend came to me for advice. She told me how she wanted to get back on her feet and turn her life around. She began to connect with Spirit on a consistent basis with my support until her own connection was strong. This led her to find someone with whom she was more aligned and resulted in a new, satisfying relationship. Her marriage hadn't been a mistake. It had given her two children she adored. It had taught her what she valued. Once she was clear, she was able to fulfill her heart's desire with a new partner.

When Accidents Happen

Back in 1998, I was driving up Ladbroke Grove in West London. My home was in sight. I signaled to turn right as I saw a parking spot directly outside my condo, which was a rare find. I checked my rear-view mirror and then my side mirror. The road looked clear. But as I turned right, I heard a loud bang that startled me. I put on my emergency brake and jumped out of the car. I was horrified when I saw a young woman lying on the ground beneath her motorbike. She'd been in my blind spot. I immediately called for an ambulance and then had some people on the street help me get her into my condo. Moments later I was terrified as she sat on my couch delirious from the huge amount of pain she was in. I hadn't had a car accident for years, and I'd never hit anyone before.

"I'm a trained Reiki healer," I said. "Here's my number. Please call me, and I'll do as many sessions as it takes to get you pain free."

She took my number just as the emergency medical team showed up to take her to the hospital, but I suspected she wouldn't contact me.

For days, I was filled with self-recrimination. I asked myself, "Why did this happen? Was I distracted? Was I so out of spiritual alignment that I manifested this awful situation?"

About two weeks passed, and then I got a phone call from her. "Hi. It's Emma. I'd like to set up a time with you for a Reiki healing," she said. I was relieved to hear from her and very curious to find out why the accident happened.

When Emma showed up at my condo, her arm was in a sling.

She'd fractured it and still had a bruise on her face. As I began conducting my first healing session with her, she revealed to me that when I knocked her off her bike, she was late for an appointment to see an apartment she was planning to rent with her boyfriend and one of her coworkers. A few things stood out right away. She was working as a nurse in a hospital, but admitted that she didn't want to be a nurse anymore. Also, she didn't want to rent with this particular coworker, but felt obligated to. In addition, she told me she was terrified of moving in with her boyfriend.

As Emma's healing sessions progressed over the course of a few weeks, she decided to leave her nursing job to go and work with children, something she had always wanted to do. She stopped sabotaging her relationship with her boyfriend after she realized that she was scared of being abandoned if the relationship got serious. Several months later, she moved in with him alone, without another roommate. Before we were done, she told me it was a blessing that the accident happened, even though it was painful, as she sensed Spirit had been trying to get her life back on track.

What happened to Emma is common—particularly if Spirit has been trying to get your attention for a while. If you look carefully at accidents from your past, I bet you'll be able to see that there was a purpose to the pain.

There's a way to get to your big miracle breakthrough faster. Over the upcoming weeks, set an intention to have the purpose of all of the accidents you've experienced over the years revealed to you. After you do, you may find yourself getting spontaneous insights at random times, like while driving, shopping in the supermarket, or taking a shower, because your mind has the opportunity to wander then. As your conscious mind relaxes, your unconscious thoughts can rise to the surface and into awareness.

You may also find yourself waking up in the middle of the night feeling fully awake with insights or having dreams that give you a deeper understanding. Ultimately you may see a pattern in your life and sense that the cycle of the pattern is being broken. Then the next step you need to take to transform the accident into a miracle will become clear, and you'll feel confident in taking the necessary actions. For me, the car accident was a wake-up call from Spirit telling me to listen to my heart's desire and not compromise, as helping Emma in her healing made me aware of healing I myself needed to do.

When Spirit is at work in your life, you should expect the un-expected. Your life can be going along great, and suddenly you will be tested. It's therefore important to be grounded and present with whatever you're doing. Some circumstances are beyond your con-trol, and you have to surrender to the lesson that needs to be learned for the deepening of your spiritual awareness.

The accident made me realize that there would be times I would make mistakes, even if I did my best to prepare for success. That did not mean I was a failure.

The Mindset That Leads to Mistakes

If you want a big miracle, you have to create the right environment for it to occur. You need to recognize the limitations that keep you from adopting the miracle mindset and to recognize specific think-ing that could set mistakes in motion.

Every time someone makes a mistake, there are always red flags leading up to it. The reason you don't see these warning signs is that a part of your mind is closed off. Why?

Fixed beliefs. You might have a fixed belief, perhaps because of something someone told you that you've accepted as a fact, even though it was just that person's own perspective, and this is creating a blind spot for you.

Fear. If your fear of failure, rejection, or abandonment is strong, then this could be stopping you from being objective.

Avoidance of responsibility. You may have made several similar mistakes, and so it is too painful to accept responsibility for your part in the outcome.

Tunnel vision. You can miss the warning signs if you have tunnel vision for your desire and have not taken other factors into consideration. For instance, others' plans and goals may run counter to yours; you may need to adapt the route you take to achieve the happiness and success you desire.

Inauthentic desire. You have not been honest with yourself about your true motivation. It's not that you are trying to be dishonest; it's your fear of not receiving your genuine heart's desire that has you shooting for a different goal.

Because all these factors can close your mind to the warning signs, it is imperative to adopt the practice of meditation to center yourself, ground your energy, and connect to Spirit. It is critical that you learn to recognize the subtle energies that distinguish red flags, and meditation can give you this ability. The more aware you become, the more mistakes you will avoid. Rule 4 is built on the three rules that have come before it. If you're like me and my clients, you'll find that forgiving mistakes is much, much easier and less emotionally challenging if you're already aligned with Spirit, operating as a spiritual vehicle, and fully committed to breaking through your different barriers.

The negative mindset that emerges from some mistakes can leave you feeling terrible and thinking that something is wrong with you. Sometimes you'll make a mistake and experience repercussions for months or even years. Focus on having compassion for yourself. You won't get past the mistake you made if you haven't been able to for-give yourself or if you are blaming someone else. When you release yourself from a negative mindset that includes anything like this, your channel of abundance opens up.

Watch Your Thoughts

When you meditate, you will notice the subtle energies around and within you. These subtle energies are your thought patterns, which can give you positive momentum toward your life purpose or turn into blockages. You must question why you think a certain way. If you catch yourself making assumptions, ask yourself, "What do I fear could happen?" This will help you regain control of your mind and positively redirect your energy, because you have moved beyond denial and are aware that you need to take a new approach.

Unspoken expectations of others are like poison. They create disappointment and misunderstandings. To avoid mistakes, you must get in the habit of clear communication and expressing your true thoughts without fear of rejection. What do you need to say? What boundaries do you need to put in place? What if you be-lieve you made a mistake and cannot forgive yourself? How do you move forward?

One of my clients missed the opportunity to marry a woman whom he believed was the love of his life. On the surface it looked as if he had commitment issues, but in fact the core issue was his fear of not being enough. When he was finally ready to marry his beloved, she was already engaged to someone else. He was devastated. She had thought he was playing games and wasn't serious.

The man tried everything he could to salvage the relationship. He felt he had made the biggest mistake of his life, and he didn't date anyone for several years. As he began to look within and heal the negative way he saw himself, he arrived at a place of acceptance in his mind. He then met a beautiful woman whom he felt ready to marry. He told me he could see how the earlier relationship had been preparing him for his soul mate.

A mistake is your opportunity to learn and has the power to lead you to heal, so that you can manifest your heart's desire. Your important task is to discern when healing is necessary.

The Top Ten Symptoms of a Mistake

To be able to catch a mistake and course-correct, you have to be able to identify the symptoms of a mistake. Common symptoms are:

- You think you have done something wrong.
- You feel something bad has happened to you.
- You believe the pain will never go away.
- You fear permanent damage has been done.
- You feel paralyzed by fear.
- You don't trust your intuition.
- The circumstances replay on a loop in your head.
- It feels as though your heart is bleeding emotionally.
- You cannot move past feelings of resentment.
- You feel depressed.

The Side Effects of a Mistake

If you deny that you've made a mistake and do not forgive yourself, you'll probably sabotage yourself in one or more of the following ways:

- You'll judge yourself, which affects your ability to be confident and happy.
- You'll mentally beat yourself up. Because of this, even

when you say something positive about yourself and your circumstances, you'll follow it up with a self-deprecating statement. When you're alone, you'll simply chastise yourself mercilessly.

- You'll be defensive and assume that people are going to criticize you in some way. Your defenses can be triggered just by the presence of an e-mail, text message, or voicemail even without having read or listened to it. A fearful fantasy can be created as a side effect of not forgiving that causes you to avoid connecting—as often as not, only to find out later that there was no issue from the other person's point of view.

- You'll anticipate a negative outcome in which you won't get what you want, and this will give you a pessimistic outlook.

What side effects have you experienced following your mistakes? How much energy do you find these side effects have drained from you? If you're ready to stop sabotaging yourself and would like to become less reactive, then you must reframe your view of your mistakes. Once you do, the pain will subside. There is a silver lining to every mistake you make, and the miracle you're seeking is in the silver lining. Search for the silver lining, and it will be revealed to you.

The Spiritual Silver Lining in a Mistake

Think of a mistake as a compass guiding you to recover discarded parts of yourself. When your soul experiences a mistake, it can go into a state of shock, denial, or fear, which causes it to fragment. This can lead to a skewed perspective of the things that are happening in your life. Afterward, when you're reaching out to Spirit for guidance, it can be hard to sense if Spirit is present.

You can trust that when you make a request for guidance from Spirit, support will always be given to you, but if there are any disturbances in your energy field, you might think you've been denied. This creates a feeling of rejection, which leads to pain; this in turn can lead to denial of your problems.

A skewed perspective may also cause you, when you receive guidance from a spiritual source, to misunderstand its meaning and make additional mistakes. If this happens, it can feel as though you are being punished, even though you're doing your best to break through obstacles to the achievement of your goals.

As you begin investing time and energy into healing your soul, memories of your past mistakes or failed relationships are likely to appear in your nighttime dreams. These dreams can be rich in guidance if you pay attention to the subtle energy around you during your waking hours, especially soon after waking up in the morning. You will awaken after such a dream with a sense that miracles are about to occur, even though you do not know exactly what will happen. The energy within and around has an expectant and uplifted quality.

You are also likely to have a new appreciation for the mistakes you made, because you'll finally be able to see that the people whom you formerly believed were intentionally trying to hurt you were not really doing so; they were merely going through their own life struggles. This will give you the awareness to stop reacting or defending your actions when someone blames or criticizes you. Once you have this realization, forgiveness is inevitable, and then the pain of your past—whether it is a financial loss, divorce, loss of a loved one, or health crisis—can turn into a wealth of healing and bring you gratitude for your life and relationships.

Barbara had been working as a paralegal for a respected law firm. She was feeling dissatisfied with her job and knew she wanted to go in a different direction with her life. But she didn't know what to do—plus she didn't want to forfeit her job security. She told me that she was attending a workshop with a friend in Chicago and felt bored, so she went to a small independent bookstore across the street from the event venue. As she perused the titles in the self-help section, my book *Unleash the Psychic in You* fell off of a shelf and hit her on the head. She e-mailed me that afternoon to schedule an intuitive reading.

I knew nothing about Barbara's situation, but during her reading I received a strong impression from Spirit in which she was standing on stage doing psychic readings for an audience of approximately a hundred people. She said she didn't see how that would be possible, as she wasn't a psychic; however, she'd gone for a reading with another well-known psychic a week prior to contacting me and received the same message. Although she was, in fact, studying psychic mediumship with a teacher, she didn't see how it could become a profession for her. But she also confessed that she didn't want to be a paralegal anymore.

Soon after this reading, her brother suddenly died. Her brother was young and had a full life ahead of him. Much to her surprise, Barbara began to communicate with her brother on the other side. The message she received from her brother was to pursue her mediumship. Her brother promised he would be with her in spirit as she led her workshops. Her mistake was that she hadn't trusted the guidance she received from Spirit, and it took a tragedy for her to move past her fears of how she would be perceived before she stepped into her life purpose. She said her mistake was underestimating her ability to give people messages from loved ones who had passed over. She committed to being of service to others.

Barbara left her job at the law firm and now leads spiritual workshops. She could have plummeted into depression when her brother died and felt angry with God; instead, she sought out the spiritual purpose of why she lost her brother. She took the grief of her loss and channeled it into creating a legacy that would honor her brother by helping others to overcome their losses.

Forgiving Your Own Mistakes

In business and in our personal lives, we often make mistakes in our relationships. Use the following three steps, when you feel you've wronged another person:

Step 1: Think of a situation when you lost a relationship or friendship. What did you do that hurt the person you love/ loved?

Step 2: If you put yourself in the shoes of someone you hurt, what higher awareness do you have about why and how you hurt that person?

Step 3: What are some specific reasons from your perspective— for example, what needs of yours were not being met or in what way did you feel misunderstood—that led you to hurt the person you love/loved?

As you contemplate these questions, you set in motion your ability to release underlying guilt, pain, and shame. Heaviness in your heart or feelings of frustration will begin to lift and you'll have more energy available to align with fulfilling relationships and joy.

Forgiving the Mistakes of Others

When you are angry and hurt because you feel someone has harmed you—in business or in your personal life—use the following process to forgive the mistake:

Step 1: What is the situation in which you believe you were betrayed and that you cannot move past?

Step 2: If you put yourself in the shoes of the other person, why do you believe the person did what he or she did?

Step 3: What shift can you make in your perspective to release your pain? How can you use any feelings of resentment toward the other person to move on in your life?

As long as you hold resentment toward the person, it sits in your energy field and hinders your ability to think clearly and rationally about the next best step for your life. Remind yourself that maintaining resentment poisons your ability to experience true happiness.

As you let go of blame, you have the ability to release your focus from wanting others to acknowledge what they did wrong and to change. Seeing them in a new light with acceptance and compassion allows you the opportunity to create the life you want.

Moving Beyond Mistakes in Relationships

Whenever you are facing a problem in a relationship, focus on the big miracle breakthrough you are working toward. Ask yourself, "What would represent my big miracle breakthrough in the current situation?" Once you have reminded yourself of the outcome you desire, look for the mistakes that are creating obstacles in your relationship.

In which areas of the relationship do you keep experiencing mistakes, both yours and the other person's? Decide what kind of boundaries you need to put in place to avert those mistakes and then do so using the following technique.

This is a process you do on your own, privately. You are not mandated to inform anyone else. Begin by forgiving yourself and the other person. Get quiet and reflect on these questions as if you were speaking directly to the person and notice any feelings that rise to the surface or thoughts that come into your mind. Focus on the outcome you want to create. Open your mind to a higher state of awareness. Ask:

- "I forgive you, but should I maintain a relationship with you?"
- "How many chances do I give you before moving on?"
- "Can I maintain a relationship with you and live with the pain I caused?"
- "What expectations do I have and why?"
- "Having looked carefully at my inventory of mistakes, where was I not clear in my communication?"
- "In what way did I lack responsibility for my decisions and actions?"
- "What will I ask for that I have feared requesting in the past?"
- "What will I do next to increase my commitment to the success of this relationship?"

Mistakes will still happen, despite going through a forgiveness process, but the key is to never let them stop you. Use them as a springboard to ultimate success. In some situations, you may have to forgive more than once to clear the energy of all your misperceptions. Stick with it, because that means a great lesson is at hand.

Facing Your Mistakes and Discovering Your Miracles

To find your miracles, you have to face your mistakes. A mistake is a misunderstanding. It is also a time when you make a decision without enough information. By reviewing and investigating your past mistakes, understanding will come. Think of a mistake as a guiding force.

As long as you blame yourself or someone else for a mistake, it will stay stuck in your energy field. One of the reasons I could not generate income for five years was because I felt massive resentment toward my ex-boyfriend and I harshly judged the decisions I made regarding my finances, which led me to lose everything and plummet into debt. Several years later, I was standing at a crosswalk when clarity suddenly swept over me. I wasn't making money not because I didn't trust my ex-boyfriend, but because I didn't trust myself with money. It had always felt safer for me to have no money, even though I wanted financial freedom. As soon as I became aware of this and forgave myself for my mistaken beliefs, I began to make money again.

Retrospectively, I find it interesting that during the time I wasn't earning much income, I was always well taken care of. I'd miraculously find a great housesitting opportunity or a barter that took care of my daily needs for everything from food to clothes to a car. What was dissatisfying and unfulfilling about my situation was that my ability to help others was limited.

Every time you hear the voice in your head say, "You've made a mistake yet again," remind yourself, "I am one more step closer to creating the outcome I desire, and I'm open to guidance about where my beliefs or a lack of information is holding me back."

Here are four steps that can help you process your mistakes.

Step 1: A Mistakes Inventory

Do a mistakes inventory. Write a list of your mistakes as follows:

- "The mistakes I made today were ..."
- "The mistakes I made this week were ..."
- "The mistakes I made this month were ..."
- "The biggest mistake I made in the past year was ..."
- "My greatest regret is ..."

Step 2: Understanding Your Mistakes

Write a list of what you learned from the mistakes you identified in Step 1:

- "What I learned from the mistakes I made today is ..."
- "What I learned from the mistakes I made this week is ..."
- "What I learned from the mistakes I made this month is ..."
- "The greatest lesson I learned from the biggest mistake I made in the past year is ..."
- "The wisdom I see in my greatest regret is ..."

Step 3: Releasing Your Mistakes from Your Energy Field

To free yourself from the heavy energy of your mistakes, now that you've taken a lesson from each of them, go over your mistakes and ask yourself:

- "Why do I feel guilty about this mistake?"
- "Why do I feel ashamed of this mistake?"
- "If no one was judging me, would I still feel as if I'd made a mistake?"

Then complete the following two sentences.

- I blame _____ [name of the person] for the mistake because...
- I feel this way because...

Once you've got your answers (and there are no wrong answers— only unexamined ones), close your eyes and imagine a golden cleansing light above you entering the top of your head, flowing down into your body, and filling up your energy field. Sense how this golden light dissolves any guilt, shame, or blame that remains within you.

With each breath you take, sense every cell in your body and your entire energy field becoming lighter.

You can repeat this process as many times as you like. Each time you do it, you'll find old memories resurfacing about events in your past—even those of which you've had no prior recollection. This technique will help you to recognize the subtle energies that lead you to make mistakes.

Step 4: The Popcorn Technique

Look at your mistakes inventory again. Then close your eyes and imagine that each mistake is a popcorn kernel. Imagine scooping up the kernels and putting them in a saucepan and placing a lid on top. Put the saucepan on the stove and turn on the flame. Think of this flame as a vehicle to deepen your awareness. As the flame heats the kernels and they pop, the mistake turns into a miracle. There's no obstacle on your path. You're free to manifest miracles. Sense how the weight of your past mistakes is lifted.

Forgiveness Is the Key

When you apply forgiveness to your mistakes and to those of others in your life, you will experience a new sense of freedom. When you recognize that your past experiences had a purpose, you'll feel good about stepping outside of your comfort zone and be willing, and even eager, to take the risks you need to take to achieve your big miracles.

You must not settle! Instead, aim higher, do your healing work, and expect a big miracle breakthrough. Do not accept unacceptable behavior from someone else. Do not stoop to the level of someone else's lack of awareness. Lead by example by always maintaining integrity. This will ensure that you're spiritually aligned and prepared for ultimate success.

Transforming a Mistake into a Miracle

Mistakes are part of the human experience, but it is important to see the purpose behind your mistakes. There will always be times where you don't have experience in a situation, and you can learn. A mistake can be an indicator you tried something new and didn't succeed yet. It can also be that you suppressed your awareness because of fear. Writing stream of consciousness, without thinking, opens you up to the intuitive part of yourself and your direct connection to Spirit. Using stream of consciousness and being open to Spirit, finish these three powerful sentences to transform a mistake into a miracle:

- *"The mistake I made was..."*

- *"What I learned from my mistake is..."*

- *"Next time, I'll take the following action:..."*

5

RULE 5: **Live Without Ego**

What is the bigger picture that
Spirit wants me to see?

An evolved ego has just the right amount of self-awareness to afford you the ability to make gradual and peaceful progress toward your big miracles. Spirit wants to inspire us with a heartfelt vision for a future greater than the desire we feel for fame, flattery, money, or power for their own sake. Creating a vision is an important way to practice being a spiritual vehicle, because heartfelt visions for the future are our primary motivation to do noble things. An unevolved ego is an obstacle to developing your vision.

A vision broadens the field of our consciousness and expands our lives, but an inflated ego contracts our energy and makes our lives narrower. The ego out of balance is self-centered, defensive, and controlling. It thinks the world is dangerous, so it puts us in as small a box as we'll allow. It builds a moat around us and fills it with thoughts equivalent to crocodiles. It doesn't care that we want to explore, trust, love, or connect. It just wants us to stand still. It points out everything negative it can see, so that we willingly surrender more and more of our freedom. Because of its me-me-me focus, the ego is not good company. It creates isolation and conflict.

Having a vision will help you clarify what is truly important to you. As you get specific about the kind of life you want to live on a daily basis, including where you want to live and work, your fitness routine, your family commitments, and your social engagements, you'll be guided by Spirit to the right place for you to connect with likeminded people. If you're presently experiencing things that you don't like, examine why you don't feel good. Even with $100,000 in the bank and a loving relationship, when your ego comes into play, it will make you feel agitated and ashamed. By focusing on the power of a beautiful vision, you'll override the negativity of your ego and be empowered to create your ideal life.

There's a deeper meaning to your life. When you recognize the gift this meaning gives to you and others, you'll be able to view your current circumstances with gratitude, even if you're experiencing challenges and losses. Each day is an opportunity for you to move beyond your doubts and your fears of others' judgment. When your ego says that you don't have enough or that you're inadequate, focusing on the gratitude you feel for what you do have will elevate your awareness. Feeling grateful can give you the strength to do what needs to be done to honor your vision and create your big miracles. It can help you transcend any difficulties you're facing in your relationships, finances, career, or health.

The Power of a Vision

If you don't know what you're getting up for in the morning, you're not going to get up. Having a heartfelt vision for your ideal life gives you a purpose, and having a purpose gives you inspiration. Inspiration is what gets the impossible done. It is the fuel of miracles.

Before you can motivate yourself and others, you must be able to articulate a vision. To find your vision, you must be truly receptive. We all discover our own vision in an individual way. Some people are given their vision. Others must go find one. Your vision can come to you in a dream or a daydream. It can be delivered as a series of thoughts, as images in your mind's eye, or as a message that sounds like your own voice inside your head. You may have a strong feeling or knowing that there's something you must do.

Some people have a big vision. Some have a small vision. The vision that will lead you to big miracles will be relevant to your life. If you want to be proactive about developing the specifics of your vision, create a Vision Book by cutting pictures out of magazines of anything you want and pasting them inside a spiral-bound notebook. I've found this technique works very well for me. It's fun to bring a vision one step closer to 3D reality by translating thoughts into imagery. I made a Vision Book containing pictures of my dream car, places I wanted to live, career goals, and hobbies and experienced almost all of them (or things very close to the things I'd originally wanted) within a few years.

Some things we envision manifest in our lives faster than others, depending on how big the vision is. Growing up in London, I dreamed of living by the water. Many years later I found a wonderful residence with a view of the ocean. While I lived there, I loved walking down to the beach at night and watching the light of the full moon sparkle on the waves. One of my friends was eyeing a special handbag for months, and her boyfriend surprised her on Valentine's Day with that exact bag. No matter what your vision includes, set the intention that you'll gratefully receive it when the time is right.

Talent manager and producer Ken Kragen didn't have a vision of receiving the United Nations Peace Medal. He had a humanitarian vision of people joining hands from coast to coast across America for the purpose of ending hunger. In 1986, after returning from a trip to Africa, Kragen was asked, "What are you going to do for America?"

The answer was Hands Across America, the largest public demon-stration ever created. It brought together over six million people of all races, religions, and political persuasions in a continuous hand-holding line stretching from New York to California for the purpose of raising money and awareness for the plight of the hungry and homeless in the United States.[1]

Hands Across America directly raised $34 million and resulted in at least $1 billion more in funding from the government and private organizations earmarked to fight hunger and homelessness. And it all started with an idea that easily could have been dismissed.[2] The idea for Hands Across America was given to Kragen by a public-relations executive working pro bono with him on another well-known fund-raising event he produced.

When the executive pitched the idea, he said to Kragen, "Don't laugh, but what if . . . ?"

Kragen responded, "I'm not laughing. It's just impossible enough to be possible."[3]

He understood that what he was hearing was a vision that could inspire. He saw the bigger picture and was able to communicate the vision effectively because of who he was and the people he knew in film, music, and the news media. Without his knowing it, his soul had been preparing him to be able to successfully accomplish this project his entire life. That's why he had the abilities and contacts he would need to carry it out.

A strong vision is a blueprint for creating a big miracle using your natural-born talents. It gives you momentum personally, profession-ally, and socially.

To bring a vision to life requires specificity. You have to zero in on the specific outcome you want and be able to describe it. When you're thinking about your vision or writing about it in a Vision Book, add as many details as you need to clarify the vision.

Stop working on your vision before you feel as if you've boxed yourself into only one way of doing things. You need to have flexibility to allow space for magic to happen.

Once you have a vision that motivates you, let nothing divert you from pursuing it. You must be patient and persistent even if you don't see results quickly. Be the best steward of the vision you can be. Ask for advice from someone with the expertise that can help you succeed at reaching your goals.

After feeling low in energy for months, I wasn't a picture of health, so I developed a vision of how I wanted to feel and why. I visualized what my future lifestyle would look like, and then I searched online and found nutritionist Elissa Goodman through the website of the California-based vegetarian restaurant chain Café Gratitude. My intuition compelled me to reach out to her when I read her story on the site, because we'd had similar life experiences, such as having worked in the fast-paced world of advertising, drinking lots of caffeine, and eating a diet of rich foods. At thirty-two, Elissa was diagnosed with Hodgkin's lymphoma, a cancer for which her doctor recommended she undergo chemotherapy and radiation treatments.[4] After starting radiation, her inner voice guided her to take an alternative path. She left her job and began practicing yoga, drinking raw fruit and vegetable juices, and eating plant-based meals on a daily basis. Since making the decision to heal her body, she'd enjoyed excellent health, and I wanted the same for myself. Elissa was able to help me pinpoint the exact steps I needed to follow.

The Purpose of Your Vision

The more you focus on your vision, the stronger it will become. This will leave no room in your mind for the ego to sabotage your dreams. As you check in with your vision throughout the day and keep bringing your focus back to this heartfelt desire, any feelings of fear and worry you're having will decrease and be replaced with excitement.

Articulating Your Vision

To articulate a vision of a miracle you want to experience, you need to be in a relaxed and thus receptive state. If you press too hard to see the vision of this ideal future, it may not come.

You'll know an authentic vision has arrived when it excites you, feels right, and keeps recurring in your mind at random times throughout the day. You may also see something on TV, hear something on the radio, or read something online that reinforces the rightness of this vision. This is confirmation from your intuition that you're on course.

Put yourself in a relaxed state by finding somewhere comfortable to sit where you won't be interrupted for at least half an hour. Settle into your seat and take a few deep breaths, bringing your awareness to your heart.

At this point, it's a good idea to do the Center, Ground, and Connect Meditation (see p. 23) to strengthen your receptivity to Spirit. Then ask the following questions, trusting that whatever comes to mind will be useful. As you receive your insights from your soul and Spirit, it is a good idea to write your answers in your Miracle Journal, because flashes of inspiration and wisdom will come to you that you will likely forget the details of later.

- *"How would I like to start my day?"*

- *"Where would I like to live?"*

- *"If there was no limit on what I could spend, what would my home be like? Would I have more than one home?"*

- *"Who would I like to have by my side during the day?"*

- *"What would my activities be?"*

- *"Would I have my own business or work for someone?"*

- *"Would I travel?"*

- *"What talents would I express?"*

- *"What would I usually do for fun?"*

- *"How much money would I have in my bank account?"*

- *"How long do I sense it would take me to make my vision a reality?"*

- *"Who do I need to be today to begin living into this vision?"*

Once you're confident of the what, when, where, how, who, and why of your vision, you'll feel fulfilled by the process of living toward your goals.

Knowing the reasons you're pursuing a particular path is essential. Without serving a purpose that's meaningful to you, your vision will seem as lifeless as a deflated balloon. To succeed, you must find the right motivation, one that genuinely elicits your passion and commitment.

Take care not to allow yourself to be driven by pain, revenge, or wanting to prove someone wrong, because even if you achieve your vision, you'll feel dissatisfied. The best motivations not only make us better people and more useful to others, but on a bigger scale they create a better world. Those are the motivations that will draw people together around you.

In *Never Eat Alone,* Keith Ferrazzi shares how fulfilling it is to introduce to each other people you think would enjoy connecting. Reading about the way he does so lit a spark of joy in my heart, as it reminded me of how much I've always loved connecting people. Over the years I put many friends together on blind dates, and one of these pairings ended in marriage. I also helped people forge new friendships and receive job offers and in the process generated a ton of great memories filled with laughter for myself. But I had stopped making a habit of introducing people after I gave birth to my son, because I went through a period where I was preoccupied only with him and my work. After reading Ferrazzi's book, I decided to renew my joy in being a connector. Now every time I meet or speak with friends, I think about others they might like to know.

If you've decided you want to "get rich" or "be a millionaire," what are your specific reasons for wanting to achieve this goal? My client Stacey told me her vision was to help women become successful entrepreneurs. She wanted to become a millionaire by developing, selling, and delivering training programs. The reason she did not achieve this vision when we worked together, in my opinion, is that she was actually driven by a desire to take revenge on her ex-husband and to prove her family wrong about their poor opinions of her.

The problem with negative motivations is that they disconnect you from Spirit. You must search deep within yourself to ensure that your vision is not actually your wounded ego in disguise.

My friend Ted McGrath grew up in an environment in which he learned that you got approval only when you made a lot of money. It's no wonder he made it his mission to earn a lot of money or that he was the youngest person ever to be offered the position of partner at one of the top insurance companies in the United States. When he reached this pinnacle of success, he thought it would be the magic bullet for feeling happy, so he was surprised when happiness didn't come. He turned to alcohol and drugs to generate positive feelings, but the highs he experienced with substances gave him only a fleeting false happiness. One night Ted overdosed and came close to death.[5]

In coming to terms with what he'd done, Ted realized that the vision he'd been chasing was not his. What he truly wanted more than anything was freedom of expression and creativity. He left the insurance business and pursued a vision of inspiring others on stage as a motivational speaker and actor. In fact, I originally met Ted while attending one of his talks. He lit up the stage with his presence.

Before his overdose, Ted was consumed by a vision of making money. Today money is only one aspect of his life. Speaking recently, Ted told me that his big miracles came when he developed the awareness to recognize his ego and deny its demands. He now searches for his personal truth on a daily basis and lives by it, so that he can set an example of love and connectedness for others.

When we are centered in love, we can work miracles. Agnes Gonxha Bojaxhiu's father died when she was only eight, leaving her family with no income. She could have fallen into a life of despair and misery and been a bitter victim of her circumstances. Instead, she joined a community of Catholic missionary nuns at eighteen and received the name Sister Mary Teresa. After her final profession of vows several years later, she became Mother Teresa.[6] Her vision was to serve the poorest of all. She washed the wounded and cared for the sick and dying in the slums of Calcutta, India. In 1979, at the age of sixty-nine, Mother Teresa was awarded the Nobel Peace Prize, and by the time of her death 4,000 sisters in her order worked under her leadership at 610 foundations in 123 countries.[7] Later she was recognized as a saint for miraculous healings.[8] Her story demonstrates that love in its purest form can inspire hope and effect a positive change in those who sincerely seek it.

Which would you rather be motivated by, love or anger? You must find the true purpose of your vision. Look at the vision you articulated earlier ("Articulating Your Vision," p. 106) and check your heart to ensure that you are peaceful and grounded and that the limitation of your ego is in no way driving you. Even once you have established a clear vision of the happiness and success you desire, as you move closer to it, step by step, your ego may try to take you hostage by telling you that it is impossible to succeed. This is where your commitment to being a spiritual vehicle can help you stay on course. Incorporate a daily prayer to keep you focused on an outcome that is for the greatest good of all and practice meditation to clear any subtle negative thinking.

Also find ways to reinforce your faith in your vision. To make your vision real, you must believe it is possible. Like a child playing pretend, go through an imaginative process in your mind, seeing yourself in the outcomes you wish to make real in your life. Surround yourself with supportive mementoes, artwork, and messages.

When I was invited to the home of investor and entrepreneur Tai Lopez in Beverly Hills, he gave me a tour of his private gym. I was impressed that he had hung a framed picture of his dad, a professional bodybuilder, on the wall along with photos of many other athletes and models, so that every time he exercises he'll be inspired to create his ideal body. Those pictures are proof that others have achieved what he wants, which reminds him that it is possible.

Set up your personal space to help you remember that your goal is achievable. If you are unsure of how to inspire yourself, sit quietly and let impressions come forth in your mind. Then ask yourself, "What is a simple way I can remind myself of my vision?" Your reminder could be a sign, a photo, a song, a flag, or anything else that holds personal significance for you. Meaning is motivational.

Be realistic about the amount of time required for the achievement of your objectives. If you set unrealistic goals, you'll trigger your ego to start barking negative messages at you. It's easy to become despondent and quit under these conditions. Keeping your goals simple will help you build your confidence until you receive signs from Spirit that you are on your right path. The ego can quickly send you into a tailspin, so you must be vigilant in case it strikes.

The Danger of the Ego

The unevolved ego always comes from a wounded place within you. The unevolved ego's primary purpose is self-preservation. It sees itself as unworthy and wants to avoid having others figure that out. One way it deflects insecurity is by making others feel guilty so it can get its way. Thus, it can leave a trail of destruction behind you and irreparably damage your relationships. The ego has a deep need to justify its goals, no matter how much damage it does. It has to prove that it's right. This makes it an obstacle to genuine heartfelt connection and mutual appreciation and compassion. The ego will create complications and problems to suppress your pain and sadness and keep insecurity away.

Because the ego uses twisted logic, it wants there to be a struggle. Its outlook is limited. It has already made up its mind that the odds are stacked against it. This is why it tells you that what needs to be done *can't* be done or that the only approach that may work for you is to put up a fight. If the ego senses that it isn't getting its way, it will cause you to become forceful and aggressive or tearful and needy, depending on the situation. It always wants you to be assertive without consideration for others.

If you give it half a chance, your ego will do everything in its power to disconnect you from your heart and limit your vision of what is possible in your life. If you are acting from your ego, you'll be motivated for the wrong reasons and might hurt yourself and others. Your ego could also prevent you from taking necessary steps to fulfill your vision. It may try to stop you from picking up the phone to call someone you'd love to get to know better, applying for an interesting job, investing in your continuing education, making an appointment with a doctor or dentist, apologizing to a loved one or a friend, setting a clear boundary with an ex-lover or former spouse, creating a spending plan, or clarifying a realistic time frame for making your vision come true.

The ego can interfere with the harmony of our personal lives. Perhaps you made a choice to exclude someone from a decision-making process or an event because the ego said you should be in charge rather than the other person. Grabbing the microphone at a wedding to give an impromptu speech, when really the bride and groom should be the center of attention, is an egocentric way to behave. Letting a parent be openly critical toward your boyfriend because you fear a loss of favor is also an ego-driven choice.

I once introduced two friends who ended up falling in love and were considering marriage. Unfortunately, the two had been raised in different religions. The man's family had given him an ultimatum: if he continued dating the woman, he would be eliminated from his parents' wills. Although he loved her, he was scared he wouldn't be able to make his own living, as he had always relied on his parents for money. The woman was brokenhearted. So many people's egos were in play in this sad scenario.

Coping with someone whose ego is out of control can be very difficult, so you must do your best to center yourself in your heart when this happens. Step back if you need to until your energy stabilizes. You must be sure that when you interact, your own ego doesn't get triggered, or else you could find yourself caught in a cycle with this individual for years to come, assuming a posture in relationship to him or her that does not serve your vision.

Sometimes people are not overtly forceful. They manipulate others by being passive-aggressive. One of my friends seemed caring, but I always came away from our time together feeling drained. I took a break from spending time with her, but after a few months she pressed me to meet up with her again. I said yes, thinking that perhaps my own attitude had been the problem, and tried to have an open mind. She asked what I'd been up to in a chirpy tone of voice, but when I shared my latest good news, her tone dropped, and she said, "I'd never want a life like that." I was immediately triggered to assume a defensive posture with her, but I caught myself before I slipped into justifying why I wanted what I wanted and explaining why the things I had were good. I recognized my ego wanting to take over the conversation, went quiet, and made a mental note not to see her again for a very long time, if ever.

The ego can interfere with our professional lives as well. Perhaps an opportunity seems to be below your skill level or doesn't pay enough, and your ego cannot see the advantages in taking it on, for example, as a chance to meet someone who could help you fulfill a nobler purpose later. If you use your career to define your self-worth (an ego-based mode of operating), it can be easy for your ego to trigger feelings of inadequacy, competition, or the dreaded impostor syndrome, believing you are in a position you are not qualified to fulfill and taking advantage of others. Remember to center yourself in your heart, ground your energy, and align yourself with Spirit every day.

Catherine, an accountant, often complained that her job was making her miserable, she couldn't stand her boss and coworkers, and her work was boring. When I pointed out that her current job was giving her the means to finance her training to become a Reiki healer, which was her passion, she stopped resenting her situation. After that she kept her head down at work and did her job competently without complaining. A year later, she left her job amicably and made Reiki her full-time career, picking up several clients from among her former coworkers.

Feeding the ego is draining. No matter what you do, the ego cannot be satisfied. Its nature is to be hungry. It is always on the lookout for threats against you and will do anything to justify its existence, including making things up. The unevolved ego says things like, "When you make more money, everything will be okay," "Lose more weight, and he'll want you back," "Get a better car, and you'll be respected," and "Have the dream vacation, and you'll feel relaxed." Notice that these statements are all conditional. If you heed the ego, the satisfaction you might feel will only be temporary, because the ego motivates through fostering a sense of deprivation or unworthiness in you.

People who use tactics such as fearmongering, shaming, manipulation, and bribery are bullies whose egos feed on the fears and weaknesses of others. Sadly, most people are primarily motivated to take action when they want to stop pain or fear losing something. This is because at some time in the past they experienced a loss or trauma that they didn't understand.

A wound like that creates fragmentation in our souls and a disconnection from Spirit. After sustaining that kind of emotional injury, a part of us will always strive to "fix it"—subconsciously spending a lot of energy looking backward, trying to figure out what went wrong. The wounded part of the self, which underlies the ego, thinks, *If I can figure out how the pain happened, then I can remove the pain from my past.* But because we cannot actually change the past, the subconscious mind creates circumstances in our present lives where we see if we can fix the old problem now. And the pain is reinforced.

When I was eighteen, I was really into this one gorgeous guy. Our date was going great until I saw his purple briefs. At that moment I decided there was no way I could be with someone who didn't wear boxer shorts. It was a ridiculously superficial reason not to date him, but I was afraid of being judged by my new friends, who could be unrelentingly cruel. You see, when I began socializing in South West London, some people considered themselves superior to me and wouldn't talk to me because I came from North West London. I felt so awful when they rejected me that I bought into their reality and tried to play by their rules. That meant I sometimes snubbed great people who wanted to be my friends. My skewed reasoning was that they didn't eat at the right restaurants, go to the coolest clubs, weren't on the cutting edge of fashion, maintained friendships with the "wrong people," or worked in industries considered boring to the people with whom I wanted to associate. That's why Mr. Purple Briefs had to go.

Many of my new friends had luxury cars, and I dreaded having them see my more economical car. I wanted to impress them, so I wasn't grateful that I had been given a car by my parents. I felt entitled to something better. In my twenties, I attracted people who also felt entitled to be given things. I began paying for my friends' meals and buying things on credit to win them over instead of allowing real friendships to develop and being honest about my financial limitations. When I ultimately went deeply into debt, it was because I had been desperate to preserve an aura of success that I believed would make me acceptable to the people in my social circle. Then I felt so ashamed of my debt that I ate much more than my body needed in order to stuff down my feelings of inadequacy, and I put on weight. My ego just kept creating new problems that illustrated my core wound.

If you look for the subtle signs of your ego in your motivations and decision-making processes, you'll find a wound created by an event and reinforced by a story that you're maintaining in your mind. This impacts your ability to live from your heart and in alignment with Spirit. Furthermore, if your wounds are motivating you, you may either put yourself into unwanted work scenarios or toxic relationships where you are on the receiving end of someone else's negative behavior or you may carry out those behaviors yourself by not respecting your body.

Six Character Flaws That Come from Ego

Being aware of the following common negative ego traits will help you to catch limiting patterns within yourself that stop you from living a consistently fulfilled life.

Greed. When the ego always needs more, you are dealing with greed. Whatever you do to satisfy it, it doesn't seem to be enough. The glass is always half empty. There is a sense of entitlement and high expectations, and you believe that the more possessions you have, the better you will feel, but any sense of fulfillment is short-lived. It doesn't matter to the ego if you win or get what you want at another's expense. The more that can be gained, the better.

When you feel greed, there is such a sense of urgency to get what you want that you don't care how it will affect you and others in the long term. To heal greed, ask yourself, "What happens if I don't get what I want now?" and "How will getting this watch, car, meal, pair of shoes, and so on impact my life ten years from now?" Focus on making your relationship with Spirit a priority over possessions that give you false payoffs.

Narcissism. A narcissistic focus says, "Look at me! What can you do for me? Why aren't you doing that for me?" Your ego has an interest in others only if there's a benefit to you in the connection. If you're motivated by your ego, you'll be interested in people only if they make you feel good and give you what you want. The ego is an opportunist.

It's a sign that you may have narcissistic tendencies if your conversations are one-sided, always turned back to yourself. Have you ever ignored someone after the person gave you what you wanted? Have you ever ditched a friend or cancelled plans because another person more to your liking came along? Being friendly toward someone until you get a specific business introduction or membership referral to a club and then dropping that person is a typical narcissistic behavior.

Check in with yourself and make sure that no selfish motivations are driving you. Listen to others' needs and practice putting their needs ahead of yours to build your character.

Manipulation. Presenting a situation favorably, often as a win-win, with selfish intentions is a form of manipulation, as is feeding people misinformation about a business competitor or a prospective romantic partner to give yourself an advantage. Knowing a person's weak side and then saying or doing things that you believe will trigger a reaction you want is manipulative. So is using someone's fears and needs to achieve your desired outcome. Telling lies to get others to give you the things you want is also a form of manipulation.

To heal your own manipulative behavior, center yourself in your heart and search for any hidden motives behind your actions. Adopt an attitude of detachment toward the particular outcome you want. If Spirit intends for you to get what you want, you can trust you'll get it.

Betrayal. It's betrayal if you reveal secrets told to you in confidence or if you use confidential information as a weapon against the person who told it to you. Gossiping is a form of betrayal. Promising to tell the truth and then lying to a person who trusts you is as well. An affair is an obvious betrayal.

To stop yourself from betraying someone, imagine yourself on the receiving end of the action you are about to take. How would you feel if someone said or did those things to you? Would you feel hurt if someone revealed one of your confidences?

Revenge. A desire for revenge comes from feeling wronged. When it is triggered, it is one of the most toxic demonstrations of the ego there is, because it can entirely consume your mind. Revenge signifies an obsession to make someone suffer, and you will never achieve freedom and peace if you're hell-bent on causing pain. If you're focused on revenge, you'll be blind to the consequences of your actions, which can lead you to do impulsive things. In its mildest form revenge is telling a white lie, and in its most devastating form it can lead to murder.

To heal your desire for revenge, ask, "How important is it for me to be right? What benefit do I believe will come from 'teaching someone a lesson'?"

Victimization. Vulnerable people who don't have the means to defend themselves from an attack, such as children, can be considered true victims. Being the target of fraud, a physical attack, or bullying by an individual or a group makes someone a victim. But some people see themselves as victims just because their unevolved egos have taken offense. Self-identified victims won't take responsibility for their difficulties even if they're capable of solving their own problems.

Watch out, because your ego can imprison you in the perception that you're a victim. It's hard to see the good in your life or create anything when you're in this mode, and you often go to great lengths to solicit other people's affirmation that you are a victim. Do your best to reframe the way you see any past relationships that left you feeling hurt. What can you do to move on in your mind? It is a choice. You have the ability to live the life that you want. Someone else doesn't make you miserable. You make yourself miserable. Make the empowered choice!

The Voice of the Ego

Look for signs of the ego by its tone. It can be whiny, complaining, tense, intimidating, condescending, persuasive, or angry. The ego may speak with self-righteous authority. Actions that could move a career path forward, for instance, are dismissed. The ego says, "I'm above that; it's a waste of time." Actions that could take a relationship to the next level are avoided. The ego says, "I'm waiting for someone better to come along."

You will be able to resist the voice of the ego once you realize that everything an unevolved ego says and suggests makes you feel inadequate, unhappy, or afraid. The ego will naturally anticipate a terrible outcome. It says, "He must be having an affair as he hasn't replied to my text," sending you into a spiral of doubt and mistrust that can only damage your relationship. It says, "I won't have enough money for rent," draining your energy as you imagine living in an undesirable place—or, worse still, being homeless and alone. It says, "She didn't reply to my e-mail; she's ignoring me," generating hurt and resentment in you instead of concern and patience for a friend. One of the primary objectives of the unevolved ego is to control others, so it may cause you to be cold and aloof if you're not getting what you want. Its goal for you is to make others feel bad by withdrawing approval, projecting guilt, and laying blame on them.

If you are about to break free from a limiting pattern, your ego may say, "Who do you think you are?" until its state is no longer threatened, because it has pushed you into a mindset of mediocrity, complacency, and unworthiness. When you feel critical of yourself and others, it is your ego at work. When you feel the need to blame someone or beat yourself up for something that went wrong, that is your ego. This inner voice, which makes comparisons and judgments, contributes nothing to your process of creating a great life. The ego believes it is always right, and its arrogance prevents you from taking the necessary action to achieve what you truly want. Being aware of the traits of the ego is the first step in encouraging it to evolve. Keep checking in with yourself to see if the voice of your ego is compelling you to act against your higher nature.

Six Simple Steps to a Healthy Ego

A healthy ego comes from a sense of self that is derived from your higher awareness. When your ego is healthy and balanced, you feel calm and connected to Spirit, to your higher self, and to others, but detached from turbulent emotions. As the urgings of the ego subside, your perceptions of others and of your own actions and motivations gain clarity.

When the ego is in charge of you during a conversation, for example, it is hard to listen and be receptive to the truth of the interaction. As the ego drops away, however—as it will when you connect to your higher self and draw insights from its wisdom—defensiveness stops and compassion replaces misunderstandings. If you can listen fully to what someone else says without jumping to a conclusion, you may learn something valuable about that person and unearth your core beliefs.

Freed from the tyranny of a controlling ego, you'll be able to see you've been living a story created *by* your ego and that this story repeats itself in different parts of your life, always resulting in an ending that your higher nature does not want. As you change your story and take new actions, your ego evolves and its effects are replaced by confidence and peace.

Here are the six steps to move the ego toward higher awareness. Don't worry about forgetting specific details of the story you are about to write in these six steps, as you can do this exercise as often as needed. Its purpose is to reveal and remove energy blockages in your mind that will lead you to a healthier view of your life and relationships. If you use this tool on a daily basis, it can bring you a lot of inner peace.

Step 1: Empty your mind. Set the intention to free up room in your head so you can be more creative and focused. Get out your Miracle Journal and set a timer for five minutes. Write a description of anything bothering you today. The things that are troubling you could have happened an hour ago or ten years ago. No matter what comes into your mind, write about it.

Step 2: Write down your old story. The ego has a story, the details of which may change in different situations, but if you look carefully, you'll see a theme running through many of the things you've experienced. Is yours a story of melodrama, loss, betrayal, heartache, prejudice, fear, failure, reinvention, being the black sheep of the family, being misunderstood, being unloved and unlovable, being unfairly accused, being rich and alone, or being poor and invisible? Write a one-page summary of your life story that includes your childhood and a description of your life today.

Step 3: Review your old story. Reviewing will help you regain control of your mind, your life, and your career. Answer these questions in your Miracle Journal:

- "What is the main theme of my story?"
- "Given that I could choose any theme, why did I choose this theme?"
- "Why do I see my story this way?"

Step 4: Find the motivation behind your old story. In investigating motivation, you'll find the limiting beliefs that have kept you stuck in a pattern of recreating unwanted circumstances in your life. What comfort do you get from sharing your painful stories from the past? Is the story you share accurate or do you adapt the details depending on whom you are sharing it with? Did you tell your story in a certain way to make an emotional connection with someone else that you didn't think you could have had otherwise?

Step 5: Reframe your old story. Shine a positive light on your old story. Write out a one-page outline of a new story using the same facts. For example, in Daniel's old story he said, "My father bought me a secondhand bike for Christmas because he thought I didn't deserve a new one, and I felt ashamed around my friends who got brand-new bikes." He rewrote his story: "My dad got me a bike and stayed up all night to fix it, because he wanted it to be awesome. I see how much he loved me."

When you can see the good in your life, it's a sign that your ego has evolved. Ideas like, "The other shoe will drop," "Things will fall apart," and "Hardship lies ahead" are figments of your imagination. Why fuel your imagination with fear when you can fuel it with a positive emotion?

Being willing to view circumstances from a new perspective will ignite a flame of gratitude in your heart. You may have a sense that you're regaining control of your time, energy, and resources. With a new perspective, you can gain the momentum you need to fulfill your vision. There will be room to focus on the bigger picture that Spirit has for you and to see it clearly, once your ego is no longer standing in your way.

Step 6: Invite your higher nature to help your ego evolve. Your energy is constantly evolving, and it can express itself as more abundance, love, and life or contract and see the world filled with lack, pain, and loss. You may have come to believe that the dreams you have are farfetched, because past events in your life seem to have demonstrated that. Here is your opportunity to explore and believe even more deeply that your vision for your life is serving a spiritual purpose. Ask yourself:

- "If money and status were not required to lead the life I want, what would I do with my days?"
- "If nothing could go wrong and I could not be hurt or rejected, what would I give a go?"
- "If I were to demonstrate one of these ideas today, what is a first step I can take to set it in motion?"

After their egos have evolved, many people feel a surprising sense of emptiness or detachment. This may be uncomfortable if you've had a lot of chaos, struggle, and drama in your life up till now. You may have the feeling that something isn't right. But please do not be thrown off course by this sensation, as it will pass. You must be vigilant not to slip back into the familiar territory of your ego. Question the voice of the ego. The more you question its motives, the less power it will have over you. Soon you'll stop trying to please others. You'll no longer care what others think of you. You'll be able to express yourself authentically. This is how miracles are created.

What we authentically want for our lives is subjective. Therefore, remember always to seek your own truth and lead the life you genuinely want to live!

Embracing Your Truth

You want what you want for a reason. Go inward to discover this truth. It is not selfish to want. Wanting is your soul's desire seeking creative expression. It doesn't matter what people think of your desires; it only matters that they are aligned with what your soul intends. Reminding yourself of your higher intentions on a daily basis will help you avoid being swayed by the fears and negativity of your ego or the people around you. If the judgment of a loved one triggers doubt or anxiety within you, release your need for this individual's approval. Once you stop seeking approval, you'll discover an inner motivation that reinforces your certainty that you have the right to a beautiful life.

Self-discovery takes time. It's imperative that you keep peeling back the layers of your motivations to better understand the drive of your ego. The evolution of your ego expands awareness of your heart's desire and the ability to live into it. You are the guardian of your vision. To be the best advocate for yourself, focus on your vision. Imagine the good it will do for you and others. When you can express the purity of your vision from a standpoint of compassion, many people will resonate wholeheartedly with you and your purpose. Open your heart to connect to your excitement. Then talk about your vision. Express kindness. Smile. Soften your eyes. Let yourself be seen. In this way, you'll build trust one heart at a time.

6

RULE 6: **Believe in Your Ability**

What am I capable of achieving if
I trust my own guidance?

A heartfelt desire is a sign that you already have within you the seed of the skill you need to accomplish a goal. The only thing that stands in your way of becoming successful is your lack of belief in your ability. Without belief, you'll give up when the going gets tough. With it, you'll stay the course no matter what. Even if your ego is evolved and you have developed an authentic vision, if you don't believe in yourself, you won't be able to see your vision through.

If there's something you want to do, you can do it. Your inner guidance will show you the way. It doesn't matter if you're the only one who perceives your ability or thinks you have a shot at success. For a big miracle to occur, you must give yourself permission to follow through on what your heart desires. If your vision of what you want is not purely for selfish gain and won't cause pain or damage to others, then, spiritually speaking, it's perfectly acceptable and honorable to pursue it. The negative outlook of others—their criticism, doubt, ridicule, rejection, or lack of support—is not a reason for you to push aside your heartfelt dreams.

Belief is very powerful. It can make miracles happen in your life.

The Power of Belief

Being able to clearly see what you're aiming for and believing that it's possible to achieve lead to taking action. Years ago, my friend Zoe was an associate editor at a large book publisher. Her vision at the time was to become a full editor, but she wasn't sure how to make it happen. She asked her boss what it would take to be promoted. He gave her an assignment that she was certain he thought she'd fail at: to acquire twelve books in one year. Because her desire was strong, she was willing to give it a go and test her ability, although acquiring books for the company wasn't in her job description.

Zoe sat down with a pen and legal pad to list possible ideas for acquisition. She had recently learned to meditate and found it increased her ability to focus, so she first centered herself by taking some deep breaths. Once she felt grounded and connected to Spirit, she asked for support in coming up with twelve great ideas. As ideas came to her, she wrote them down. Then she set about finding projects that matched her ideas.

Zoe had already made up her mind that her strategy was going to work, because she believed in her ability as an editor. During each phone call she had with authors or agents from then on, Zoe presented her ideas and asked for any book proposals they'd like to show her. Not every phone call resulted in the acquisition of a book, but the totality of her actions during the very first month that she employed this strategy led to a lot of interesting new-project submissions, several of which her editorial director permitted her to acquire for the company. Within twelve months she met the quota her boss had set for her. One of the books she acquired hit the *New York Times* bestseller list when it was published the following year. Afterward, her career took off.

At the time Zoe's boss gave her the assignment, she could have been disheartened by its magnitude or found herself hung up on the details of how she would succeed; instead, she saw it as an opportunity to demonstrate her ability—and to have an adventure. She felt she was being given permission to try to succeed. When she looks back on it now, it's the clarity of purpose she had on the day she drafted her first twelve acquisition ideas that she remembers most vividly as the key to her big miracle.

Soon after her success, a friendly colleague at another publishing company called Zoe for moral support. She had been given the assignment to meet a similar quota and feared it would prove impossible. When Zoe told her friend how she'd achieved twelve acquisitions in a short span, her friend's mind opened to the possibility. The friend's belief in her own ability was strengthened sufficiently, which allowed her to overcome her doubts and take action. When they next spoke, Zoe's friend happily reported that she had gotten the assignment done, and "it wasn't as difficult as she imagined."

Belief in your ability can translate to all areas of your life. If you have a desire to run a marathon, become a certified yoga instructor, heal a misunderstanding in a friendship, master your finances, or buy your dream home, you can do it. Your belief that it's possible for you is the starting point to satisfying your heart's desire. If you believe you don't have the skill set to do something or that it isn't possible for some other reason, you won't be willing to do what needs to be done to achieve your goals. You won't even leave the starting gate or choose to invest any energy in it. Fortunately, you don't need to know how to do something perfectly to begin working toward a goal. Begin by believing that you have the ability to learn, and then show up and do the right and necessary things when the time comes. Believe in the person you are and in the rightness of your desire, and others will start believing in you too and lending you their support.

How will you know the right things to do? Talk to others who have successfully walked a path before you. Ask them how they did it. Take a course. Carefully read the autobiographies of people who've had success in accomplishing goals similar to yours: couples with successful long-term relationships, leaders in your industry, and athletes who've done incredible things, such as climbing Mt. Everest. Look for clues in their stories to the kind of things you can implement to achieve your goals.

Search for commonalities between these successful people, and then think about how you can apply the characteristics you've identified to your own situation. Also review your own past successes to see what you have done right. Could those same steps and approaches help you achieve what you're envisioning now?

Spend fifteen minutes every night writing in your Miracle Journal about things you've done to move toward the miracle you're envisioning for yourself. Use this time for positive reflection and self-reinforcement. Pray for guidance from Spirit about the places where you still feel stuck.

Getting specific about the skills you need to fulfill your vision and making the choice to develop them will help remove any obstacles to your belief in the possibility of success. After that, reinforce your belief by feeding your mind with positive visualizations about your success on a daily basis. Use the Center, Ground, and Connect Meditation (see p. 23) frequently to fortify your faith in yourself. Steadfast belief will translate into ability.

When you face an obstacle or feel overwhelmed by doubt, stepping away from your work for an hour, setting a timer, and journaling about all the things that are upsetting you can disrupt a negative thought process. You may find it beneficial to imagine sitting beneath a shower of golden light that resembles a waterfall and letting it cleanse your mind. If you're passionate about your purpose, you'll find that you have the willingness and stamina to get through your internal blocks. But you must be vigilant about resolving, releasing, and forgiving past resentments, as these can distract you from doing what needs to get done to reach your miracle.

Be mindful and do your best to make good choices. Check in with your emotional state on a consistent basis and align with Spirit to make sure you're centered. Make the decision that you deserve success, love, health, and happiness. Believe that the tools you need to create your miracle already exist within you and then hone them as you take the necessary steps to fulfill your vision. If you're serious about wanting to achieve the desired vision for your life, you must believe in yourself—and developing your capability to do something well through consistent practice is key.

The History of Your Negative Beliefs

As long as you expect a negative outcome, your subconscious mind will continue trying to find experiences in your memory to match and reinforce your limiting beliefs about yourself. To increase your belief in your abilities and your chances for success and happiness, you must examine and overcome self-denigrating ideas. If you review your history, you should be able to identify recurring negative patterns of belief, such as:

- "I am not smart enough."
- "I am not attractive enough."
- "I don't know the right people."
- "I am not funny enough."
- "I am a bad/undeserving person."
- "Nobody like me stands a chance."

These ideas have their origins in our negative or traumatic life experiences. It is therefore important to search out when in the past you would have formed such beliefs.

A Time Line of Life Events

In your Miracle Journal, write a time line of major negative events that occurred from the day you were born to the present day. For example, your parents divorced when you were eight years old, your best friend died in a car accident when you were sixteen years old, you were fired from your first job when you were twenty, and so on. Go all the way back to your earliest memories.

You may find that your memories are not revealed in chronological order, because the most traumatic memories are the ones that typically come to mind first. Some significant events may be buried deep within your subconscious and will only rise to consciousness when you make a request to recall them. Center, ground, connect, and ask Spirit for support.

To fill in the gaps, it may also be useful to review occasions in the past when you didn't demonstrate faith or confidence in your abilities and experienced the pain of failure due to your personal inaction. Letting yourself down may have been extremely disheartening, but you can learn from it now. Be patient with yourself as you fill in the gaps on your time line of life events. This exercise of reviewing your life can bring up a lot of intense emotions.

After your basic time line is established, make a note of the primary feeling associated with each event. For example, you were fired from a job and you felt shame, your girlfriend broke up with you and you felt heartbreak, or you accrued a large debt and felt fear. Once you have a list of at least ten events and have uncovered the emotions associated with them, look for the similarities both in the events and how you felt about the events.

Look for a pattern of recurring painful or traumatic events. Until you clear the pattern, the energy from those events will sit stagnating in your energy field. Your subconscious mind will lead you to keep recreating similar events, so you can try to make sense of why they happened. To accelerate your success, it's imperative to disrupt negative patterns of thought and emotion.

Use the list you compiled as a tool to separate your emotions from the objective facts of what occurred. For instance, an objective fact might be that you offered up an idea at work and were shot down. Your emotion was embarrassment. But on twenty similar occasions everything went well and you felt accomplished and appreciated. This will help you gain a clearer perspective on what happened and diffuse your painful emotions and negative beliefs about yourself.

The soul constantly reaches for something more expansive in our lives. We were born to grow. When we are inspired to take action, we need to be ready to follow through, which we can only do if our energy fields are clear and our minds are open. Reviewing past events and emotional triggers helps us to clear our energy field and restore a foundation of belief and confidence.

It's imperative, every time you feel doubt arising, that you ground yourself in the present moment, turn inward, and find your spiritual center. Let your soul guide you to the truth of who you are and what's possible. As soon as you notice yourself feeling incapable of doing what needs to get done to achieve your miracle, ask yourself, "What can I do today?" Then write down three action steps followed by three character strengths you need to develop to get those things done. Keep focusing on your positive traits and refining your action steps. Everything positive you discover in yourself, from patience and generosity to optimism, can be built upon to manifest your dreams.

When you make the decision—and it is a decision—that you're able to do whatever you set your mind to, you'll meet every day with new appreciation. Instead of groaning when you wake up, anticipating the worst, you'll perceive life in a different way—as an adventure! When this started happening for me, I found I had so much energy that I would wake up naturally without an alarm clock.

Over time, this is how you'll close the gap between what you can do now and what you need to be able to do, until you can do everything necessary for success.

Create a Foundation of Belief

Those activities you love doing—the ones that give you joy and increase your energy—are an expression of your spirit. Often, they are activities you have loved from a young age, but never pursued fully, usually because of a lack of belief in yourself. But if you feel a love for something and want to do it, you can always improve your ability. The key is practice. The more you do, the more you'll believe in your ability.

If you want to do something, you can. But you must not let anyone dissuade you from doing what you love. I can attest to how much time can be wasted if you stop following your heart. I can speak to this personally. When I was four years old, I fashioned a cardboard box so it looked like a TV, climbed inside it, and pretended I was on camera. It's one of my happiest childhood memories. In elementary school, I was always cast as the lead in school plays. I loved being on stage. But then once when I was performing, I got laughed at and was told I was no good. It rocked my belief in myself. By high school, I had become extremely self-conscious and stopped performing. I envied my friends who went to the famous British performing arts school for youth, the Sylvia Young Theater School. When I started seeing them regularly appearing on TV, I became sure that I could not act. Not believing I could become a professional actor, I chose to give up on performing. It wasn't until I turned forty that I felt brave enough to once again listen to my heart and actively develop my skills as a performer.

My husband introduced me to his teacher, acting coach Howard Fine. I enrolled at his studio, while continuing to run my coaching business, with the goal of improving my public speaking on stage. Early on in the course I volunteered for an exercise, stepped confidently onto the stage, and did an emotional recall practice. It did not go well. Howard pointed out where I went wrong, and I felt terribly embarrassed. I couldn't connect to the depth of emotion required in the exercise, because I was numb from suppressing painful memories that I'd been unaware of. I could also see how it had been holding me back from advancing in my career.

That night I went home and practiced the exercise alone. I discovered that a huge amount of shame was blocking my potential, shame that began when I'd been laughed at on stage and snubbed when I was enthusiastic and sharing my heart with people I cared about. Before the next class, I put a great deal of effort into preparation, and I made a big improvement. I had a new goal: to make it into Howard's master class. The support of my classmates and Howard's mentorship gave me an opportunity to feel safe enough to have a breakthrough.

I learned the necessity of adopting a neutral mind to be able to receive the constructive feedback—what actors call "notes"—I was given. Instead of taking Howard's notes personally, I was able to step away and work them, without allowing them to trigger any feelings of shame or worthlessness in me. Eventually, I achieved my goal of getting into Howard's master class. If you can focus on doing any skill to the best of your ability without needing to be liked or approved of, you'll improve. The more you practice, the more you'll improve. You can train yourself to do just about anything, given enough time.

Taking an acting class has been invaluable for my business, especially when I am giving a speech or making a media appearance. Every time I go to speak on stage or appear as a guest on a radio interview, I notice that I no longer feel fear. The stage feels like home. My confidence allows me to be fully present with my message and convey my belief in what I'm saying to my audience. Doing so has given a sense of significance to my life.

When you tell others with conviction what you'll achieve, yet there's no solid core to back it up, your belief is empty. You must develop a solid core of belief within you; otherwise you'll feel as though achieving your vision isn't possible, or worse, that you're a fraud. Be a person who is okay with learning. Seek out people who are doing what you want to do. Watch and listen to them. They'll be your proof that it's possible to find love, make more money, ski a diamond run, or reach your ideal weight. You don't have to say affirmations. Another person can be a role model and living affirmation for you.

Never forget that achieving your desires requires preparation. Anything is possible if you develop skills to support yourself in realizing your vision. You can transform an empty belief into something real that gives you a rock-solid footing. A fantasy is something that you never intend to make real, whereas a vision generated by your higher self in connection with Spirit and fueled by your heartfelt desire can become a reality. Absolutely. Without doubt. You simply must be realistic about whatever is required to close the gap between where you are now and your goals.

Tim Ferriss is the first American to hold a Guinness World Record in tango dancing. He went from his first Argentine tango class to the semifinals of the world championship in Buenos Aires in about six months. In his blog, "The Four-Hour Work Week," he shared that he had no special predisposition for dancing the tango. He advanced quickly because he was methodical.[1]

Make an honest evaluation of your ability to achieve your intended goals. Ask:

- "What are my strengths?"
- "What are my stretches?"
- "Do I need to invest in studying some more? If yes, what do I need to study?"
- "How much do I need to practice before I'll believe fully in my ability?"

Your willingness to learn will bring out the natural abilities you possess. As you keep practicing the skills you need to manifest a big miracle, your belief in your abilities will be strengthened, as will your emotional resilience. Every time you feel you've failed or your mind tells you that you aren't good enough, detach and recommit to building your skills.

The best yoga teachers have trained for more than five hundred hours and continue to study as well as teach. World-class teachers know the importance of having a student's mind. They do not believe they are experts and therefore above learning. They know they'll benefit from careful observation followed by thoughtful application of the key ideas they are learning. Ask yourself:

- "What is my soul calling me to do that I am not creating space for in my life?"
- "What would I love to do, but believe is a waste of my time and money because I think I'm not capable of pulling it off?"

- "How many hours of study would be necessary to get good at this?"
- "Would I be willing to put in those hours?"

The Voice of the Inner Critic

The major obstacle to belief in yourself is the voice of the inner critic. The good news is the voice of your inner critic has several distinctive traits that you can learn to recognize—and thus shut down. First, the voice of the inner critic is relentlessly judgmental. It will always make you feel you've done something wrong or that there's something wrong with you. It will belittle you and ridicule your lack of ability. It will teach you to resent others and make you angry and insecure. It will terrify and paralyze you, and it will never stop complaining and criticizing. It will tell you to blame others. It will tell you that you can't. It will tell you to give up. It will make your heart heavy, create an ache in the pit of your stomach, and cause stress in your body.

If you grew up in an environment that was not emotionally supportive of your dreams or where you were constantly told to "face reality," you may have developed guilt about your aspirations. It's common for people whose talents are different from those of their family members to be treated as though they're misbehaving or being irresponsible. A family of police or lawyers may not understand a child whose talent is sculpting or ballroom dancing. A family of artists or writers may not understand why a child would want to become a police officer or lawyer. If you're that child, over the years your attempts to fit in at the expense of your dreams may have led to despondency. You may have unconsciously taken on the beliefs of those around you. Every time your soul nudges you to take another step toward your vision, your inner critic quickly interjects, "You are going to fail. You're not cut out for it. You'll go broke. You'll hurt your family. You're being irresponsible and selfish. You don't have what it takes."

You'll know your inner critic is succeeding if you feel constant tension and anxiety or obsess over negative thoughts. When you have a strong relationship with your inner critic, it will leave you feeling terribly drained and lacking in inspiration. In time, your inner critic will even persuade you that your visions are ridiculous and a waste of your effort.

The goal of the inner critic is to shame you and drive you into a state of humiliation and embarrassment. The critic wants to make you feel small and unworthy. Its motivation is to crush your inspiration and rob you of your belief in your abilities. It wants your enthusiasm to wane quickly. You can be sure that your inner critic is talking to you if every time you read or hear about others' success stories, you think, *That's them, not me. They managed to do it against the odds, but I can't. Even if I could, it would be irresponsible. My parents wouldn't approve. They're probably right.* Even though your heart skips a beat with excitement at the possibility that you could do something you love, your inner critic wants you always to assume that there's no point in reaching for success.

To break the spell of the critic, you'll have to muster up great inner strength and courage and then send the critic away. If you stand up to the inner critic, it may put up a fight and become hostile, trying forcefully to shame you or prove that you're a worthless loser. It's imperative that you ignore this voice and never stop doing all you can to strengthen your belief in your ability. Refocus on your vision, and your talents will prevail.

Counter your inner critic with an inner cheerleader. Ask yourself, "Why do I lack belief in myself and my abilities?" Write down as many reasons as possible. Read your list carefully. What truth is there in this list? If there's any truth to it, what can you do now to create a different outcome for your life? If you decide that you don't have the ability to succeed, you won't have the ability to succeed. If you have zero evidence of success in your life, let today be your turning point. Decide to go out and create some.

In time, once you're peaceful inside, others' negative judgments, rants, or gossip will no longer upset or paralyze you. You'll find yourself bouncing back faster and faster from rejection and malice. You'll no longer feel the need to engage with those people or defend yourself, because you'll know the truth—that you are capable, deserving, lovable, and on a spiritual path that is beyond their pettiness.

Belief in your ability is what enables you to see your vision through. Disbelief or a lack of confidence in your ability to do what is necessary is a major obstacle to manifesting your vision. There are two main ways disbelief shows up in our lives. The first is through the voice of your inner critic, which regurgitates criticism that you have adopted as true. The second is through people who are critical or make it their purpose to point out your lack of ability—the sources of your inner critic. Disengage from critical people as soon as you recognize them for what they are.

Naysayers come in different forms, but they share the conviction that you do not have what it takes to achieve your dreams. They may outright say that you lack talent or are stupid or predict that you will never amount to anything in the area of success you desire. Take this and use it as rocket fuel to break through the barrier of your inner critic. If you are very empathetic and find yourself absorbing other people's words into your energy field, it means you also have the ability to be a great inspiration to others that living your dreams is possible. The most ignorant people will tell you that you'll fail because of your race, your gender, your sexual orientation, or your religion. You must not believe any of them.

Sir Sidney Poitier was the first African American to win an Academy Award for Best Actor, in 1963, and in 2009 he received the Presidential Medal of Freedom, the highest civilian honor in the United States. He was raised on a farm in the Bahamas. When he started out as an actor back in the 1950s, he did not have any social connections or money that would help him get ahead. After his first audition, the casting director told Poitier, "Why don't you stop wasting people's time and go out and become a dishwasher or something?" Because he believed in his abilities and in the possibility of achieving success in film, he ignored this naysayer.[2]

Poitier has lived an amazing life. Because he continued on his path, he became famous and was able to draw attention to civil rights issues, inspiring millions with his poise and grace. Grace is a sign that Spirit is moving through someone. As you live your life to the best of your ability, expressing your gifts and talents, Spirit will use you as a spiritual vehicle to transfer them to others.

The Voice of Inner Guidance

Actor Chris Pratt, star of *Guardians of the Galaxy* and *Jurassic World*, shared an inspiring post on his Instagram account:

> Fifteen years ago I felt the same passion I feel today, but I had very little opportunity. I had to hustle hard and go hungry. I had to eat sardines and figure out how to get gas money. And I never had a plan B. I never stopped believing. Ever. Don't give up. Apply constant pressure for as long as it takes. It will break before you do. Go get it.[3]

Inner guidance is always present. At first it may not seem so, but it is there. We carry a lot of competing voices in our heads, such as the voices of our family and our culture and, of course, the inner critic. It can be hard to hear the voice of inner guidance amid so much noise. Learning to single it out from the chatter is a process of discovery. Although at first it may seem quiet to you, as soon as you stop inviting the critics to the inner room of your mind, you'll be able to hear it loud and clear. Listen for it. You'll know it when you've heard it, because it feels calm, loving, and grounded. If you deliberately build a strong, heartfelt relationship with the voice of your inner guidance, you'll discover the belief you need to make it through adversity until you attain your goals. No obstacle will hold you back.

Even if you're lucky enough to be surrounded by people who are incredibly optimistic about your potential, belief in your success must start with you and your connection to your inner voice of guidance. Several years ago I had a wonderful mentor in Los Angeles who taught me much about success and balancing the personal and the professional for a fulfilling life. Witty, practical, and brilliant, she simplified many things for me that I'd long found difficult to understand. I diligently implemented her advice, and she helped me to quintuple my income in a single year. I am incredibly grateful to have found her, and to this day I believe she was an angel sent to guide me. Even so, I knew I had to trust the voice of my inner guidance more than hers when the two were at odds.

After several months of speaking to my mentor almost daily, a very strong instinct told me that I needed to relocate to Miami. The feeling got so intense that I felt my heart was going to burst out of my chest, and the sensation just wouldn't go away. Within days of being guided to make this change, I moved with my husband and son to the Sunshine State. My mentor insisted that I was making a big mistake and then stopped talking to me because I was taking an action with which she disagreed. I was devastated, as I valued her opinion greatly. Despite losing her approval, I knew I had to trust my inner guidance.

At first when Nick and I arrived in Miami, I wondered if we did in fact make a mistake. We had nowhere to live and no plan for how to make a living locally, yet miracle upon miracle happened. We swiftly found a gorgeous home to rent right on the ocean. I then met a fantastic music producer who helped me create an online program in which many people participated and that got them—and me—great results. I also hosted a number of live workshops from which I gained wonderful clients I would never have met if I hadn't moved to Miami and done those events. When I returned to Los Angeles nine months later, a number of people in my social circles assumed I was coming back because I'd made a mistake. They didn't know that my business network had expanded considerably in Miami and was now more profitable than ever.

From that experience, I've learned to trust that if I'm guided to live somewhere or do something specific, it may be for a reason that I am not yet aware of. I must take the leap and trust that Spirit has a plan. I do this by asking Spirit who I must reach out to when I arrive in a new place. This may mean, based on the voice of my inner guidance, I pick up the phone and call someone to whom I've never spoken before. I am attentive to the next steps being revealed. It's important to live your life without regrets. If you have a calling and don't act upon it, you'll never know what opportunities you've missed. You could end up with nagging disappointment that taints your other experiences.

Muster the courage to believe in your inner guidance. Spirit moves in mysterious ways. Let's say you follow your inner guidance tomorrow and things don't work out as hoped in the short term. Ten or fifteen years from now you may learn that there was a hidden purpose to that step in your journey. Maybe you met someone you needed to know. Maybe you learned a skill. Maybe you healed in some manner. Maybe your presence impacted someone else in a beneficial way. There's a lesson for you in instances like these that can help you break through a lack of belief.

The voice of your inner guidance has several distinctive traits that you can learn to recognize. This voice is calming. No matter what type of chaos or difficulty is occurring in your life, the voice will reassure you that all is well. It offers a nuanced understanding of your circumstances. It will remind you that there's a purpose to the pain you're experiencing. If you pay attention to it, the voice of inner guidance will give you insights into how best to move forward—what behaviors to abandon and what new paths to take. It will often leave you feeling uplifted, with the sense that anything is possible and life is wonderful. It will also give you repeated confirmation that you're going to have a successful outcome.

This voice is loving, kind, supportive, and nonintrusive. It will never focus on what you're doing wrong. In a gentle and matter-of-fact way, it will point out the things in your life that require closer examination, usually by presenting you with a question upon which to reflect. The voice may say to you, "There's going to be a delay because another piece of information is needed or someone else needs to take an action before you can do your part." Or, without being harsh, it may point out another way of doing things, so that you don't have to wait to act. The voice of inner guidance is encouraging and patient. It can feel like a wise and loving parent, grandparent, or best friend. Since its source is Spirit, it will make you feel centered, grounded, and connected.

You'll know that your inner guidance is succeeding if you feel a sense of deep inner peace and gratitude for everything. You'll feel happy, light, and ready for miracles.

Use Visualization to Build Positive Belief

Your imagination is a powerful tool for building a foundation of strong belief in yourself. Of course, it can also produce fearful imagery that paralyzes you—so it's vital to continuously fuel your mind with positive imagery that inspires and uplifts your soul. After you've programmed your mind for love and abundance, you'll always have the inner strength to remain calm and follow through on your plans—even when challenged by naysayers or your inner critic.

It's best to do visualization on a consistent basis, ideally twice a day: first upon waking and again before going to sleep. Here's how to do it.

Visualizing the Future

Begin by closing your eyes to find your center. Bring your awareness to your heart. Then imagine yourself moving forward ten years into the future. Imagine that you have already achieved a key goal. What is it like to be the future you? Run through events and outcomes in your mind that you associate with achieving that goal. Visualize yourself at the center of those events and experience them as if they're happening in the present moment. Use your physical senses. Remember to assess what you're seeing, hearing, smelling, tasting, and touching.

Ask and then write in your Miracle Journal:

- *"How old am I?"*

- *"What do I look like?"*

- *"How am I dressed?"*

- *"Where do I live?"*

- *"Who are the loved ones in my life?"*

- *"Who do I spend time with?"*

- *"How do I feel about my achievements?"*

- *"What skills do I have?"*

- *"Have I won any awards?"*

- *"What am I paid for my expertise?"*

- *"Am I well known or a celebrity in my industry?"*

- *"What are my qualities?"*

- *"What is the state of my health?"*

- *"What do I do in my leisure time?"*

- *"Where have I traveled?"*

Once you have played out the details of the miracles you've enjoyed in your mind's eye, ask yourself:

- *"What are the ingredients of my life that make it fulfilling?"*

- *"What primary emotion supports my vision?"*

- *"How did my big miracle come about? What were the steps I took?"*

Next, get detail oriented about the steps required to arrive at your vision. Once you feel emotionally connected to your vision, add more details to build it out.

Then, take these details and turn them into small actions to make your vision a reality. This will guide you to your big miracles.

If you wanted to move abroad, let's say to a Caribbean island, you'd perhaps begin with research on the Internet followed by several vacations there before becoming a local resident. There's always a simple starting point, a practical step to take that's easily within reach. When you believe, you won't doubt your ability to take the steps Spirit reveals to you, and you'll do them willingly, even though you don't have evidence of your vision.

If you feel a sense of disbelief or hear the voice of your inner critic getting in the way of your visualization process, take a deep breath and then recommit your focus to seeing as many details of the scenes around you as possible. This is how to reinforce your vision of success and program your mind to believe that what you want is not only possible, but inevitable. In fact, you may have begun manifesting your big miracle—you just may not recognize that you're already in motion and on your way to the breakthroughs that will take you there.

Breaking Through Is a Creative Process

A writer can write, an actor can act, a singer can sing, an inventor can invent, a mother can take care of her newborn baby. Whatever your soul's calling, you have the seed of ability within you. You have to water that seed and, once it sprouts, use your time, energy, and focus to nurture it fully. You also have to be willing to do what it takes, whether that's a lot or a little, hard or easy for you, and no matter what others say.

You'll know you are ready for a breakthrough in reaching for your miracle, because every time you're faced with an obstacle, you'll keep moving through your resistance. There may be a time when an authority figure you respect pushes you in a way that feels oppressively critical.

The 2015 movie *Whiplash* demonstrates this phenomenon brilliantly.[4] Student drummer Andrew, played by Miles Teller, dreams of being the best drummer in the world. His music teacher, Fletcher, played by J. K. Simmons, is harsh and critical. If Andrew does something right, Fletcher does not compliment him. He is expected to do it right. If he is the slightest bit out of rhythm, however, Fletcher hurls verbal abuse at him.

Everyone in Andrew's class fears Fletcher, but Andrew fights back. He stands up for himself, yet he doesn't stop practicing the drums. He practices with even more vigor. He channels his energy into developing mental toughness. He's so clear about his goals that he views the sacrifices he makes as necessary steps to make his dreams come true. Belief in your vision will help you rise to the occasion and meet the challenge.

On one hand, watching this movie, you could say that Fletcher is a bitter and narcissistic music teacher. On the other hand, you could say that it takes his pushing his students to their darkest places of shame and fear to get them to break through their barriers and shine. I agree with the second assessment. In the film, Fletcher helps his student become great. Andrew transcends the pressures Fletcher applies to him, while his classmates cave in. He is fueled by passion and focus to achieve his goals—and he does. He cultivates belief in himself.

Although the movie *Whiplash* isn't *overtly* spiritual, it is still spiritually resonant. Andrew's determined belief was that he had the ability to be the best drummer in the world. His big miracle was the solo piece he practiced over and over that led him to playing at Lincoln Center for an audience of thousands of people.

Do not internalize the fears and judgments of others and make them your own. Having a breakthrough is a creative process, so you must believe in your ability to survive it. With skill comes ability. Write down the skills you have. Commit to developing the required skills that you don't yet have. Put them into practice daily.

If you take action without judging yourself, the results will take care of themselves. Show up, be present, and do your best. If you didn't do your best on one occasion, forgive yourself and move on. Figure out what you need to do next to advance your vision, and then go out and do *that* as best you can. When you believe you can do things, you will.

7

RULE 7: Accept Responsibility

What am I resisting? Why?

Acceptance is the key to breaking through your resistance to the ultimate life you desire. Spirit is limitless power and wants to you have an abundant supply as well. When you overcome your resistance, you can plug into this energy source and create all manner of things. When you lack responsibility, it is difficult to be open to new ideas and opportunities that will add benefit to your life. Accepting responsibility for your choices means you can see your circumstances with new eyes and shift from feeling overwhelmed to being aligned, followed by the appropriate action. Difficult relationships and decisions become manageable. When you accept responsibility, you are no longer reacting to life and putting out fires. You are not praying for guidance in emergency after emergency. You are the artist painting the pictures you most want to live.

Take a moment to close your eyes and imagine what you'll create today. When you make creation a priority, you'll have the necessary energy that you need to handle the difficulties in your life. You'll find excellent solutions. Accepting responsibility is a powerful strategy to create your big miracle. It is a vital rule that enhances all the other rules.

Start with simple acts of accepting responsibility for your life, like flossing your teeth even if you feel tired, putting the dirty dishes in the dishwasher, and doing the laundry routinely so that you have enough clean clothes that you like wearing to choose from every day. Responsibility for these simple actions well equips you for bigger responsibilities. With friends it means you call them back when you said you would and you show up on time to social engagements, even if you think other people will be late. It doesn't matter what irresponsible people do. Never use other people's lack of responsibility to justify your behavior.

Accept responsibility for your relationships. This means setting good boundaries and making clear agreements. Toxic people may throw tantrums when you put a boundary in place, because their own boundaries have likely been crossed and they were never taught how to care for themselves emotionally. If a loved one reacts or a friend gets uppity when you state a boundary, have enough self-esteem and commitment to yourself to walk away instead of walking on eggshells or getting into an explosive fight.

You have the ability to express your emotions responsibly in your relationships. Perhaps you've been a high-drama person in the past. As you accept responsibility for yourself, your soul will no longer be willing to tolerate the energy of destructive and chaotic people. You'll find yourself saying no to them calmly or disengaging from their negativity and keeping your distance. If you've suffered from worry or anxiety, you'll find yourself becoming more relaxed and happier, like a different person, after accepting responsibility for how you feel. As you become more responsible, you'll find that successful people want to be around you. You'll receive invitations to fun events and be taken more seriously in your work.

In my role as a spiritual life coach, there are four main areas that people want to talk to me about: career, money, relationships, and health. These are overlapping. When you begin to accept responsibility in one area of your life, the other areas begin to improve too. You'll find that you have more energy available to you for self-improvement. Here's an example of what this looks like.

Let's say you take responsibility for your health. As your health improves, your energy level rises. Therefore you can invest more energy into your work and become more productive. You begin to earn more money and feel more fulfilled by your accomplishments. Because you feel less stress, you're uplifted and begin to enjoy your relationships more. It makes you happy when you can be present with friends, loved ones, and your significant other. If you were exhausted, you wouldn't have the same availability and openness. Accepting responsibility means you do not wait for a health crisis to pay attention to your body; instead, you pay attention regularly, as needed.

Let's say you accept responsibility to remove blocked energy with regard to your finances. As you boost your income, a weight is lifted off you, enabling you to work less and play more. Creating abundance gives you time to address parts of your life that you love to focus on, which formerly may have seemed like a luxury, such as creativity, self-care, and a daily spiritual practice.

Accepting responsibility sets your mind free, because you know in your heart that no matter what anyone says, you've done your best. With a sense of freedom comes the miracle of living an unhindered life. You're grateful for your interactions with everyone, even people with difficult personalities, because you recognize interactions as opportunities to be of service and to model a better way of life.

Accepting responsibility begins by adjusting your own attitude first and being open-minded and present with others. Being attentive to their needs and visualizing from their point of view can help you build greater trust in your relationships.

Responsibility will bring you greater opportunities. As you take on more exciting roles in your life, for example, as a parent, teacher, mentor, service provider, or reliable friend, miracles will flow into your life, and your days will become richer than you ever imagined.

Spirit is everywhere! Our money, career, health, and relationships are a map of our internal reality and our energy. If we align with Spirit and accept responsibility for our lives, we are being proactive cocreators. We are energy, and Spirit is energy. If we express positive energy, then the patterns we see in our lives will be positive. If we see patterns in our lives that we don't like, we need to change the energy we're putting out. You always have choices about how to apply your energy. You simply need to know where to invest your energy. This is a creative process that each of us ultimately must master.

Reimagining Your Relationship with Spirit

Spirit is neither a parent nor a dictator. Spirit doesn't reject, abandon, or hurt us. Spirit is a partner and collaborator, a friendly supporter. When we begin to view ourselves as equally important to Spirit in the creation of our days and the shaping of our lives, then we become better spiritual vehicles.

Although people have certain desires, they often don't realize the responsibility that comes with asking for them. If you say, "I want to get married and have kids," and this scenario ensues, then you have to show up in the marriage and for your kids. There are consequences.

If you want to be famous, then you have to accept responsibility for having influence, such as being a good role model. People begin looking up to you. A pop star who says, "Drugs are cool," may influence a teenager to try cocaine. If you are misaligned with Spirit and act irresponsibly, you can lose your fame. Actor Mel Gibson, who was once everyone's favorite movie star, ruined his career by making sexist and anti-Semitic slurs and driving under the influence of alcohol. Although he later apologized, the consequences of his irresponsibility have left a shadow hanging over him.

If you want a lot of money in the bank, accept responsibility for managing it. Power comes with money. Apparently, nine out of ten lottery winners burn through their earnings in five years.[1] Those winners are not taking responsibility. If we aren't responsible, our finances will suffer. Money is not the problem; our behavior is. That's how energy works.

If you want optimum health, be responsible for your diet, hydration, exercise, sleep, and doing all the things that contribute to optimizing your well-being. Nobody else can care for your body in the same way you can. It is up to you to book your dental appointments, show up on your yoga mat or the treadmill, and drink at least eight glasses of water a day instead of four glasses of wine. Shirking responsibility won't lead to happiness or create good health.

People who get angry at Spirit rarely see the poor habits they themselves need to address. Spirit can only help us once we take an honest look at ourselves and the life choices we've made, such as the way we treat people, how we work, and our financial affairs. Spirit offers us loving guidance, yet because we have free will we have responsibility for the outcomes in our lives.

If you've been irresponsible for a long time in many areas of your life and you suddenly experience a spiritual awakening, resist the urge to fix everything at once. It's better in the long run to right the situation in increments, while holding a positive intention. Tiny steps can result in big miracles. If you've been haphazard in relationships and finances and neglected your health, it can be overwhelming when you decide to be responsible. You may be tempted to go back to your old ways when faced with the reality of coping with the people you have upset, the money you may owe, or the excess weight you want to lose. A gentle approach is required. Focus daily on strengthening your connection to Spirit, and you will find your circumstances steadily improving. When we seek an honest relationship with Spirit and ourselves, we can put the past behind us, whether our mistakes were small blips on life's radar screen or monumental breakdowns.

In your Miracle Journal, write about the new ways you're accepting responsibility and how good they feel. Write about the problems you need solutions for. You won't figure everything out in one session. This will be an ongoing process of healing, but it's well worth it. If you want to be a role model to others, the most valuable thing you can do is embody responsibility in all your actions. To do that, it helps to begin by forgiving yourself for what has already happened that cannot be changed and focus on how to move forward with integrity.

A spiritual awakening can happen suddenly or slowly. When it happens quickly, you will no longer be able to avoid your responsibility to creditors who are phoning you, for example. You may not be able yet to pay them what you want to make the pain of the debt go away entirely, but you can figure out an amount to offer that is responsible. You may have to reach out to several creditors from whom you borrowed money to set up realistic repayment plans that won't jeopardize your ability to support yourself and family. This may be necessary if you have dependents, such as children or elderly parents, relying on you. Behaving responsibly is how you can maintain your spiritually awake state.

Money comes and goes. If you put yourself in spiritual alignment, you'll be empowered to build a sacred relationship with your finances. You will come to see money as a tool that—when you act responsibly as its guardian—you can use to work miracles in your own life and the lives of others.

You may recognize where you dropped the ball in a friendship. If you're at fault, accept responsibility and apologize without making excuses before expecting a wounded or neglected individual to be super friendly. If you treated someone poorly in a romantic relationship and you want to get back together, make a sincere apology. Accept responsibility to safeguard your heart before reaching out, because you may not get back the love you're hoping for. If you don't want to be in a relationship anymore but feel bad about how things ended, accept responsibility for your part, but don't require forgiveness as a necessity for your future happiness. If you don't receive a warm response, don't make the person wrong; let it be. Just make sure that you act with integrity from this day forward. Make the decision to take care of managing all the outcomes created through your past actions. Understand, however, that it may take a while to heal, once you wake up to and thus feel the pain you've caused yourself and others through your past denial and irresponsibility.

It's beneficial to look for the hidden motivations that led to irresponsible behavior, which usually come from the ego. Make your request to Spirit and trust that the motive will be revealed to you gently so as not to stir up shame. Perhaps you must come to terms with the fact that you wanted something you didn't believe you were worthy of receiving. Perhaps you wanted love yet didn't truly believe yourself worthy. Perhaps you disliked your job or continued a relationship that was unfulfilling. If these things cause you pain, know that the shame does not represent Spirit, but your ego. Do your best to focus on what can improve your situation rather than on whatever seems lacking.

When you shift from being asleep to being awake, you'll experience feelings that were suppressed. Despite any pain, this is good. This means you're coming to terms with those areas in which you've lacked responsibility. It means you're healing and realigning with Spirit.

The Importance of Self-Love and Worthiness

Accepting responsibility can initially be overwhelming. Ultimately, the only way to move beyond that state is to be kind to yourself. Surrender your point of view to a higher perspective. In the eyes of Spirit, you're perfect. You are a miracle. As long as you remember that, you'll treat yourself with greater love and kindness. You'll find yourself drawn to responsibility without feeling as though you're missing out on something or being restricted. You'll also have the ability to be mindful going forward.

Ideally, now that you are accepting responsibility, you are showing up in everything you do and for everyone you know with an open mind and heart. In relationships that means listening for the needs and desires of others and imagining how you can bring joy and happiness to them. With regard to health, showing up means being grateful for your body and feeling awe for the incredible things it can do. You don't have to think about how you breathe or how your heart beats; they just do. It's a miracle. If you tune in to the miracles that already exist, you'll get into the space of creating miracles.

Choose awareness. Look for the bigger picture beyond the way a situation or event will affect you. Notice the subtle details of your reactions to others. Watch for when something sets you off and triggers annoyance within you. With awareness it's easier to course-correct. Listen for what's really being said, not what's being said on the surface. For example, in a relationship if someone says, "I'm fine," when the accompanying energy clearly demonstrates that's not so, address it. If someone is disgruntled and you pretend there's no issue, you might accidentally engage in behavior detrimental to your well-being by agreeing to do things that you don't want to do because that person's disapproval or rejection of you is unsettling. If the person won't take responsibility for his or her feelings by acknowledging the situation, take a step back. Taking responsibility for your self-worth also means not indulging other people's manipulative behaviors.

Own your truth. We don't always get what we want, but if we don't speak our mind, we likely won't get what we want anyway—or if we do, it won't be in the form that would be ideal for us. In a significant relationship, owning your truth could mean having a tough conversation. On a small scale, you may need to discuss where you want to eat. If you want Chinese food and your companion hates it, you must be willing to accommodate one another's tastes and build consensus, perhaps by taking turns choosing the food or eating separately. Wherever you and your companion decide to eat, whether calmly, passive-aggressively, or angrily, remember that you chose it. Don't pull faces and spoil your companion's meal when it's not your turn to pick the restaurant.

My husband loves NASCAR races, but the noise and crowds give me a headache. My refusal to attend NASCAR events doesn't mean I don't love him. It also doesn't mean that he should never go to the races in order to please me. It means his race day gives me an opportunity to go to the spa instead! We can do some things separately. The responsibility we share is to be truthful about our desires and figure out an alternate way to have fun and maintain our bond.

From a core of self-love and commitment to developing your sense of worthiness, you can act with open eyes, improving the choices you make and actions you take. That's empowerment. Stop trying to control others by placing stipulations on what you give, including your love. Release your expectations and take care of your needs yourself. As you do, past resentments will evaporate. This will lead you to have much more compassion for yourself and others and help you to maintain equanimity.

Accepting Responsibility for Your Finances

Money often gets blamed for the problems in our lives. *Money is the enemy,* we may think. If you feel this is the case, remember that money is an inanimate object. It's what we do with money that creates unwanted outcomes. The state of our finances reflects our life choices, so it is those choices that do good or cause harm, not the money itself. As accepting responsibility becomes the foundation of your behavior, you'll intuitively know the best things to do with your money—even if loved ones have a different opinion.

A dysfunctional relationship with money can be repaired by working from the inside out, as it is the nature of our thoughts and a general lack of mindfulness that lead us to make poor financial choices. Psychologically, money is a symbol of security, freedom, love, and power. Spiritually, it is a symbol of giving and receiving and the flow of energy in our lives—whether open or impeded. To transform the financial landscape of your life, you must diligently observe your spending patterns and try to understand your relationship with money. This will be your key to having an abundant bank balance and eliminating debt. Meditation and writing exercises can increase your awareness of your earning, spending, and saving habits. If you take responsibility, you'll have fewer money-related crises and conflicts.

When I've attended workshops on creating wealth and making your dreams come true, the thing I've heard other attendees share most frequently is their desire to earn a million dollars. It's as if the people expressing this hope think that as soon as they've brought in that million, all their problems will disappear, all their needs will be met, and their lives will be perfect. Why is one million the magic number? What will a million dollars specifically do to make life amazing?

When I turned twenty-one, I took a vacation with my friend Christina, who had a villa on the Mediterranean. She also had a chalet in Switzerland, a condo in Miami, and a multimillion-dollar home in one of the most affluent neighborhoods in London. Her closet was filled with the most recent season's designer clothes. She had a BMW convertible and access to a chauffeur if she didn't feel

like driving. She had signing privileges on her billionaire father's unlimited American Express charge card and never carried less than
$10,000 cash in her purse.

As we sat by the villa's spectacular pool, Christina looked troubled,
even though her eyes were covered by designer shades. I could sense
she was miserable. There was no shortage of people who wanted
to hang out with her. She got invited to every A-list event and was
treated as a VIP wherever we went, but she didn't care. This was the
life she was born into, and she didn't know anything else. We often
sat up until sunrise talking about the day's events, but one time, at
around 3 A.M. as we sat out under the starry night sky, she told me
she just wanted to feel happy.

"You've got everything. So many people would love to live your
life," I said encouragingly, trying to get her to see that her life was
truly amazing.

"I don't," she snapped back. I'd hit a nerve and wished I hadn't
said what I had. There was a long, uncomfortable silence. Then she
leaned over, reached inside her Chanel handbag, and pulled out a
small packet of white powder; she poured its contents on a glass
coffee table, separated it into line with the edge of a credit card, rolled
up a 1,000 franc note (worth approximately $100), and snorted a
couple of lines of the powder. She took a moment to feel the effects
of the cocaine and then held out the rolled-up banknote for me. Not
being a drug user myself, I did my best to decline as politely as possible.

Christina took another hit of coke, and my heart sank. This gorgeous young woman had everything going for her—resources, abundance, beauty—but it was not enough. She was using that rolled-up
bill to abuse herself. Symbolically she was saying, "Money, you are
worthless. I don't care about you. I don't need you. I hate you. You
make me miserable." She wasn't able to see that money was not the
thing making her sad.

The problem for my wealthy friend Christina was she was never taught to have a healthy relationship with money or with herself. Money was always there for her, but her parents were mostly absent from her daily life. She was sent to boarding school at a young age, and when we were teenagers her parents were rarely at home, as they were usually traveling. She craved the presence of loving parents. Money and the buying power that comes with it replaced them superficially, but it could never provide her love, no matter what she bought.

Becoming a millionaire does not bring us happiness. We bring ourselves happiness. In reality, we don't suddenly wake up one day and feel our lives are perfect because we've finally made a million. We aren't our bank balances or the amount of money we've made in our lives. We're human beings. We make a series of choices, and our finances reflect those choices.

You may imagine that your stress would be vastly reduced if you had a few more zeroes on your bank balance, but freedom is about more than how much money you can make and keep. It's about doing things because you want to rather than from a sense of obligation. Accepting responsibility for your true feelings in connection to your relationships and finances is a powerful way to reveal and release patterns that control your happiness—or lack of it. For example, you buy designer clothes to fit in with a particular group of friends, you stay at a hotel out of your price range to impress someone in a new romantic relationship, or you undercharge for your services when you are around people you don't think will value them. As you practice responsibility, Spirit will guide you to a better understanding of what will lead you to happiness. The more you study your finances, including both the way you handle money and the way you interact with people when you're exchanging money with them, you'll get to know yourself in a whole new way. This can set you free from compromising your core values.

If you're unhappy with any aspect of your relationship with money, you can change it now. You have the power within you to do that.

How to Form a Healthy Relationship with Money

Imagine that you were watching TV and saw on the news that twenty people had died in a plane crash. You'd probably feel a pang of shock and sadness before resuming your activities, right? But if those twenty people were members of your family and close friends, your feelings would be intensely different. The news would be devastating because of your intimacy with the people involved.

The same principle applies in other areas of our life. To shift the energy underlying the patterns in other areas, it helps if we can relate to the energy in a more tangible and intimate way. By putting a face to it, we gain insights that help us accept responsibility for the patterns. The energy of money is abstract, so we have to find a way to transform the image of it in our minds. That's what this exercise is designed to help you to do. Take this opportunity now to build a healthy relationship with money by asking the following questions. As you create a clear picture of what money means to you, you'll be able to identify the relationship you want to have with money and accept responsibility for it. Your new clarity will enable you to quickly and easily address imbalances in your life that are affecting your finances. You'll develop a new level of focus that helps you stay on track with your financial goals in a manner that feels harmonious to your soul.

Record your answers in your Miracle Journal:

- *"Do I have a love or hate relationship with money? Why?"*

- *"Am I indifferent toward money? If yes, why don't I care?"*

- *"Am I obsessed with money? If yes, why do I think money is my solution?"*

- *"Do I see the need to earn money as an obstacle to my happiness?"*

- *"How could money help me? What amount would help? Why?"*

- *"What is money's role in my life?"*

- *"What type of conversations do I typically have about money?"*

Then, finish these sentences:

- *"The relationship I want with money is ..."*

- *"The reason I want this relationship with money is ..."*

- *"My commitment to creating this relationship with money is ..."*

- *"The benefits I will experience are ..."*

Accepting Responsibility for Your Relationships

Love is the most amazing feeling. It's as if time stands still. There's no resistance or judgment. Love gives you the energy to create miracle upon miracle and bestow them upon others.

Love isn't for a few special people. Love doesn't choose one person and reject another. Love wouldn't blame someone for a broken heart. Love isn't cruel or manipulative. That is the ego. Love is a form of energy that's always accessible to you when you choose to center your energy in your heart and open up to your connection with Spirit.

A desire for love underlies many of the things we do in life, because love has the ability to inspire us and create happy memories we believed were impossible. My client Tim was feeling frustrated. He didn't believe he could get married and start a family until he was financially secure. He thought of love as a carrot dangling in front of his nose, just out of reach, because he wasn't farther along in his career. "If I could just make $500,000 this year . . . ," he said when we first met.

Over four years of coaching with me, Tim increased his income. During those years, he moved to a bigger home and purchased a flashier car, but remained single and unhappy. He was still sure that doubling his income once more would be the solution that made him feel his life was complete—and that only then would he be ready for the woman of his dreams.

I had Tim do an exercise in which you add up what you've made in total during your working life and then divide the amount by the number of years you've worked to find your average annual earning. Tim took his first job at sixteen and was now thirty-nine. He'd worked for twenty-four years, taking one year off. He was amazed to learn that he'd already made a million dollars, $1,137,800, to be exact. His average annual income was $47,408. He *had* already achieved his million-dollar goal! This insight was a turning point for him, because he realized that reaching a specific financial goal wasn't going to give him confirmation that he deserved to be in a loving relationship. He saw in that moment that if he changed his viewpoint about love, he could find love and share it with someone else.

Tim's relationship with money had become a distraction. He was constantly chasing money, and it was never enough when he got it, so he spent to relieve his disappointment. His relationship with money could be expressed by the phrases, "I don't trust you. You're going to leave me." As we dug deeper, we found that he felt the same way about women. When his childhood sweetheart had married his best friend, his heart was crushed. From then on, his motivation for success was proving she'd made a mistake and winning her back. On an energy level, this fantasy was blocking him from forming a lasting romantic relationship with anyone else. Tim finally saw that his drive to make a certain amount of money was to prove he was worthy of a loving relationship, that when he was in a relationship he lived beyond his means, and that as the relationship broke up he lost his drive and fell into a cycle of depression and inertia.

To heal and feel whole, seek the source of your feelings. By accepting responsibility for them, patterns that have held you back in your relationships will be revealed. Do the meditation exercise "How to Form a Healthy Relationship with Money" (see p. 159), substituting the word *love* for the word *money*, to help you perceive and clear your energy blocks.

Accepting Responsibility for Your Career

Meaningful work leads to a feeling of great satisfaction and a sense of purpose. If you're aligned spiritually, you're doing what you're destined to do, and this keeps you happily focused on your work. There are no chores or burdens in your career, as you understand that the work you do is not only generating income and fulfillment for you; it is also benefiting those around you.

Work is not a punishment. Work is not humiliating. Work is not keeping you from having fun. As you accept responsibility for creating a career path that you feel passionate in pursuing, doors will open for you, leading to flow and prosperity.

Growing up, I was friends with two brothers. One brother ended up on unemployment. He had an attitude of entitlement and believed that he shouldn't have to work for what he was given. The other brother believed in hard work. He understood that he could build a bright future for himself. He established several companies, one right after the other, and became a multimillionaire. His goal was to always take care of his staff, customers, friends, and family. He was very generous, but not flashy or wasteful with his money.

If you ever look at someone successful like the second brother and think, *He's successful because he came from money,* or look at someone like the first brother and think, *He's broke because he grew up in poverty,* you need to take another look. The circumstances we're born into are not the reason why we are rich or poor in the end. Regardless of your circumstances, you can overcome any challenge, whether it is a lack of finances, an abusive upbringing, a poor education, or a physical disability.

There is much evidence of this throughout history. At the Auschwitz concentration camp during World War II, Elie Wiesel was surrounded by murder and death on a daily basis and could easily have fallen into despair. He could have given up and succumbed to the psychological scars of the Holocaust. Yet he survived and went on to become a humanitarian, sell over 10 million copies of his book *Night,* and receive the Nobel Peace Prize. There are many other life stories of those who have overcome adversity and gone on to great achievement and wealth, because they found their connection to Spirit and understood that no one is their source for money, security, or opportunity. When you form a direct relationship with Spirit, you can create what you desire.

Abundance is accessible to us if we relinquish any underlying guilt that, in wanting and providing for ourselves, we are depriving someone else. The level of wealth we ultimately attain after overcoming any deficits in our circumstances at birth stems from our soul's essence and the different experiences we had when we were growing up. Some of those energy imprints are positive, others negative, and you can overcome the latter.

For example, Michael Edwards, a.k.a. Eddie the Eagle, dreamed of being an Olympian since he was six years old. He was riddled with knee problems as a child and wore leg braces. He also had poor eyesight and wore thick-rimmed glasses. In his working-class British family, his dad repeatedly shot down his vision of becoming an Olympian and urged him to become a plasterer. Edwards was obsessed by his vision and resisted his dad's plea to follow in his footsteps. He made it onto the British national ski team, but was rejected from the Olympic team. He didn't give up. Instead, he adapted his vision and chose the dangerous sport of ski jumping as a path to compete in the Olympics. Edwards said, "When I started competing, I was so broke that I had to tie my helmet with a piece of string." He leveraged his minimal resources and combined them with pure determination to make it to the 1988 Winter Olympics in Calgary, Canada. He won the hearts of the people and press. He became one of the biggest stories that year, inspiring and bringing joy to millions. In 2016 a movie, *Eddie the Eagle,* was made that tracked his journey from childhood to the realization of his dream.

Through examining your beliefs about work and uncovering the underlying limiting patterns of what you believe work and a career mean, you can free your mind and begin to live the life of your dreams without the energy of obligation. Do the meditation exercise

"How to Form a Healthy Relationship with Money" (see p. 159), substituting *my career* for *money*, to help you perceive and clear your energy blocks in this area of your life (skipping questions 4 and 5).

Accepting Responsibility for Your Health

Health is a miracle. Health gives you the ability to have a wonderful life. Health is your legs carrying you up a mountain trail. Health is your body floating in the ocean and swimming alongside dolphins. Health is being able to look into the eyes of your loved ones. Health is being able to touch and feel the delicate, yet strong energy of a child. Health is being able to accept responsibility for your energy levels, knowing when to rest and recharge and when to push your pedal to the metal. Optimum health is having an outlet for your emotions, so you'll always treat those around you kindly with love and care, keeping stress away.

Health is not a bearer of bad news, and health is not impeding death. Health isn't something to be taken for granted or another thing to "manage." Focusing on your health is an opportunity for you to practice self-love and to take pleasure in your physical body.

If you don't accept responsibility for your health, for instance, by putting nutrient-rich food in your body, drinking plenty of water, and exercising on a regular basis, you'll get sick. To stay healthy, you also must manage your energy. Your body will give you warning signs, such as tightness, headaches, a tugging feeling in your tummy, or exhaustion, when you're moving out of spiritual alignment and the flow of your energy is imbalanced or stagnant. As you meditate, recognize the language of your body, follow that with actions to make your body feel better, and your health will improve.

A few years ago, when my life got very busy and I was on the road a lot, working long hours and getting only three to four hours of sleep each night, I would fuel myself with sugar for comfort, carbs to keep my brain working, caffeine for focus, and alcohol to destress. Then I'd be wired at the end of the day and find it hard to fall asleep, so I'd wake up feeling sluggish. I kept making excuses for why it was not a good time to integrate a healthy lifestyle until I began to feel nauseated on a daily basis. My body was speaking to me loud and clear.

I finally accepted responsibility for my health and lifestyle. I altered my diet, got more sleep, quit drinking caffeine and alcohol, and worked fewer hours. In the process, I learned that prevention is much easier and takes less energy and effort than recovering from an illness. Today I feel much better, because I accept that everything I put in my body and do affects my energy levels. I don't do things perfectly. Occasionally I still have days when I'll drink a sugar- and fat-laden chai tea latte or eat some chocolate lava cake, but there's a major difference. Now I course-correct quickly by returning to consuming a daily cold-pressed raw juice and wholesome green salad. When I slip out of alignment in my workload, I can quickly get back to feeling great, because I am not making excuses.

Do you make excuses for eating unhealthy foods or skimping on exercise? What simple changes could you accept responsibility for that would increase your well-being today? Do the meditation exercise "How to Form a Healthy Relationship with Money" (see p. 159), substituting *my health* for *money*, to help you perceive and clear your energy blocks in this area of your life (skipping questions four and five).

Cleaning Up Your Past

You can't change what's happened in the past, but you can clean up how you feel about it. This will help you improve the flow of your energy. For miracles to occur, you must seek to eliminate the psychic debris that lies between where you are and where you want to be. First, acknowledge the gap between outward appearances and your inner feeling state. Make a request to Spirit to reveal everything within your energy field that's blocking your ability to create financial stability, loving relationships, career success, and optimal health.

Looking at each of the key areas of your life, what are ways you could make immediate improvements? A financial block might show up as clutter in your office or home: piles of paper containing invoices, payment reminders, expired coupons, and catalogues of things you are considering buying, but really shouldn't, based on your current bank balance. Accept responsibility for what you can do. Picking up a pile of those papers and deciding what can go in the trash and what needs to be addressed can lighten your mental load. Do it.

A relationship imbalance might show up as gossip or drama in a group of friends or between family members. Accept responsibility for what you have said and done, and do not believe hearsay, because there's a good chance that it isn't true or is none of your business. If relatives are accusatory or critical, you don't have to accept their judgment. Don't spend time on the phone engaging in unproductive conversations and obsessing over text messages. Have direct conversations with people when misunderstandings arise rather than talking behind their back.

Clearing blocks in your career means that if you make a mistake at work, you admit you made a mistake. You don't try to cover it up, but learn how to do a better job the next time.

If you committed to a healthy eating plan and diverted from it, you don't berate yourself, which would add to the imbalance in your energy field. Instead, accept responsibility for your choices that day and get back to your commitment tomorrow.

Accepting responsibility is a willingness to say yes to preparing taxes, listening to people who need your help, paying bills on time, starting work at 6 A.M., even if you're tired, in order to make your deadline, sacrificing time with a friend if a loved one needs to be picked up at the airport, and replying to a client's e-mail in a timely manner, because not doing these things means that other parts of your life will become more challenging. Willingness to accept responsibility is saying yes when you want to say no, because it is good for you in the bigger picture.

Clearing Karmic Debt

Karma is the result of your actions. You are energy. There's an energy connection between you and each person you've ever come into contact with. Some of these connections are long-term. Others are short-term. They may be strong or weak, healthy or toxic, loving or abusive. Every kind of action has an effect on us and the people we're connected to. Depending on whether your actions are good or bad, you will create good karma or bad karma. An accumulation of misaligned actions results in karmic debt. The more you accept responsibility for your actions, whether they are proactive or reactive, the better your life will be, because you'll produce positive karma and harmonious relationships. Use this exercise to clear karmic debts in your life. You may be surprised by the results you get. Doing inner spiritual work can lead to a miraculous breakthrough in your outer world that may have long seemed impossible.

For this exercise, you'll need two sheets of paper and a pen or pencil.

On one page, create two columns. In the left-hand column, make a list of anyone you feel owes you something. In the right-hand column, write down why you believe they owe you. For example, you fronted services to a client and were not paid, or you invited a close friend to your birth-day dinner and she didn't show. As you reflect on your list of people and reasons for their indebtedness, forgive those debts. Release the story of what happened and set them free. Send their energy back to them and bring your energy back to you.

On the other sheet of paper, again make two columns. In the left-hand column, make a list of those you feel indebted to. In the right-hand column, explain why you feel indebted to them. As you reflect on these two lists, forgive yourself. Release the story of what happened and set yourself free. Send their energy back to them and bring your energy back to you.

As you shift your awareness from denial to responsibility and release the stories you have created about each circum-stance, you'll be releasing stagnant energy in your body, mind, and spirit. Don't be surprised if, after doing this exercise, out of the blue you hear from an old friend you fell out with or someone who owes you money sends you a check in the mail. Do not underestimate the power of this exercise. Give it a try!

Intention Leads to Actions

If you intend to be a proactive creator, you need to be able to look at your actions and see their consequences. Actions are always linked to consequences. If you aren't getting the results you want, you need to make an adjustment in your actions.

Because actions stem from intentions, you need to specifically reflect on what was happening internally that led to the results you got. What were you feeling at the time you took the action? What was your intention? What were you hoping would happen? What were you afraid would happen?

Often we create what we fear. By undergoing this process of reflection, you can begin to clear the blocked energy of misunderstandings in your relationships and get back into the flow of the responsible use of your energy.

Be sure that going forward you are proactively putting out the right energy. Let Spirit partner with you to help you manifest the miracles you need and want.

The Miracle of Responsibility

The miracle of financial responsibility is, among other things, having enough money to cover your expenses, take great vacations, contribute to charitable causes, and leave a legacy for your children. Guilt is unheard of, because you know you're doing the best you can. You're mindful. You check your bank balances on a regular basis and promptly pay bills that come due. You spend within your means and save for the future. You're free to focus on your vision.

The miracle of a committed relationship is in focusing on what you can do to make your beloved feel loved every day. You're grateful, honest about your true feelings, and respectful of your partner; you honor your promises. There's no sense of obligation. You never wonder if there's someone better for you or compare your loved one to anyone else.

The miracle of a fulfilling career is in loving what you do so much that it doesn't feel like work. You are inspired when you wake up in the morning to make a difference in the lives of others with your gifts and skills. You are actively seeking opportunities to contribute to your community. There is no sense of hardship or competition, because you know your purpose. You love solving problems and helping others.

The miracle of excellent health is being alive and having an abundance of energy to do all the things you'd love to do, which may include traveling the world, playing sports, and engaging with amazing people.

In reality, there are things we don't have much, if any, control over, such as the weather and the people around us. Everywhere we go there are laws in place that must be adhered to by law-abiding citizens. Yet we do have an abundance of control over our thoughts and our actions. When we accept responsibility for the creation of our lives, miracles can and do follow.

Responsible Actions with Spirit in Mind

To reclaim power over your finances, relationships, career, and health, connect with Spirit and ask yourself the following questions to bring awareness to your decision-making processes. If you do, the next time you have a choice to make, you'll find it easier to accept responsibility.

Ask why:

- "Why did I buy _____ [item]?"

- "Why did I get into the relationship with _____ [name]?"

- "Why did I take the _____ [kind] job?"

- "Why did I eat _____ [food]?"

Ask when:

- "When didn't I take responsibility for my finances?"

- *"When didn't I take responsibility for actions in my relationship with _____ [name]?"*

- *"When didn't I take responsibility for my job?"*

- *"When didn't I take responsibility for my health?"*

A message from Spirit will be revealed to you as you investigate your activities (or lack of activity). As you form a responsible relationship with yourself, you'll enjoy what you have more and feel sure that you have all that you need. You'll trust that you're enough.

8

RULE 8: **Aim High**

*If I could imagine a better quality
of life, what would it be?*

When you aim high, you're saying *yes* to the gifts of the universe.
Spiritual awareness leads to more gratitude. You know your value.
People are drawn to you, because they see you place a positive value on yourself. You aim high, because you know there's something
beyond your current circumstances worth reaching for. Your desire
comes from inspiration rather than wanting to escape deprivation.
You also believe you can reach what you aim for. People who aim
high are in search of a bigger life. People who aim high have a strong
desire to learn more, be more, do more, have more, and give more.
They have a hunger for joy.

   You can't fail when you aim high, because you're focused on being
the best version of yourself. Aiming high means you'll never have an
average or mundane life. When you aim high, you learn what's truly
important to you. You define your core values and laser-focus on visualizing the details of your vision with enthusiasm. Through aiming
high, you'll know instinctively where to channel your energy on a
daily basis. You'll recognize when distractions arise and easily filter

them out. A person who aims high is focused on quality experiences and depth of connection with other people. You're confident about where you're meant to be, what you're meant to do with your time, and with whom you're meant to connect. Your clarity allows you to take action with confidence.

Aiming high leads to all sorts of miracles, because you're open and embodying a high-energy vibe. This makes you a magnet for love, friendship, abundance, success, and well-being. Aim high, and you'll leave past experiences of failure and struggle behind. You'll become more resilient. As you aim high, you free yourself from toxic people who don't reach for what they want. Put this rule into action, and your life will improve by one hundred percent. Make a commitment to aim high in each area of your life, and you'll create many miracles.

A Better Quality of Life

Everyone deserves a better quality of life. If you want it, reach for it. If others tell you that you can't achieve it, this indicates that they don't believe it's possible for *them*.

In 2014, I was invited to a VerdeXchange dinner at the Consulate-General of Japan in Los Angeles, where I had the good fortune of sitting next to Ron Finley. VerdeXchange is an organization promoting the green economy. Ron grew up in South Los Angeles, where purchasing a fresh tomato required a forty-five-minute drive. He therefore planted vegetables in the curbside dirt next to his home. Unfortunately for him, the City of Los Angeles owns the neglected dirt areas where he was planting, and he was cited for gardening without a permit.[1] Feeling this was unfair, Ron circulated a petition demanding the right to garden and grow food in his neighborhood. This caught the eye of the media and some of the more influential people in the community, and the city government backed off.

Ron is on a mission to transform South Los Angeles from a food desert to a place where fresh produce and healthful foods are abundantly available and affordable. His actions are focused on educating and inspiring, on feeding body and soul. He has a vision that children in South Los Angeles should grow up with the option of fresh healthy foods instead of processed and convenience foods. He began on his street. He carried this vision to his neighborhood and wants to help communities everywhere to create edible gardens, one city at a time.

Working to create a better life for yourself, you can be a model inspiring others to create a better life for themselves. A better quality of life doesn't necessarily mean a bigger house, faster car, or more money. Your concept of a better quality of life might be living in a creative community or a sustainable environment.

We often think we have to make big changes to get the results we want, but sometimes adding or subtracting one element can greatly improve the quality of your life. In truth, a small permanent change can create a big miracle. One of my friends said when he cut out drinking alcohol, he no longer woke up feeling groggy and stopped getting headaches. Another friend said that incorporating a twenty-minute daily walk has eliminated her back pain.

Creating a better life could mean ensuring that you have things you love to wear in your closet instead of items that make you feel less than wonderful. It might mean living near a gym or setting up a workout space at home. It could be treating yourself to a larger collection of books, a bigger tea selection, periodic bubble baths, or new underwear and socks. These simple things can inspire a feeling of abundance and contribute to big miracles over time.

For you, inviting friends over for a good meal on a weekly basis or having a meal out at your favorite restaurant once a month might substantially add to your well-being. Getting a regular spa treatment like a massage or facial or taking two vacations a year might make life better. Creating a better life could be allowing yourself to go to bed an hour earlier (particularly if you have kids who need to be gotten ready for school Monday through Friday) or sleeping in for an extra hour on the weekends. Everything we do matters when we're reaching for a miracle. Buying a new bed could help you get a better night's sleep. If you had more sleep, you'd have more energy. If you had more energy for the things you'd love to do, what would that be worth to you?

If there are a lot of things you'd like to change in your home, for example, focus on making one room better at a time. Start with one corner of the room or one drawer and then move on to the next corner or next drawer, knowing that you're continually improving the quality of your space. Even though she loved people and had a big heart, one of my clients wouldn't invite people over, because her home was cluttered and not well kept and she was ashamed of it. Having a maid service come and clean her home improved the quality of her social life. It also took a weight off her mind. She said that when she got home from work, because she didn't have to think about cleaning, she could put up her feet and relax. She hadn't taken this action sooner, because she believed it was indulgent to have someone else do what was her responsibility, even though she was coming home tired after a full day of work.

Adding a regular meditation practice at the start of your day or writing a list of three things you are grateful for before you go to sleep can lift your mood and energy. It doesn't cost you anything to do these things except time, and they can help clarify simple action steps you can take now to improve the quality of your life.

Treating your body well is aiming high. Having a high standard for your health is the greatest gift you can give to yourself. Incorporating fresh organic fruit and vegetables into your diet adds to the quality of your well-being. To take exceptional care of your body may require a financial investment, but if you decide that improving the quality of your life is a priority, Spirit will assist you in closing the gap to make it possible. Perhaps a monthly yoga class membership and the special nutritional supplements you want to take are beyond your current budget. If so, look for alternatives. What about getting a monthly membership to a series of online yoga videos for approximately $10 per month? My favorite online video sites like this are PowerYoga.com and MyYogaWorks.com. You could also save up so that you can treat yourself to a special retreat or ask about scholarships at your local Y. Many communities offer public recreation options.

Some people feel guilty for wanting a better quality of life when others in the world are suffering. They believe that having more for themselves is keeping others' needs from being met. If you're afraid this is the case for you, do a mental reframe. When you improve your life, with a focus on aligning with Spirit, it is abundance, not greed. You can do much more good for others if you yourself are healthy and in a stable position mentally, emotionally, and financially.

One of my clients felt guilty for coming from a wealthy family. I pointed out that her affluence gave her the opportunity to travel and share her talents and gifts with those who were less fortunate and also to teach others to do the same. The irony is that, in some parts of the world where people have a fraction of what my client has, the people are much happier and grateful for what they have. They don't feel deprived, because they already possess things they care about more than money, such as family, community, music, nature, and their spiritual practices.

If to you a better quality of life means living in a multimillion-dollar home and owning several sports cars and a private jet, search for the truth of why you desire those things. What is the spiritual purpose? If aiming high means being a celebrity and winning awards, what is the spiritual purpose? Search deeply and honestly within yourself, so that you are not driven to aim high to compensate for insecurity, loneliness, or low self-esteem.

Whether you choose to reach a little higher or a lot higher, always remember that the purpose of aiming high is your spiritual growth. Whatever you achieve or receive from a place of spiritual awareness will produce gratitude rather than a feeling of "not enough."

Are You Ready for More Goodness?

Improving the foundation of your life starts with creating a peaceful mind, a healthy body, and a supportive home environment. When you address these issues, you'll find that your life is better. Use this exercise to identify issues that need your attention when you're looking to stretch yourself. What is a simple action you can take? Something to add? Something to subtract? As you aim a little bit higher, you declare to Spirit that you're ready for more goodness in your life.

Begin by closing your eyes, centering your awareness in your heart, and checking in with the quality of your thoughts. Ask yourself:

- *How do my thoughts feel?*

- *Would I like my mind to be filled with better ones?*

Next, use your awareness to feel into your body, and ask:

- *Is my energy high or low?*

- *Am I achy or pain free?*

- *What action could I take to feel better?*

Now, open your eyes, stand up, and go find a mirror. Look in the mirror.

- *Am I happy with my appearance?*

- *Is there a small change that would make me feel better about myself?*

Take a look around each room in your home. In each, ask yourself:

- *Does this room reflect the quality of life I desire?"*

- *If not, what is one simple thing I can do right now to make it better? (This could mean that you take out the trash, put in a load of laundry, light a candle, or sort and put away a pile of papers.)*

Aiming high is meant to feel good. As your mind, body, and home begin to feel more harmonious, you'll find yourself appreciating your environment more. If you have to force it, aiming high will feel overwhelming and turn into an obstacle. But as you reach higher and raise your standards, which is what happens when you seek a more aligned relationship with Spirit and reside in an environment that reflects the joy of your soul, there is less stress. You find yourself living in flow and bringing more goodness into your daily life.

Nonattachment

How do you create a big miracle? You imagine it, feel it, and think it. And then you let go and let Spirit move the energy! There's a period of time between the imagination of what you want and the realization of it. During that span, trust that Spirit is working on your behalf. It may look as though nothing is happening, but if you could see everything as Spirit sees it, you'd see that a lot is taking shape.

It can feel terrifying to let go and trust that things are working out during this period, especially if you've aimed high and invested your time, energy, money, and resources into a vision for a better life. Nonattachment takes deep faith. Nonattachment allows you to live without regret in the present moment, no matter what's happening. You can take an action without being bogged down in fear or worry. Nonattachment allows you to maintain integrity and do what's best, including aiming for higher ideals. It also helps you to set healthy boundaries with others.

If you can enjoy the journey without being attached to reaching the destination, you'll feel the freedom of aiming high. If your intentions are pure and you're seeking a closer relationship with Spirit, you have nothing to lose in aiming high. You may need to make a sacrifice. You may feel as though you are going backward. But you don't need to be afraid. The preparation you do when you're aiming for a high mark is like pulling back on a bow to give an arrow enough power to reach its destination. Aiming high is your declaration that you deserve a big miracle. When you declare that you want excellence, doors that were formerly locked will open for you. Freeing your mind from limited thinking is a milestone that you must reach before you can experience a miracle.

If you have a bigger scale vision for your life, make sure to apply Rule 1, Align with Spirit, before putting Rule 8, Aim High, into action. It's best to have a solid spiritual foundation before reaching for new and exciting challenging experiences. As you maintain centeredness, you'll be able to see who supports you and whose judgment and fears hold you back. Surround yourself with uplifting people who encourage you to go after your dreams.

Many people are only dreamers. They talk about what they want to do—whether it is meeting a soul mate, getting fit and healthy, achieving a career goal, or changing the world—yet they don't back up their dreams with concrete actions. The nearer you get to your goals, the more likely you are to be faced with the temptation to spend too much time with dreamers who only make you feel good and never push you outside your comfort zone. The truth is that other people aren't responsible for your progress, so being complacent can block a miracle.

If you're aiming for an intimate committed relationship, you must be vulnerable and reveal your true feelings. If you're aiming for a better body, you may need to decline dinner invitations for now or take fresh fruit to a family meal if your family will be eating cake and ice cream for dessert. If you're starting your own business, working longer hours is expected. You might also need to invest your clothing budget in research and development for the next six months. These are the types of trades everybody makes when focused on a goal.

Be nonattached about getting the approval of friends and family. When you aim high and make changes, people will judge what you're doing. The friend you've been going to the local burger joint with for two years may do everything to deter you from going to a health-food spot. A friend with a failed acting career may tell you that investing in acting classes is a waste of your money. A parent who had an acrimonious divorce may be cynical about anyone you date. This is where practicing nonattachment will help you keep sight of what you are aiming for.

Most people aren't really trying to deflate your dreams. They just don't believe in miracles. They call it luck when they see someone leading a magical life.

As you aim higher, you may find yourself losing your balance temporarily. Suddenly everything that previously felt easy and familiar seems foreign and difficult. You could have been top of the class in your school, but as you enter a new workplace, you find yourself at the bottom of the ladder in your dream industry. The climb may look insurmountable from the bottom rung, but it's not. This is a good time to remember that you'll create your big miracle via a series of small action steps. Take the actions, trusting that whatever Spirit wants you to learn is a piece of knowledge or an insight necessary to hit your mark.

Spirit will put the right people in front of you in the most unexpected ways and at the most unexpected times. Spirit will also put you where you are meant to be. This is your destiny.

Actress Vanessa Marcil grew up in a violent home in a gang-infested area in Indio, California. Nobody had high expectations for her. Her dad told her straight up that she shouldn't aim high, because none of her dreams would come true. As a teen, she was kicked out of high school and had some trouble with the law. While she was on probation, she saw Oprah Winfrey's show for the first time and thought that she'd like to become friends with her. This was when the notion of aiming high took root within her. She might not have called it that and had no idea how it could happen, but the idea set her in motion. She started to study successful people and began reading inspirational books. Getting out of Indio was her main goal.

In the meantime, she began cleaning houses and washing cars in her neighborhood for free to show the people in her community that she could be trusted. Her girlfriend had an audition at a local theater for the classic Tennessee Williams play *Cat on a Hot Tin Roof* and needed a ride, so Vanessa offered to be of service. As she waited in the theater, the director came up to her and told her she was up next. "I'm not auditioning. I'm here for my friend," she said.

"Have you ever acted?" the director asked.

"Only in classes that my mom put me in to keep me out of trouble," she replied.

"Don't think of it as an audition. Do it for fun," he said.

Vanessa did a cold reading that day and got the part. A couple of months later, when the show opened, an agent saw her performance and told Vanessa she wanted to represent her. This was a major coup. Every aspiring actor knows how hard it can be to get an agent. Spirit clearly wanted Vanessa to go to Los Angeles to pursue acting.

Vanessa worked three jobs just to pay her rent. Just before her first big audition, her agent told her she needed to get a $500 head shot taken. When Vanessa explained she didn't have the money to pay for photos, the agent took a Polaroid photo of her and attached it to a fake resume that he put in front of the casting director. With that single audition, Vanessa was cast as the iconic character of Brenda in the soap opera *General Hospital,* a role for which she went on to win an Emmy Award for Outstanding Supporting Actress in a Daytime Drama.

Vanessa did not know how to aim high per se. But as she focused on feeling good and on doing good for others, miracle upon miracle occurred that helped her progress against the odds. Her dreams began coming true. She eventually was a guest on *The Oprah Show* and became Winfrey's friend.[2]

More recently, Vanessa was told by people in the film and TV industry that it wasn't possible to cross over from daytime television programs to movies. She then landed a costarring role opposite Nicholas Cage in *The Rock,* a movie that grossed $335 million at the box office worldwide.[3] She was subsequently cast as one of the leads in the primetime TV show *Las Vegas* and costarred in over one hundred episodes.[4]

Vanessa is proof that you can aim high and meet your goals if you're not attached to particular outcomes. Vanessa doesn't define herself by recognition or the awards she's won. She simply aims for what brings her the most happiness, makes her feel the most alive, and gives her the most peace. She has never focused on success or failure, because she's always known that the idea she has for her life is smaller than what the universe has in store for her. Vanessa is a very humble free spirit who moves through life without fear. It is the journey itself that gives her the most joy.

Don't pigeonhole yourself by believing there is only one kind of success out there for you—and don't try to control how the miracle of the life of your dreams will manifest. Instead, always bring your focus back to spiritual alignment by placing your awareness on your heart. Be yourself and walk the path you're called to walk. Let destiny take your hand and lead you wherever you are meant to go.

The Power of Imagination

Your imagination is a powerful tool that can assist you in creating your big miracle. You have access to your imagination twenty-four hours a day, and it will show you how to solve any problem or move beyond any unwanted circumstance in your life if you give it half a chance. Whatever you imagine over and over will eventually manifest for you if you want it enough.

Take a moment now to imagine what a better quality of life would be like for you. What details spring forth in your mind's eye? Key words may pop into your head. You may also get a strong feeling about what you're visualizing. Use all of your five physical senses to make your image of a better quality of life as tangible for you as possible. This step solidifies your vision and is the step before grounding your vision in reality.

Imagining your best life will send a message to your subconscious mind and to Spirit. This process of putting energy toward your vision through your imagination will eventually transform your life into the best one possible. The key to achieving the outcome you desire is consistent actions that aim in the direction of the vision you have for your best life. When you keep using your imagination to direct energy toward your vision, you eventually cross a threshold that brings your vision into a visible form.

You're constantly manifesting reality with the power of your imagination. Whatever your regular primary thoughts are about will be the very thing that will manifest in your life. The good news is that if you focus your imagination on what you want and aim high, you will create miracles. It is amazing what the human mind can do.

Professional athletes know to play out a success in their minds until it feels real to them. They run the course, make the toss, or execute the putt over and over until it is ingrained in them. Whoever has the strongest imagination and has practiced exercising it the most will be the winner in life too. A big part of aiming high and succeeding is practice. The more you practice, the more normal an action becomes. What seems difficult at first eventually becomes easy. For example, driving a car or making a serve over the net in tennis is hard initially, but later becomes almost automatic.

The more a dancer practices the routines she's taught, the better she gets at picking up new choreography. An actor good at the art of memorization can learn his lines faster. A chef intuitively knows exactly what ingredients and their quantities to put in a recipe to make it taste exquisite, because he has mastered the art of cooking.

Before you do things, it's beneficial on an energy level to imagine them first. If you focus on the things you plan to do with conscious attention, you'll get a better outcome. The process is relatively simple. Here's how to do it.

If you have a party to go to, for example, imagine trying on three different outfits, visualizing both how you will look in them and how you will feel at the party. Imagine the people you'll be talking to when you're wearing the outfit and how they respond to you as well as the mood the outfit puts you in. Depending on the energy you want for the party, let the imaginary experience help you decide what to wear.

When you use your imagination, you can align yourself with the energy of what you want faster, because you are alert to finding it. For example, if you want to create your ideal body, first find an image that is a good representation of how you want to look. Start looking for images in magazines or on social media that inspire you. Watch for when you judge your current body image or feel disheartened that what you want to achieve isn't possible. You can put a simple plan in place to make healthier food choices and exercise several days a week. Every time you feel as though you're falling short, recommit to aiming high and implementing your vision. Seek a balance of imagining your desired result, reaching for your goal through action, and letting go of your idea of the way you will arrive at your goal. As you review the evidence of your results, the necessary action steps will become clearer and the attachment to faster results will subside as your faith moves toward certainty that a big miracle is on its way.

The Big Picture

When you aim high, it helps you look toward the future and see the big picture of your life. The big picture is your life in broad strokes accompanied by the awareness of how those strokes are connected, for instance, how where you live affects your relationships and career track. As you aim high with the big picture in mind, you cultivate the mental toughness to stick with what needs to be done, because you understand there is a purpose to it. By contrast, when you look at your life from the perspective of the past or present challenges, your sight is automatically limited, making it virtually impossible to aim higher.

When you're aligned with Spirit, you're able to get a bird's-eye view of your life. If you have a clear vision of the big picture for your life, you'll understand the amount of time outcomes are likely to take. You can find the courage to break free from your routines to gain greater perspective. As you get serious about aiming high and committing to your big picture, you understand that preparation is necessary and not a punishment. Research helps you gain more valuable information. If you want to move to your dream home, permission is not required from someone else to make that change in your life.

See yourself living in the home you desire. Do online searches to find out what exactly it costs to move into your ideal space. Remember that Spirit wants you to have what your heart desires. Ask yourself, "What can I do to generate income today that will give me the means to move into my ideal home?" Do this consistently for ninety days and a higher quality of living will arrive.

People who understand the big picture know they must be patient and consistent in their activities. Their relationship with Spirit is highly integrated into their lives, so that their intuition can give them strong guidance. Besides seeing the big picture for your life or visualizing a specific goal or achievement, understanding the purpose of your soul gives you the necessary energy and momentum to aim high and achieve your dreams.

Big Dreams

Big dreams are beautiful. If you have a big dream, go for it! It is a disservice to your soul not to do so. If the desire is within you, you can trust that a part of your spiritual essence wants to express itself. Big dreams are personal. One person's big dream may be to travel the world and teach yoga retreats, while another person's big dream is to live with her handsome husband and three kids in a gorgeous farmhouse by a river.

What is your big dream?

What big vision makes your heart skip a beat?

Make sure the big dream you're pursuing is yours alone or that it's a dream you believe in wholeheartedly and want to be a part of or support. Most big dreams require the collaboration of many people.

Perhaps you don't know exactly what you want, but you know you want it to be special and fulfilling. Some people know from a very young age exactly what they want out of life. Others have a strong desire, for instance, to help others, but don't know how best to put that desire into action. If so, ask Spirit to show you the path. Seek purposeful experiences, and you'll find your life becoming more meaningful. As you do this, each experience builds upon the prior one and creates a richness and depth in your relationships and career path.

Spirituality has been a deep passion of mine since I was a child, but it wasn't until I turned twenty-one that I felt the desire to write. Then I began journaling daily and attending writing workshops on the weekends. While waiting for appointments or meeting friends, I'd pass the time by pulling out my journal and writing. However, during my twenties I couldn't see the path to becoming a writer, so I kept writing for myself alone until Spirit showed me the next step, how to go about publishing a book. It then took more years of putting into practice what other authors had done successfully to produce my first manuscript for *Unleash the Psychic in You.*

I used to be very impatient and expect immediate results, as if waving a magic wand would get me the outcome I wanted on demand. Eventually I understood that the big picture Spirit was trying to show me is achieved through a series of actions that move and shape energy until it is fully formed, and this process can take some time. It doesn't mean something is wrong when there aren't immediate results from actions. I relaxed and embraced the rule of aiming high. I got motivated and committed to my big-picture vision for the long haul regardless of the discomfort I felt or the lack of support from others. I learned that it was up to me to create my vision.

Some big dreams take years to develop, but if you stick to it, they happen. Spirit will always help you have small wins along the way to keep you moving forward toward that better quality of life you seek. I had imagined speaking on stage in front of hundreds of people so often that when it finally happened, I felt very comfortable because I expected it.

This wasn't an entitled sort of expectation, mind you. I was grounded in my body, centered in my heart, and connected to Spirit when it happened and viewed the lecture as an opportunity to serve my audience. In the past, when opportunities came along and I wasn't centered, grounded, and connected, my self-esteem would get bruised and I'd recoil from aiming high again anytime soon if I didn't get the outcome I imagined. Then I would have some small wins that steered me back on course.

If you experience a setback or disappointment, the best advice I can give you is to keep going! Pause to review what worked, what didn't work, and why in either case; then focus on moving beyond where you were before the setback; otherwise you'll end up living a smaller, narrower life.

Don't confuse a simple life with a small life; there's a distinction. Amanda de Cadenet did a fascinating interview with comedian and actress Sarah Silverman for *The Conversation,* in which they spoke about the principle of living within your means.[5] Sarah could have chosen to live in a big house in the Hollywood Hills and instead opted for an apartment. She also owns an older car. For her, aiming high means creative freedom. She wants to be able to choose the projects she works on instead of letting her finances lead her decisions.

High-Energy Living

To aim high and create a better-quality life, you need to be in a high-energy state. There are several things you can do to reach and maintain a high-energy lifestyle, so that you can create miracles with your energy. Experiment with the following suggestions:

Listen to music that makes you happy. Music is one of the best mood enhancers. It touches our souls and can move us from inertia to ecstasy. Create a go-to list of songs that raise your energy when you need a boost. I often listen to music when I'm writing and especially when I'm working out. Years ago I attended a workshop hosted by author and speaker Jack Canfield during which he used the *Super-*

man theme song to inspire the attendees. Think about how you can use music in other ways to increase your energy.

Eat quality organic produce. Nourishing food will help you fine-tune your energy and reach a heightened state. The expression "You are what you eat" couldn't be truer. The higher the quality of food you put in your body, the better you will feel. Eat this way every day, and you'll quickly find that you have the strength and stamina you need to aim high and go after your big dreams. One of my favorite things to do before I begin working on an important project is a green-juice cleanse. I can sense the appreciation in my mind and body as I get into a greater state of alignment with Spirit. If you eat well, your internal organs will be grateful too.

Surround yourself with positive people. Nothing can bring you down faster than negativity from friends and loved ones—especially your loved ones. Their opinions can crush your dreams and lead you to doubt if it is even right for you to aim high. If others are critical of you and your lifestyle and you sense your energy levels dropping, take a break from them. Love them from a distance and return to aiming high as quickly as possible. Positive people will never judge the quality of life you envision; instead, they'll encourage you and want to support you in achieving your dreams.

Wear something you love. Putting on the right outfit can make you feel like a million bucks, and it doesn't have to be expensive. I wear my Pam & Gela "Happy Now" printed T-shirt and my Intentions Beads bracelet to remind me to create beautiful work. Clothes that inspire you can send strong positive energy to your soul. Some women have a power dress or suit they wear to uplift them. Others have a favorite pair of boots that gives them a confidence in their step. If you don't love what's in your closet, let it go, as wearing something you don't feel good in all day can drain you. It's better to have a few things you love to wear in your closet than lots of things that leave you feeling mediocre and possibly deflated.

Feel the Joy

You can't imagine a better quality of life if you don't feel joy. A strong positive feeling is a vital step before making what you want real. When you focus on joy, you enter a high-energy state. When you imagine what you want, backed by the feeling of joy, you align with certainty. Joy puts you in a state of mind that makes you want a bigger and better life.

My seven-year-old son, Dominick, is highly intuitive and empathetic. He loves watching the Academy Award–winning animated movie *Inside Out*.[6] If you haven't seen it, I highly recommend it. Nick and I use the film as a teaching tool to help Dominick recognize and express his emotions. Without giving away the plot of the movie, it's about a little girl named Riley, who has a control room in her head where her emotions live. One of the characters is Joy. The others are Sadness, Fear, Anger, and Disgust. Joy is responsible for creating Riley's happy memories. The film has really helped Dominick communicate, because he can recognize his range of emotions. He understands that he has control over his feelings and that he gets to choose how he feels. Sometimes he'll tell me, "I'm angry," and I'll suggest, "How about putting Joy back in the control room." He doesn't always do it, but suddenly he's aware of his emotions.

If you find yourself feeling sad or angry, before you can reach for joy you need to acknowledge what you're already feeling. It does no good to try to suppress negative emotions. Don't try to shift the negative emotion before acknowledging it, because that makes it stronger. Instead, observe the emotion and then request that joy come back to you.

After acknowledging whatever mood you're currently in, go ahead and shift that mood. Put on a comedy or look for the funny side of whatever is getting you down. On many occasions I've been able to look back later on something that made me so upset and laugh about it.

Joy always makes you feel good. If you don't feel that way, it's because anger or fear is temporarily dominating your mind and heart. Remember that you have a choice. If you opt for a better quality of life, anger and fear will need to take a backseat and let joy drive your spiritual vehicle.

Acknowledge Your Miracles

I love that the word *present* means both "this moment" and "a gift." Both meanings are relevant to your situation when you're aiming high. When you chose to aim high, the ego will advise you against doing so now. It'll suggest that you aren't ready and should wait a little longer. "Aim high? You'll be ready tomorrow," it tells you. But the next day comes and the ego says the same thing again: "Wait." So if the ego wants you to wait, what does your soul want? It wants you to take an action. Use the gift of this moment to stretch yourself and reach for miracles. Reaching will attune you to the prospect of receiving more.

If you feel a desire to reach beyond your current circumstances, trust that this is your soul seeking growth. Aiming high will teach you things about yourself that you didn't realize. You'll see that you're much stronger and more resilient than you've ever imagined. Aiming high will reveal your unexamined abilities and assist you in transforming your weaknesses into strengths.

Miracle Thinking

The more you focus on miracles, the more often they'll happen. Miracle thinking is a mindset in which you expect miracles and you don't let worry and fear take control of your mind.

To practice miracle thinking, begin playing out in your mind everything you want, but letting it be even better than you've previously imagined. Think of the best outcome that could happen and then imagine more. Ask yourself, "If there was an even better outcome than this, what would that be?"

Get out your Miracle Journal. Let your mind go still. Center, ground, connect, and then finish these sentences:

- *The best outcome that could happen in my love life is . . .*

- *The best outcome that could happen in my sex life is . . .*

- *The best outcome that could happen with my health is . . .*

- *The best outcome that could happen on my career path is . . .*

- *The best outcome that could happen with my finances is . . .*

- *The best outcome that could happen with my family is . . .*

- *The best outcome that could happen for my home is . . .*

- *The best outcome that could happen in my friendships is . . .*

- *The best outcome that could happen in my travels is . . .*

- *The best outcome that could happen in my education is...*

There is no wrong way to answer these questions. If you write without censoring your answers, your soul will reveal your next best steps for aiming high.

9

RULE 9: Take the Right Action

*If I trusted that Spirit was guiding
me, what would I do now?*

Spirit's intention is to guide you to your highest state of spiritual expression. If you're aligned with Spirit, when you focus on your vision, the next right action to take will be made clear to you. This is when you enter a flow state. A flow state is when one good thing lines up after another. There is no force required to get the outcome you desire. To find your flow, you must trust your connection to Spirit to travel the path of least resistance. If you keep taking the right actions, more things will align for you. You'll be introduced to the right people and stumble upon the right resources. Happy accidents, strokes of luck, and coincidences will occur. Someone may surprise you with a gift that advances your progress. None of these things will be something for which you plan, but all will be welcome and helpful.

As you continue to take the right actions, you'll naturally connect to Spirit and tap into a flow state that's almost effortless. When it clicks for you that what you imagined is becoming real, you'll know the rightness of your path. A hunger for proactivity will fill your belly and propel you forward. Then your big miracle is inevitable.

Action Is Essential If You Desire Change

Fear of taking the wrong action and possibly failing can lead to pro-crastination. The more often you procrastinate, the more clouded and chaotic your thinking will be. Your mind will start to feel heavy and conflicted with all of the unmade decisions weighing on it.

Interestingly, you won't have evidence that you've taken the right action until after it's done. For this reason, taking action involves a degree of faith and risk on your part. However, if you believe every-thing will work out, the action steps you need to take on the way to fulfilling your vision won't *feel* as risky anymore. Instead, they'll feel like exciting opportunities to learn more about how to achieve your vision, empowering you to take even more informed and confident actions as you progress. Because you understand that Spirit wants you to learn something from every action you take, you'll act without fear beforehand or regret afterward.

The right action is never a flippant remark or impulsive behavior. It is deliberate speech and deliberate decision making. To find your right next action, faith, mixed with commitment and consistency, is required. You must listen for guidance from Spirit, which will come through as intuition. You may see, feel, hear, or simply "know" the voice of your intuition. Its messages may emerge from any of the senses. For example, you may "hear" the same word repeated over and over in your head or have a feeling of urgency emanating from your solar plexus.

When you're committed to taking the right actions, you'll have a strong sense that you are embodying your true self. You'll have weeded out the unhelpful thoughts and beliefs that used to prevent you from being authentic with others. You'll make certain that ev-erything you do is for the greater good as well as good for you. And you won't get attached to unrealistic expectations or put pressure on yourself to be perfect. Once you've followed through on an action, you'll be able to look back and see there was a lesson in it. If you don't get the results you hoped for, you'll evaluate your choices, adjust as necessary, and make progress when your next step is required.

Action is necessary. If you stand in the same place forever, you can't move forward personally, professionally, or spiritually. Your opportunities will be wasted and you won't blossom as Spirit intends. However, if you focus on being a shining example of a true Spirit-led vehicle, you'll instinctively know the right actions to take. You'll be guided. I can promise you that Spirit won't let you down.

Four Steps to Recognize Your Next Right Action

It's critical to maintain momentum once you begin moving toward a goal. This means you must act as soon as possible whenever an opportunity that aligns with your values and intentions presents itself. Following hunches is imperative.

To receive clear intuitive guidance from Spirit when you're facing a decision or choice, take the following four steps. This process will be particularly beneficial if you're feeling unsure or sense the need to clear an obstacle in your path. It can help you figure out what to do at a fork in the road: are you headed up the on-ramp of a superhighway or about to turn down a dead end? It can help you to shut off the noise of unsupportive friendships and unproductive busywork and see beyond the clutter of unaddressed papers on your desk and unhealthy food in your kitchen cupboards. It will help you feel in your bones exactly what Spirit wants you to do. As you clear your thoughts and emotions, knowledge of the right action will effortlessly emerge.

Step 1: Watch
No matter what decision you're facing, from where to live, to what to eat, to whom to marry, to what job to pursue, there's an abundance

of information right in front of you that can help you recognize the right action to take. Spirit populates the world with clues to our next right actions. My friend Mike was on a hike in the Red Rock canyons of Sedona, Arizona, when he saw that a tour guide setting up lunch for a group needed a corkscrew to open a bottle of wine. After Mike offered him the use of his utility knife, he was invited to share in their meal. During the hour he spent with the group he watched everything the guide did and said, coming away inspired to begin leading metaphysical excursions to geological energy vortices. He had received a message from Spirit related to his next right action.

The more often you ask Spirit to show you the next step, the more information Spirit will reveal to you. Look carefully at your surroundings. How does what you're seeing make you feel? Observe how people are behaving and the choices they're making. Ask yourself:

- "What do I see in my current environment that inspires me?"
- "Who do I see around me living a life similar to what I want?"
- "What resources do I recognize in my immediate environment, neighborhood, or social circles that could support me in taking the right action?"
- "What experiences do I want more of in my life?"
- "What is the best next action to take?"

Step 2: Listen

Listen for the voice of guidance in your head and heart. Also listen for loving words of wisdom spoken by other people. Guidance may come through a lecture or a song playing on the radio. It may also be found in a natural setting. Pay attention to calming, uplifting nature sounds you hear. For example, if you go down to the beach, close your eyes, and listen to the waves crashing on the shore, you may hear a message about getting into flow. If you hear chattering birds outside your house, they could be delivering a simple message from Spirit to you, such as "Lighten up," because their calls sound like laughter. When I lived in Arizona, Spirit often sent me messages though the whistles of the chatty and insightful gray-tailed grackles that lived near my home.

You'll be able to hear your inner voice better if you are able to stop the stream of chatter in your mind, so make it a regular practice to empty your mind. Clear it of thoughts of criticism, judgment, worry, fear, and anger. If you find that your head is full of negative thoughts, write them down so you can identify and let go of obstructive feelings. Ask yourself:

- "Who have I been listening to that speaks negatively of others?"
- "Why am I letting other people's fear, criticism, or judgments enter my energy field?"
- "What is the probability that the things I fear will actually happen? And what would I rather have happen?"

Also put questions to Spirit and listen for the answers. Keep asking variations on:

- "Spirit, what should I do today?"
- "Where should I go?"
- "Who should I talk to?"
- "Is now the right time to respond to _____ [name]?"
- "Spirit, what do you want me to know about this situation?"
- "Is now the right time to take action to get the best outcome?"

You may need to ask the same question a hundred times before you get the answer you're waiting for if you aren't listening intently for it. Not getting an answer may mean that you need time away from people you love who have negative mindsets or whose energy is intrusive. Such people could have good hearts, but limited outlooks that interfere with your decision making.

Asking a series of questions can help you pinpoint very specific and detailed information. It's not unlike playing the children's game Twenty Questions. For example, when I was looking for a school for my son, Dominick, I asked, "Should we choose a public school or a private school?" I got the answer "Public." Then I went online and did a search for the "best public schools" in our area, backing up my intuitive guidance with concrete research.

I found five public schools that were all rated as excellent on educational merits and teaching quality. I read all the reviews. At that point, my intuition came back in again. As Nick and I were discussing the options, we balanced them against other aspects of the lifestyle we wanted to lead, such as being able to walk from our home to the school, being near the ocean, and thinking about where I needed to be to be able to meet people for my business. These were all logistical considerations.

The feeling of the neighborhood was a factor as well. All neighborhoods have their own energy. We drove around and checked out how we felt viscerally. When we walked through the various schools and their neighborhoods, we imagined what it would be like to see our son in those settings and living the reality of the choice. Would he be happy? This process led to our ultimate decision about where our son would go to school and feeling good about our choice.

It's amazing the amount of wisdom that is available to you when you can open your ears. TED Talks have been a wonderful source of inspiration to me. Spirit can speak through anyone. And it's not only the words that are being spoken that can deliver the message; it could be a person's energy or the tone of voice. Listening is an impressionistic experience. A hundred people can be sitting in the same audience hearing the same lecture but receive different messages. Spirit ensures that you hear what you need to hear when you are receptive.

If you've missed some words of wisdom that you were supposed to hear, the words will be revealed to you whenever you ask Spirit to elaborate or clarify.

Step 3: Feel

When you're faced with an important decision or can see that you're at a crossroads regarding your career, relationship, or living environment, close your eyes, focus, and bring your awareness to your heart. Tell Spirit you want to connect to your soul. Then ask yourself, "Does this choice/decision/option feel right or does it feel wrong?"

Spirit will never lie to you. The only way you can be fooled by your feelings is if you stay on the surface of them. At first, you might experience resistance as you try to go deeper into your feelings. You might have to travel through several layers of internal resistance. But if you stay with the feelings, you'll find yourself moving through the layers and entering a deeper zone of peace.

If you've been feeling conflicted, the best way to feel the entirety of your feelings is to stop whatever you're doing and pay attention to them—even if it's anger, frustration, or fear you feel. Reduce activity. Go somewhere where you can be alone. Busyness can exhaust you and cloud your judgment in decision making. A lot of times taking on other people's judgment, fear, or resentment makes choosing the right action hard. To create stillness, ask yourself:

- "What hurt am I carrying in my heart?"
- "Who upset me whom I haven't told how I really feel?"
- "When was the last time I felt betrayed? And what happened?"
- "How are my hurt feelings holding me back from taking action? For instance, am I being more cautious because I was hurt?"
- "Have I ever rushed into business deals, relationships, or

moved to a new home without doing due diligence, because I
was feeling wounded or vulnerable?"

- "Are my painful feelings or regrets inhibiting my ability to take
action?"

Step 4: Know

When you're fully connected to Spirit, you know what to do. Knowing is a sign of alignment with truth and verifies the absolute rightness of your decisions and actions. Knowing means you can remain
grounded and connected to Spirit even if in the presence of someone
else's emotional storm. Accusations may be thrown at you, lies may
be told about you, and yet you know the truth. You are aligned and
have pure knowing about the right action.

It's common for people to project their own feelings and thoughts
on you as if they were yours. The obvious example of this is when
parents want their children to behave a certain way, because it's
what they themselves would do. Projection crops up everywhere
we go. When I got engaged, for instance, a friend I respected told
me I was making a mistake and that she wouldn't come to my wedding because she "couldn't support my poor decision." Of course,
I knew the rightness of my relationship and got married anyway.
Because this woman had cancelled her own wedding ceremony the
night before it was supposed to take place, it seemed obvious to me
that her remark was a projection of her own thoughts and feelings
onto me.

Keep your authentic personal truth in the forefront of your mind
during challenging times. If you understand that you've done nothing wrong, even when you're under attack or people are criticizing
you, you can continue taking action to the best of your ability.

If you sense that you're meant to take an action, then you can be
sure that you're meant to take that specific action. Spirit doesn't lie
to us. If you feel a sense of urgency, as if a clock is ticking inside you,

pay attention and act upon it. If you find yourself procrastinating, do some internal clearing: *clearing* would be your next right action. Everything we do begins inside.

If you apply this four-step process regularly—multiple times every day, if necessary—you'll enter into a flow state, boost your productivity, and be satisfied by the quality of your life. Everything in your life will improve, because you'll know you're doing the right things to reach your highest aspirations and most heartfelt goals, and Spirit will be right beside you, nudging you along, which is fun and exciting. It also feels peaceful. You'd be surprised how quickly you can make an important decision if you watch, listen, feel, and let yourself know.

Three Signs that You're Taking the Right Action

Confirmation that you're taking the right action may come in three forms:

Pure knowing. Although you may not have physical evidence to show that your action is the correct one, you trust that it feels right. Pure knowing usually comes only after we've done a good amount of personal work to clear out anything blocking our inner guidance.

The right people are responding. You have a vision and a specific plan for how you want to implement it. After allowing your mind to empty, ask yourself, "Who would be aligned with my idea/message/product/service?" Reach out to people whose names come to mind. Some will respond favorably. Some won't. If just one influential person says yes to you, you've got evidence of being on the right track. Many wait for a seal of approval to respond.

Synchronistic events. When synchronicities start happening, it's a sign that you're taking the right action. There's an energy propelling you toward the realization of your vision. You may have put out a request to Spirit for specific resources to move a project forward, and the next day you meet someone who can help you. My client Sharon was looking for a unique event space. The next day I had a call with another client, Catherine, who was an events coordinator. As she told me how excited she was about a new space she would be promoting, I thought it would be the perfect fit for Sharon. I brought them together.

Sometimes when you make a request for insight, it will come quickly. Other times it may arrive more slowly. When the outcomes you want aren't being achieved at the pace you'd like, you may question whether or not you're on the right track. That's why it's so important to be vigilant for signs from Spirit nudging you toward right action. For instance, you may see an unexpected social media post in your newsfeed that resonates with your vision. That inspires you to get on a plane and attend a conference at the last minute. At the conference you establish a new business relationship and from that a deal emerges that moves your vision forward—none of which would have happened if you hadn't recognized the synchronicities at work. In a case like that, you've experienced pure knowing (resonating with the post), the right people responding (making a new business relationship), and synchronicity (everything coming together to move your vision forward).

Right Action Has No Real Risk

When you take the right action, there's no real risk. Fear that you'll get rejected can cause you to play it safe, but then you aren't living a full life. If you don't reach out to someone, you'll never know if you'd have been compatible. If you aren't honest about your feelings, you'll never know if a relationship could have blossomed into a marriage. If you don't try your idea, you'll never know if it could have been profitable. If you don't commit to and follow a fitness plan, you'll miss the opportunity for optimum health and your ideal body. In these instances, there's no risk that you're taking the wrong action. As you act, you grow.

If you've taken the wrong action a number of times, however, look to improve yourself. Once the pattern is revealed to you, you can figure out the next right action to take. Discovering your behavioral patterns is a game changer, in fact. This can give you the ability to move forward with grace rather than tiptoe through your life in fear.

If you're trying to avoid something or someone, don't. Address the tough stuff head-on; otherwise it will catch up to you later and cause you to be reactive rather than proactive. Resistance to right action comes from the ego and not having the willingness to do what needs to be done—to go the extra mile. When people say they don't know the right action to take, it's usually because they fear judgment or rejection. Being responsible is foreign to them. A person of this mindset always ends up living a small life and is usually drawn to codependent relationships.

Taking the right action may mean being humble. Sometimes doing things you don't enjoy or ones that you see as below you can lead you where you want to go at a faster pace—and result in an even better outcome than imagined. The example that leaps to mind is how the talent agents at William Morris Endeavor in Hollywood are trained, starting in the mailroom. Many college graduates have taken a job in the mailroom, knowing that it's the first stop on a path toward the career of their dreams. If you fear criticism, rejection, or loss of reputation for agreeing to work in the mailroom—or do comparable work—you could blow a rare opportunity.

Your family members may think right actions aren't necessarily prestigious. Thoughtful people know that every action leads to important learning that will increase their success in the long run. That's why they are willing to pay their dues in their careers. Spirit can help determine which actions are valuable for your situation. But you have to ask for guidance.

When I was thirty-three, I got a TV hosting job in London that paid well, but my heart called me to America. I left that job and started over from scratch in Los Angeles. Upon arriving, I had no home, no car, no savings, no job, and knew only a couple of people, yet moving was the right action to take—I knew this. Within days Spirit had guided me to take other actions that improved my situation immensely. I watched and listened attentively for signs and found a beautiful place to live in Santa Monica for a low rent, was offered use of a car for a small monthly fee as the driver was locked into a lease and barely using it, and got work as a Reiki healer. Within several months, I'd established a strong foundation for my new life and never needed to use my return airline ticket to London. A mutual friend introduced me to my husband, Nick. We got married a year later, which truly was a miracle, as my history of dating was disastrous!

For some, high risk leads to high reward. For others, the right action may be playing it safe and being consistent. The right action to take depends on your current situation and your threshold for risk. Your ability to handle the unknown is a factor in how well you do. If you're doing the right things most of the time, then regardless of your highs and lows, you'll eventually arrive where you're supposed to be. So don't give up.

Family and friends may tell you that your head is in the clouds because you're a dreamer or that you're doing the wrong thing and will fail. If so, remind yourself that it is not irresponsible to have a big dream if there's purpose to it. Your passion for a particular vision is the very factor that will help you to recognize the right actions to take.

Right vs. Wrong

A right action in its simplest form is an action that does not cause harm and leads to a beneficial outcome. However, sometimes an action you take will hurt a person. For example, you may need to fire someone or break up with someone. In such a case, that person's feelings could be hurt or the person may experience a financial shortage. Even so, these decisions could absolutely be the right ones for your life and well-being. Making a decision like this doesn't necessarily mean you took the wrong action. If someone gets angry or hurt and refuses to forgive you for an action you took, center yourself in your heart, ground your energy, and connect to Spirit. When you feel aligned, ask Spirit for guidance on how to handle the situation. Once you've received the guidance, do not second-guess the action step that has been revealed. Simply take it.

A wrong action is when you do something that doesn't feel right, but you do it anyway. It takes you off course from your heart's desires. Most of the time people make ethically wrong choices due to fear and pain. It is therefore valuable to check in with your heart when making a decision that directly affects other people. Ask yourself:

- "Who will be affected by the action I am about to take?"
- "Is my motivation pure?"
- "Could my plan hurt anyone? If yes, how?"
- "Should I go ahead with this or do something else?"

There are varied viewpoints about what is ethical in different situations, creating a lot of gray areas in life; so when you're in a gray area, it's important to weigh your options carefully. Remember that you have to be able to live with the consequences of your decisions. Would you steal from the grocery store if your children were hungry? Would you shoot a weapon if your country were at war even if you were a pacifist?

The framework of beliefs you grew up with will forever influence your decision-making processes unless you consciously reprogram your mind. You must keep peeling back the layers to find your personal truth about how to act. Develop your own set of personal and business ethics to help you align with your moral intuition followed by taking the right action, which happens when you are in alignment with Spirit.

Tapping into your inner guidance system will help you avoid ethical pitfalls. Many success stories throughout history have occurred because people were convinced that the actions they were taking were the right ones and would not harm anyone else or were necessary for the greater good of their families or the world.

One of my clients, a graphic artist, was having a tough month financially, because more money was going out than coming in. A prospective client asked him to build a website to sell a synthetic drug that, though no law against its use or possession exists, is illegal to sell. Gray area. The job would have paid him $15,000 in cash for only a couple of days' work. He phoned me because he needed a sounding board.

I thought about it for a second and then asked him, "If you knew money would come in from another job, would you still take this one?"

"No way," he replied. "It doesn't feel right."

He knew the right action to take was to decline the job and trust that Spirit would guide him to another, better opportunity. The idea of making money from that job pushed the boundaries of his integrity. Shortly afterward, two job requests came in that were aligned with his core values and added up to $10,000.

Spirit will always guide you when you make a sincere request, but Spirit cannot force you to exercise your integrity, because you have free will.

Do your best to remember that your decisions have an impact on others, especially if you are married, have children, or have hired employees. When you make a decision, you have to think beyond the effect it will have on you alone. How will it affect your loved ones? Will the action you are going to take have a short-term or a long-term impact on them?

Why We Fail to Act When We Should

If you know the right thing to do, why don't you always do it? Watching yourself fail to act can be like watching yourself in a movie—there's a sense of being at a distance from your own body. Despite knowing that by not following through in a particular situation you're taking the wrong action, something stops you. You may protest that you've experienced unforeseen circumstances, that someone you're interacting with is difficult to handle, or that you're too busy, but if you look closely at the situation, you'll find that the root cause is either feeling inadequate or undeserving. These kinds of thoughts and emotions derail us from taking the right action at the right time.

To identify whether you are procrastinating or an action isn't appropriate for you, read the following list of common patterns and see if you are acting out any of them in your life.

Overpromising. Usually we overpromise because we want people's approval, fear their rejection, or think we're going to gain something from them that we want. Do your best to maintain awareness of your own mental and emotional triggers—the ones that often cause you to say yes when you should say no or to say yes to doing too many things at the same time—so that you can make commitments you can responsibly follow through on.

Avoidance/procrastination. It doesn't matter if you're avoiding action because you're feeling intimidated and afraid, busy and overwhelmed, or not up to the task and undeserving, putting off doing what needs to be done today blocks opportunity. It's procrastination.

Diane received a request from a TV talk show to be a guest expert. She felt terrified because she was unprepared, so she sat on the invitation for a month. By the time she mustered up the courage to reply with a list of speaking points, the producer, who had needed to move quickly to maintain his production schedule, had filled the spot with someone else. The irony is that Diane wanted more visibility. She was terribly disappointed in herself.

Upon self-examination, Diane decided she deserved a bigger life than she was leading. She was able to overcome her pattern of avoidance by holding herself accountable for becoming better prepared. The next time a press request came in, Diane was entirely ready to say yes.

A friend of mine was offered membership in a very prestigious club for which she had to have excellent credentials and references to be accepted. Only a limited number of spots were open. Although the membership director reached out to her several times, my friend kept putting off responding to the director. Two years later she felt ready to join the club, but by then it was too late, as the membership quota was full. My friend told me she wished she'd taken action when she first was contacted, as the club would have been a great networking environment for her.

Worry. You think the sky may fall. You experience a constant low-grade energy drain, because you can't stop thinking about what could go wrong. If five things go well in your day and one goes badly, you focus on what didn't work and expect it to happen again. You focus on the evidence of lack in your life, forgetting that it has come from your past actions or things beyond your control, instead of focusing on positive actions you're taking and being optimistic.

If you have a pattern of worrying, your first thought when you wake up will be negative. You can feel the presence of fear in your body, and it causes you to waste time on things that don't advance your vision. My client Danielle, a habitual worrier, would focus during every coaching session on not having enough money to pay her bills. She was certain she wouldn't be able to pay them and seemed to want me to agree that she was likely to fail to meet her responsibilities rather than talk about how to generate earnings. The first three weeks of the month would be filled with panic and doubt, and then, in the final week of the month, she'd feverishly launch into action and exceed her financial goals.

"Imagine if you hadn't expended all your energy worrying about how you'd fail. Do you think you could have generated more income?" I asked her.

"Yes," she said.

After several months of consistently meeting her financial goals and seeing that her bills routinely got paid on time, her worry subsided and she was able to enjoy more of her life.

People pleasing. Doing things for others is wonderful. You may experience more joy in giving than receiving, except if you're giving and doing things for others for the wrong reasons. Have you ever found yourself saying yes when your body and soul were saying no? If so, rather than being generous, you were trying to please others. In the end, when our prime motivation is pleasing other people, we feel emotionally drained by the tasks we do and the resources we expend, which blocks us from taking the right actions in our lives that would help us reach our goals.

Dan kept receiving counsel that he needed to pay down his debts and save for his future. Everywhere he turned, he received this message—from people, from advertisements, even from his dreams—but Dan ignored the guidance. He liked the way people looked at him when he would pay for their drinks or dinner, so he was always picking up the check when he went out with friends. His people pleasing led him to max out his credit cards. He was failing to take the right actions that would lead him to pay down his debts.

When have you agreed to do something beyond your means or that interferes with your own well-being just to make other people think highly of you? This could be something as small as eating a cookie that someone offers you, even though you're on a diet. People pleasing can take many different forms, all of which cause us to override the actions that are in our best interest, such as reining in our spending or saying, "No, thank you," to a cookie.

Dishonesty. Telling a white lie can sometimes seem like the best thing to do in the short run, but lying is a slippery slope. In my experience, people who don't express their true thoughts, feelings, and intentions get found out, and it causes them a lot of guilt and heartbreak. For example, promising fidelity when you know you'd rather be with someone else is dishonest. It's unfair to string along someone who has strong feelings for you while you're waiting for a "better relationship" to show up. As long as you're expending energy to maintain even a small lie, your energy isn't fully invested in those things that you're authentically interested in. The universe will be confused as to your intentions and deliver chaotic results.

When you're attuned to Spirit, you cannot lie in any shape or form and expect to make progress. Acting without integrity will weigh so heavily on your conscience that it will block your intuition. Fortunately, being aware that there will always be consequences to your actions, you'll think very carefully about your choices from now on and choose to do the right thing. That may mean having the courage to end a marriage or let go of a best friend. Taking the right action is not always easy, but you'll sleep better at night for having integrity.

To discover your limiting patterns, look back through your actions that led to undesirable outcomes over the last several years. This will help you to pinpoint where you went wrong and also where you stopped short of a breakthrough. If you find yourself having ongoing difficulties, go back to Rule 4, Forgive Mistakes, and put it into practice so you can stop recreating the same tired old patterns of pain.

As you step outside of your comfort zone and begin taking consistent, diligent actions to achieve your dreams, you'll figure out that the wrong actions may have been impossible to avoid because they were a part of your spiritual growth. When you stop fearing mistakes, you'll take more right actions and find a positive momentum building. As you start being the person you want to be, life will become miraculous because you'll experience gratitude for simple things.

Your Vision and Values Will Give You Stamina

If you look at the entirety of your vision for your health, happiness, career, and relationships and get overwhelmed about the next right action to take, break the goal down into smaller, simpler doable steps. For example, if you are contemplating a career change, first research the industry, follow several industry leaders on social media, and then attend an event that one of them is speaking at. Find out what you need to do to qualify for entry into the industry (courses, certifications, etc.) and what level of financial investment could be expected to get started. Remember, if you make a mistake, you can course-correct. Just keep making adjustments.

Open your heart and mind to Spirit. If you have a hundred steps to take and you're only on step two, at least you're moving forward. Take another step.

Don't look ahead to what hasn't happened yet and feel bad because you aren't "doing enough." Keep taking one step at a time. Take a step or two on a daily basis. Surrender to being present with the step you're on. One day you'll arrive at step seventy, then at step eighty, and sooner than you think possible you'll find yourself at step ninety-nine.

You'll grow from every action, whether it is the right or the wrong action. It may take your consciousness a while to wake up to the higher truth that there is something to learn from every action, and if you continue to be centered in your heart, you'll eventually break through everything that limits you from living your ultimate life.

When you experience a true miracle and reach a goal, it may feel very different than you expected it to feel when you first wanted it. This is because our motivations impact our results. If you're motivated by feeling betrayed, wanting to get even, or seeking approval, you may gain outer recognition, which can include fame, honors, awards, and money, but you won't experience inner peace. To fully enjoy the achievement of a goal, you must chase out any negative motivations within yourself along the way.

There are no shortcuts or quick fixes in the game of life. If you delve deeper into how those around you have achieved their meaningful success and happiness, you'll see that they walked their talk. They equipped themselves with tools and used those tools on a daily basis.

You must find a pure motivation within yourself to ensure you take the right action. As your momentum reaches a critical point, you'll feel as if you're being tested. The stakes may be much higher than when you set out on your journey. As a result, you may feel there is more to lose at this point than you did originally. When you find yourself in this place, know that you're not alone. Spirit will be with you.

Do your best not to allow yourself to be diverted from your center by what others think is right for you. If someone else thinks you're doing the wrong thing, it could create a dilemma for you. Avoiding confusion is exactly why you must be clear about your personal motivations, morals, and limiting patterns of thought, emotion, and behavior.

To walk your talk, you must know yourself. I once studied with a business coach who told me that business must always come before family. She said, "It doesn't matter if your child is sick. You should continue to do what needs to be done to succeed." This guidance didn't sit well with me. It was a turning point for me in which I realized that our core values weren't aligned, because I knew that if my child were sick—or any child, for that matter—I would always place the child's interests above my business interests. My moral compass told me not to compromise. Recognizing my truth helped me know the right thing to do.

Think for a moment about your vision. Ask yourself:

- "What are my core values?"
- "What value is most important to me?"
- "What am I prepared to do to realize my vision?"
- "What am I not willing to do?"

Sometimes two actions compete for our attention. If you've made a commitment and you realize you need to change your plans, it's important to have the courage of your convictions. You may feel it's wrong to change your commitment, especially if others are counting on you, but if you make the decision from the standpoint of considering what will create the best outcome for everyone concerned, this principle will help you accept what you have to do. Making course corrections is a necessary part of life. It's as if you're a pilot who constantly needs to adjust the flight path of your plane to arrive at your ultimate destination.

Do your best to look at the action you are about to take from as many perspectives as possible. You may need to sleep on a decision. It may even take several weeks before you feel clear about the next right action step in some situations. Make the decision to adhere to the rule of right action no matter how long it takes, and a new awareness will set in. Once you do, patterns that caused you problems in the past will no longer hold you back. It may feel as if a spell has been broken, and you may wonder why you weren't able to shift and break through your challenges sooner. Everything has its own right timing.

Sometimes when we think things aren't getting done fast enough, in fact, more information will be revealed soon or a course of events apart from us is working itself out that will affect our outcomes. As you take the right action and resist the shortcut or quick fix, in time the feeling of peace will overcome temptation—you'll have evidence that giving in to temptation only creates a false sense of progress. There's a time to act quickly, but if you feel any sense of urgency or desperation, that's your cue to take a step back and move more slowly. When you're driven by impulsive behavior, things generally do not work out well.

Melissa was trying to decide whether to take a business trip for a potential collaboration that would require her to spend more money and take more time away from her family. She was feeling the pressure to make a decision soon. One night, shortly after she went to sleep, she dreamed that the person she was going to visit had lent her his phone. She had arrived at the correct destination, but she was terribly lost and going around in circles. Toward the end of the dream, she realized that the GPS on the phone was outdated and didn't have the correct information to get her where she wanted to go. The phone also couldn't send text messages.

As we reviewed her dream together, it became apparent to her that there was a breakdown in communication and she needed to find her own way to reach her goals, using her own resources—not by collaboration. Spirit was using the phone as a metaphor to communicate a message to her. Once she accepted the guidance, she knew what to do.

Taking the right action may not always be easy, but in the long run it will get you to your desired outcome more quickly and with less effort and fewer mistakes than other actions.

10

RULE 10: **Be of Service**

*If all my needs were already met,
whom would I help today?*

Imagine having everything you need. You can eat whatever you want and live wherever you want. Your buying decisions for clothes, travel, and lifestyle aren't dictated by the amount of money in your bank account. What if you had unlimited freedom like this? Would you sit on a tropical beach being waited on hand and foot for the rest of your life? Would you have a desire to help people? In an emergency would you go above and beyond to help a loved one or a stranger? After all your own personal needs were met, what would you do to serve in a bigger way?

The desire for true service comes from the heart. It is a willingness to help another person, an organization, or a cause with your energy, time, skills, and talents. When you're being of service, you're helping others achieve *their* goals and dreams. No matter where you are in your journey to your big miracle, you can contribute and make a difference to the people in your community. Service is being there for people—friends, aging relatives, vulnerable neighbors—in their times of need. It is doing something generously without expecting anything in return. Your love and compassion, your head, heart, and hands could make a real difference in the quality of someone's life, whether that's by offering to cook for a homeless shelter, building a Habitat for Humanity home for flood victims, or mentoring a young person in your spare time. On a professional level, your skill set and expertise could be the "missing link" that individual clients or the employees in your company need to achieve success. Your expertise and enthusiasm could help someone attain a goal that at the moment feels like an insurmountable mountain.

Helping people inspires us to do more and gets us out of bed in the morning. When we're being of service, our hearts are opened. Service is an expression of love, which is the driving force of the universe. Love keeps energy circulating and puts you in the flow of abundance.

My friend Manny Diotte is a great example of someone who does heartfelt service. He began his career as a motivational speaker and business coach, but it wasn't until he followed his inner calling to serve sick kids on a daily basis that he achieved his ultimate success. At just seven years old, he was himself diagnosed with cancer. He spent the next three and a half years of his life in and out of the hospital, undergoing fifty surgeries and hundreds of radiation and chemotherapy treatments. When he could, he would go from room to room visiting the other kids with cancer with the goal of putting smiles on their faces. The silver lining of Manny's childhood illness was the love and graciousness he exchanged with others.

Later, when Manny was a teenager, he was told that one of his legs would need to be amputated. Before agreeing to the operation, his father flew him from Texas to Los Angeles to see a renowned surgeon for a second opinion. In the pickup zone at LAX Airport, Manny spotted a Ferrari and asked the owner if he could have his photo taken next to it. The owner agreed to let him sit in it, then said, "Son, you seem so happy. I wish I had the time to give you a ride."

Manny never forgot how special this encounter made him feel—like a celebrity. Sitting in the Ferrari and having his photograph taken was so significant to him, in fact, that twenty years later he has made it his purpose to give other sick kids the ride of their life and more by founding The Ferrari Kid, a charity whose sole purpose is making children with cancer feel like celebrities for a day. The organization helps reduce their suffering and bring them joy by helping them forget about the needles, doctor visits, and chemotherapy treatments for a little while.

Manny has received many letters from parents saying things like, "That was my child's best day ever," and "It was the first time my kid smiled in two years." Ferrari owners love the sense of purpose that loaning their cars to these singular events gives them, because, as Manny says, "A Ferrari is a piece of metal, but we give the cars a soul by doing something special with them."

Manny has been recognized by *Business Journal* as one of the top seventeen people to meet and the number-one nonprofit leader in his hometown of San Antonio, Texas, yet he honestly doesn't focus on money, awards, or fame. Until he figured out how to fulfill his spiritual purpose by establishing his nonprofit, The Ferrari Kid, Manny pursued a speaking career that focused on business, but didn't have much success. As he followed his heart to help kids, he arrived at true success and fulfillment. Having undergone a personal evolution, he now focuses on being of service and doing the work that he is uniquely qualified by his life experiences to do.

Manny impresses me for so many reasons, not the least of which is that I've never heard him complain despite everything he's been through. Every time I speak with him, he makes a point to ask if there's something he can do for me. He never asks for anything in return.

Service can be a very simple act of kindness like listening with compassion to a friend. Often our friends don't need advice, but just to be accepted as they are. As they share their fears about the future, for instance, the act of your listening brings them clarity or comfort. Can you think of a friend to whom you could give emotional support today?

Another kind of service is connecting people. Within your social network of friends and associates, which individuals would benefit from meeting each other? What resources and knowledge do you have that could help your friends reach their goals? People often overlook the valuable network of trusted connections they already know or dismiss the special talents they possess that could be very helpful to others. What would happen if you were to embrace an attitude of helpfulness? Of offering support to everyone you come into contact with? How do you think the lives of people around you would change? I've seen an abundance of miracles happen from introducing new contacts and longtime friends to one another.

Being helpful in a selfless manner allows you to be a more powerful spiritual vehicle. You can expand your vision of service by taking on an activity that needs doing, such as helping in your child's classroom, becoming a Big Brother or a Big Sister to a lonely child, promoting a friend's event, or hosting a fund-raiser. If you're willing to commit a significant amount of time and focus, you could join the board of directors of a local nonprofit. However you choose to serve, follow your heart. Your heart will be your motivation to follow through on the service projects you commit to. Listen for your heart's desire to serve.

The Rewards of Service

Giving without expectation of return is a great way to open up the channels of abundance in your energy field. Unconditional giving creates connectedness, which can result in more opportunities coming your way, because the universe likes balance. The Law of Spiritual Reciprocity is that everything we broadcast through our thoughts, emotions, and actions—on an energy level—manifests outcomes in our lives. The return of energy you will experience could come from somewhere totally unexpected and unrelated to your original act of giving.

To practice unconditional giving, choose five people you'd like to help. Reach out to them and ask how you can be of service or, if you already know the areas in which they need support, give that support without asking. Set in motion a simple plan for helping them today. Then watch your abundance increase, noticing what comes to you.

Observe what happens if for a single day you embrace an attitude of selfless service while doing your job or spending time with your family. Stop wondering, *What can I get from this?* and simply let yourself experience the good energy moving through you. Extend the experiment for another day or two—then for a week. A consistent series of small positive actions can lead to massive shifts in energy and remarkable results in our lives.

Being of service teaches us many lessons that prepare us psychologically for a big miracle and also gives us opportunities to center ourselves in our hearts and live lives more connected to our souls. The more we immerse ourselves in the energy of the heart, the more clearly we are able to hear the voice of Spirit offering us guidance.

On a red-eye flight from Los Angeles to Miami at around 3 A.M. we hit a patch of turbulence. I felt a little bit anxious, so I engaged in conversation with the passenger next to me. Donna had recently lost her mother. When she learned I was intuitive, she asked if I could sense that her mom was still around her. It gave her comfort when I reported that I did. I sensed that she was always nearby and had a strong feeling that her mom had never complained, was a giver, and adored her family. It turned out that the woman did a great amount of charity work. She lived for service. Donna told me she thought that if her mother hadn't had the passion she did for helping others, she would likely have passed away sooner.

Being of service gives us a stronger motivation to live—a purpose.

Being of service can also take our minds off our problems. As I focused on helping Donna, it took my mind off the turbulence, and my fear passed. In addition, being of service gives us the opportunity to replace any feelings of inadequacy we may have with joy and self-acceptance. As we focus on helping others, we distract ourselves from negative feelings we have about ourselves and our situation, so we can enjoy our lives and relationships more. That energy is attractive to be around.

As a parent, one of the greatest gifts you receive is the opportunity to serve your child. When you take care of your baby, there's no anger or resentment toward her because she can't do things for herself. You don't get angry at your son for crying, because you understand that your role is to be of service by comforting him, feeding him, or changing his diaper. Imagine if you adopted this same state of mind in your work. As a result of your caring attitude, your clients and colleagues will feel supported and treasured—which would be good for your business—and you will feel less irritated and put upon, less judgmental, and less martyred on tough days.

In searching for opportunities to be of service, always remember the ripple effect. Something you did for someone else may not have seemed such a big a deal to you, but could have made a profound impression on that person and in turn, through that individual, helped others too—like ripples in a pond. Many people become kinder themselves after being on the receiving end of a kindness. It can be especially powerful to be of service to someone who regularly offers service to others, such as a nurse, a firefighter, a teacher, and so forth. When I've volunteered in my son's classroom, his teacher always expresses so much gratitude, because she can give more personalized attention and extra support to the kids who need it most. There are twenty kids sharing her attention on most days.

Simple acts of kindness can make a major difference in a person's day: holding a door open, smiling, reaching out to someone you haven't talked to in a while to see how they are. Doing small random acts of kindness for others when you're intending to be of service on a daily basis brings out the good in you and makes you a better person. Fulfilling someone else's needs is humbling and will assist you in stripping away your ego. If someone looks down on the service you provide, choose to be positive.

It is vital that you put yourself in environments that feel uplifting, where you're surrounded by loving people. Stop hanging around people who complain about what isn't working and what they don't have or who criticize the services offered by others. People who have no motivation to make the world a better place can drain your energy.

Some feel they are above holding certain positions themselves, so they look down on those who hold those jobs. Others may feel that their jobs are not considered desirable and are ashamed and embarrassed. Don't ever let someone else's judgment stop you from doing your job or being proud of how you're of service to others. Be proud of who you are and your ability to help others.

One of the defining aspects of being a spiritual vehicle is being of service. Give thanks for the opportunities you've received and set the intention that you'll be a supportive resource for Spirit to move through you on behalf of other people. Pray that those who need your help are directed to you or that you are guided to them.

Before you go to sleep, review your day. Ask yourself:

- "How did I add value through doing service today?"
- "What was my favorite part of being of service?"
- "What good thing happened today because I showed up?"

Service often opens new doorways and creates unexpected miracles. My client Selena had been feeling unappreciated in her job. She loved what she did, but some of her coworkers were manipulative, and she found the environment in her workplace highly toxic. In her spare time, she took a volunteer position at a charity and met a board member who noted her work during her several months of volunteer service and recommended her for a job that paid close to double her current salary. She was elated and took the job. The miracle happened because the individual who was in a position to help her could see her soul shining through her service.

The more you are of service, the more success you'll experience, just like Selena.

Service is the path to abundance. Any problem you seek to solve with heartfelt desire leads to abundance. Sometimes it happens quickly, other times slowly, but it always arrives. As you serve others with sincerity, life will serve you. Generosity is rewarded, because the energy of the universe tends toward balance. You will get the help and resources you need to ensure that your hopes and dreams are realized when you include the component of service in your business and life.

Furthermore, when you serve people (or animals or nature) by doing something you love, you'll find yourself wanting to do more of it. As you find your place to serve in an environment that feels good to you, respect and trust will follow.

To be of service to a greater number of people, remember to ask Spirit to be of service to you! Spirit will always help you. If you ask for guidance and resources, they'll be provided.

Where Can You Be of Service?

The deeper purpose of service is to connect you to your spiritual nature. Determining the way you want to serve others will ground your vision in such love that you'll have the strength to follow through on your goals and become more fulfilled, connected, and successful. If you're truly being of service, you'll receive so much more than you give. Your heart will open wide. Find a cause to serve that inspires you—something greater than your own self-interest. Being a spiritual vehicle aligned with a cause can lead to miracles.

If you're overwhelmed, being of service is grounding, because it brings things into perspective. Service teaches us to recognize the gifts and blessings we already have. Shifting our mindset from self-absorption and a sense of deprivation to caring and appreciation for what we have can cause abundance to flow into our lives and through us to others in many forms. The beauty is that everyone can be of service. It doesn't matter how much money you have or what your physical abilities are; there is someone you can help.

Answer these questions to clarify what cause inspires you. This could be a cause that serves people, animals, or the environment. Do not restrict your imagination. Ask yourself:

- *"Whose struggle do I most resonate with? Why?"*

- *"Whose pain do I wish I could stop? Why?"*

- *"Which historical figure inspires in me a sense of service? Why?"*

- *"If the legacy of my service were to be remembered in the history books, what would I like to be remembered for?"*

- *"Who has helped me through a difficult time? Was it a specific person, a business, or a charity? How did they help me? What could have gone wrong if I had not received this support?"*

- *"What are three problems I see in my neighborhood? Do I have a skill or ability to contribute to solving those problems?"*

- *"What is my most significant memory of someone I've helped in the past?"*

If you get stuck when choosing where to serve, center yourself in your heart and listen. Pick one act of service to do today or in the near future, even if it's small, and reach out. Just see what happens. Let it be an experiment. The thing to remember about service is there are so many people and causes that need support, you'll easily be able to find a way of helping that feels good to you. Your help would be genuinely welcomed by so many people.

I also suggest making an intention to be of service an element of your morning ritual. Each morning when you wake up, breathe consciously. Inhale love and exhale fear for about a minute. Then, once you feel that your awareness is centered in your heart, ask, "How can I make a difference in someone's life today?" Once you have an answer, get up.

After doing the ritual you may find that Spirit puts people who need help in your path throughout the day. This could take any form, from an unexpected phone call to an exchange with someone waiting in line at the supermarket or in the seat next to you on an airplane. You may sense intuitively that your help is needed. You may have a strong feeling you should contact someone you spoke to yesterday or a friend you haven't seen in years. Reach out and trust that there is a purpose to the timing. Don't let fear hold you back. Who will you be able to help today?

Being of Service Through Your Business

Businesses can be great vehicles for Spirit. Any cause you care about and any population you're interested in helping can be served through professional activities. It's easier to create a whole movement through a business, because there are more people working together. Here are a few examples of what you could do to be of service professionally.

If you run a business, align it with a nonprofit organization. If you run a nonprofit, align it with a business that has a mission like yours or could help you fulfill an aspect of your vision that you aren't yet doing yourself. For example, BritWeek is a U.S. nonprofit group that highlights areas of creative fusion between businesses in the United Kingdom and California. It hosts events that focus on the British contribution to film, fashion, music, the car industry, and science. Through events it produces that are attended by celebrities and sponsored by corporations such as Virgin Atlantic, Jaguar, and Boots, it's raised millions of dollars for humanitarian causes, including Malaria No More, Save the Children, and the Children's Hospital Los Angeles.

Attending a charity event is a great way to meet kindred spirits with whom you can collaborate and become friends. In our world of ever-increasing automation technology, there is less human contact— and we miss it. It seems that in business today we are supposed to do much more in a day than we did ten or twenty years ago. We used to say, "Hello. How are you?" to each other. Now everyone is in a rush to get somewhere, so if someone does ask how you are, it seems to be more of a formality than a sincere question. Life has become an obstacle course, and people are the obstacles. The Information Age is a gift in most ways, but it does cause overstimulation.

What's something you could do to add a personal touch to your services? Would a personal phone call or handwritten note be a human touch that your clients, customers, vendors, or colleagues would value? Hosting a regular gathering to bring your friends and associates together for fun and inspiring conversation could lead to a new creative project or spiritual inspiration.

Build a socially conscious business. Demonstrate your values within your business. For instance, be generous with your knowledge. Look for as many ways as possible to create a heartfelt bond with others through your existing services or products.

Toms is an example of a retail business that has integrated a charitable aspect into its activities. For every pair of shoes you buy, a pair of shoes goes to a child in need through its One for One program. Each time a customer purchases a pair of sunglasses, the company works with its Giving Partners, nonprofit humanitarian organizations, to restore a person's eyesight through surgery, prescription glasses, or medical treatment. For every bag purchased, the company works with its Giving Partners to provide a safe-birth kit and training to birth attendants to ensure that mothers can welcome their babies to the world under sanitary conditions, reducing the chance of infection.[1] The value-driven company continues to focus on the fusion of for-profit and nonprofit under one roof. This adds meaning and a feel-good factor to the customer's purchase. The company's motto is "Business can improve lives."

As you integrate Spirit into all aspects of your life, Spirit assists you in seeing miracles where others do not see them. Spirit is constantly giving you signs as to where you could be of service. Be proactive in creating opportunities rather than waiting for them to happen.

Taking on a new service role through your profession may require you to take a calculated risk to move outside of your comfort zone. That's what happened for my dear friend Kia Miller, who had a successful career as a TV producer on the Emmy Award–winning show *Top Chef*. She took a leap of faith and left her TV career behind to follow her soul's desire to become a yoga teacher.

Kia's turning point occurred when she overheard someone on a flight talking about teaching yoga. She had been going to classes for a while, but hadn't taken steps to get certified and become a professional. She experienced so much envy in her heart that she knew she had an inner calling she needed to follow, if she was to align with her desire to know the deepest part of herself. She believes that when we know ourselves, we gain a sense of real peace and acceptance that is priceless. She experienced this through practicing yoga. Yoga completely shifted her perspective on life, after which her main passion became answering the question: "How can I share this with other people?"

In following her soul's calling, Kia found an inspiring and compelling service-based way to achieve financial success. To pursue a career in yoga, she had to change her lifestyle, for a while downsizing to reduce expenses and paying mindful attention to her finances. Living a simple life helped her in so many ways that she decided to create a business around the concept. Today, she helps people in the corporate structure transition to leading service-based lifestyles that resonate with their souls.

Before Kia gave up her television career to teach yoga, she had lived much of her life for others, seeking their approval. She wore many masks to survive, and as successful as she was, the lifestyle was stressful. Her husband, Tommy Rosen, was a film and events producer. When he saw how fulfilled Kia was by teaching yoga, he began practicing yoga himself. It healed his back and helped him manage his addictive tendencies. Today he is a yoga teacher too, and they travel the world together leading yoga retreats. He also founded a business, Recovery 2.0, with Kia and has published a book and a couple of video programs about using yoga as a recovery tool in treating drug and alcohol abuse.[2]

According to Kia, one of the keys to her success is that her goal is to touch as many lives as possible through yoga.[3] She isn't focused on how much money she can earn, yet her abundance has continued to increase. I've always admired Kia for serving from the purity of her heart instead of being driven by the desire for recognition. She experienced a big miracle by having the courage to let go of her successful TV career without evidence that she would be able to earn as much being a yoga teacher.

Balance Service with Self-Care

Service is wonderful and highly fulfilling. However, we can overdo it if in being of service to others we forget to be of service to ourselves. People in the helping professions, such as nurses and social workers, are familiar with the depletion that comes from giving until you have no more to give. Caregivers of sick or disabled relatives often report having similar experiences of depletion if they aren't being relieved so they can take time to renew their energy on a regular basis. Being drained of energy takes the joy out of service, so be mindful of your personal needs when giving.

If your business is service based, and you're the main person providing service to the customers or clients (for example, a doctor, therapist, graphic designer, or hairdresser), remember to pay attention to your body's needs. If you're standing all day, you could end up with an aching back and feet if you aren't taking care of yourself. If you don't get enough sleep because you're taking on too many shifts in a row, you won't do as good a job and you're not doing anyone a favor.

Avoid the following four types of behavior, as they can block your ability to be of service and to enjoy the free-flowing energy exchange of giving and receiving that leads to miracles:

Don't be a doormat. Being of service does not mean that you are supposed to work for free, unless you have enough money to be self-supporting. If you are struggling financially and doing a lot of volunteer work, be aware that generating zero income not only puts you out of balance (because it means you're depriving yourself); it also means you aren't being the best volunteer you could be. If you're going to do volunteer work, make sure that you can meet your own basic needs, which includes all your living expenses, before saying yes.

Don't be a prisoner. If you put yourself in a service situation for the wrong motivations, for example, because you seek emotional validation, it will disconnect you from your ability to be of true service. It leads you to saying yes for the wrong reasons. Align yourself only with organizations and causes that inspire you and match your core values. When we volunteer, we come into contact with other volunteers and service professionals—some we like and some we don't, and we don't have to like them all. But if you find that the environment and people you're working alongside are hostile or emotionally toxic or that too much is being asked of you and it's stressful, be sure that you establish clear agreement, maintain healthy boundaries, and do not overcommit or allow anyone to abuse you. Some people with giving natures are taken advantage of. You can say no.

Don't be a martyr. You don't have to take on excess responsibilities to prove you are lovable. If you find yourself in a situation where you're always the one who raises a hand to take on an extra task or you do all the cooking at holidays for your extended family by default, remember that you're not a superhero. Ask for help and give others an opportunity to share in the experience of service with you. If your boss asks you to stay late at the office and you're exhausted or you're on vacation and a client says he needs you because he is having an emergency, think before you agree to the request. If it is your heartfelt joy to be of service on the weekend, great, go ahead. Be mindful of your true feelings and energy levels or eventually you'll burn out and stop enjoying your work.

Don't overgive. For a period of time in my coaching business I made myself available to my clients at all hours. I'd say, "Call at any time if you get stuck." Several of my clients who were in different time zones took me literally and would call me at midnight or 6 A.M., and I kept my word to speak with them. Eventually I realized that being on call and perpetually available was doing a disservice to them, as I was either tired late at night or ungrounded when woken from sleep. As a coach, there are no emergencies to address, only challenges. You only need to be on call if you are a doctor or firefighter.

Overgiving can lead to secret resentments. Express yourself when you feel your boundaries are being violated. If you don't communicate your feelings, two things will happen. First, the resentment you feel will build up and clog up your energy field; this will deplete your energy and keep you from experiencing joy. Second, you'll throw yourself out of spiritual alignment and take on responsibilities that move you away from your vision.

Make a point to recharge your energy and nurture your spirit every single day without exception. This means doing things that feel good to your body and soul, such as keeping healthy snacks in your bag so your energy doesn't crash or using an essential oil diffuser to enliven your senses, uplift your mood, and ground your energy. I love to inhale frankincense essential oil for spiritual inspiration and lemongrass to clear my head and focus. When you're inspired and your energy is high, you'll feel a natural urge to share your good energy with others.

From Spirit's viewpoint, service is an opportunity for joy. There is no shame or humiliation in any job or task when you are recognized and appreciated. Even if you aren't acknowledged, take pride in all you do for yourself and others. Keep your heart open, and those who have been praying for help will be guided to you and vice versa. Being of service means you can be a miracle agent in the lives of others. Like Manny or Kia and Tommy, you can live a bigger life through a desire to serve wholeheartedly.

Opening Your Heart to Service

Almost everyone wants to be of service to others. If some don't, it is because they feel depleted of energy or are struggling to manage the demands of their own lives. As you set the intention to open your heart, opportunities to be of service will align for you, and this will lead to abundance in all areas of your life. You will recharge your energy centers and, in turn, you will naturally feel inspired to help others without a sense of fear or obligation.

Take several deep breaths into your body. Inhale love, exhale fear.

Send your awareness to your heart to center yourself in your body.

Imagine yourself sitting in a circle of golden light. Pull your focus off any people or circumstances that are bothering you and draw your awareness inside the circle.

Bring your focus above your head and imagine connecting to Spirit.

Sense yourself moving back into alignment. You will know that you're aligned when your mind, heart, and energy feel peaceful. If you don't feel peaceful, do the best you can.

Keep coming back to these steps until you feel as if the discomfort within and around you has cleared. Then ask Spirit the following questions and stay alert for the answers:

- *"If all my needs were met, in what way could I pass on abundance to others?"*

- *"What form of service would inspire the most joy in my heart and benefit to others?"*

- *"What am I choosing not to see that is making me feel out of balance?"*

- *"What could I do to restore my balance?"*

- *"What is my core motivation for being of service to others?"*

After doing this meditation exercise, you may find Spirit wants you to be a vehicle of love. If you accept that, then you can be of service.

11

RULE 11: Get Outside Your Comfort Zone

*If I were to do something outside of my
comfort zone, what would it be?*

Would you jump out of an airplane? Apply for a job beyond your level of experience?

How vulnerable do you think you could be with your heart before it would break?

How uncomfortable are you willing to get?

Imagine what could happen if you got outside of your comfort zone on a daily basis. You'd likely achieve things you didn't believe were possible, wouldn't you? It's probable that you would. Your life would almost certainly be bigger, better, richer, and full of miraculous moments. Not only would you be inspired; your example would inspire the people around you to live fearlessly. Most important, if you went outside your comfort zone on a daily basis, you'd experience your big miracle sooner.

Living outside the box of your comfort zone is one of the most liberating feelings in the world. It's like walking on clouds and letting your heart sing from the rooftops without apology. Any sense of embarrassment or shame is gone when you decide that you're free to be yourself without limitation.

How might you expand your comfort zone? Imagine your life if fear didn't stop you from doing the things you want to do. Visualize moving beyond fear and living with heartfelt conviction. Practice being unstoppable the next time you sense yourself pulling back.

After thinking about what your life will be like once you're living fearlessly, talk about it with friends. Keep talking about it until you feel a fire being lit within you to take action. Will you travel the world, achieve optimal health, own a business, start a family, or adopt a child? If you've set the earlier rules in motion, by now you're already well on your way to creating a big miracle. This is when Rule 11, Get Outside Your Comfort Zone, is pivotal. As you approach your breakthrough moment, you'll reach the barrier we call *fear*.

Make Fear Your Teacher

Fear will do everything to deter you from experiencing the miracle your heart and soul desire. Many people quit pursuing their dreams when they get closer to the fear barrier, because fear has a painful intensity to it. Fear can stop you in your tracks even if you've been moving along quite nicely. Fear is subtle and can lead you to procrastinate for reasons that you believe are rational. As you are about to move beyond your comfort zone, fear can even transform into terror—which is why that is the moment at which most people revert to their old habits and quit. They can rationalize that it's best to stay in their comfort zone, despite the fact that it's strangely uncomfortable.

At the fear barrier, people will make good excuses for why they're no longer pursuing their dreams. They need to be financially responsible, take care of their kids, stop dreaming, get realistic about their health limitations, and so on—and who were they kidding anyway? Once the pressure is off them, they feel a great sense of relief because the tension is gone. They relax. But they also quit believing that miracles are possible for them. People who succumb to fear view fear as an enemy rather than as a teacher that has the capacity to strengthen their courage and help them create miracles.

Fear is not your enemy if you understand how to go beyond your comfort zone. If you let yourself get closer to fear and reframe the way you look at it, you'll discover that you have the power to keep moving toward your miracles when you're under pressure—and the world won't end.

Let fear become your teacher. You can learn so much from it, and it wants to give you the gift of confidence. There is a very thin line between fear and excitement. Ultimately, they're two sides of the same coin. Do something that scares and excites you every day, and you'll soon recognize that fear can guide you to big miracles. Do something that gives you butterflies in your stomach. It could be taking hold of the microphone at a conference when you're scared of public speaking or doing an activity with which you have no prior experience. Whatever it is, it should make you feel ready to turn beet red with embarrassment if it goes poorly, because it's so uncomfortable.

I watched the first season of the reality TV show *Laker Girls*, which follows the rivalry between dancers who dream of becoming cheerleaders for the National Basketball Association team the Los Angeles Lakers. The competition is fierce. In viewing the show, I felt as though I wanted to be part of the environment I saw on TV, because I was inspired by the passion, determination, and courage of the dancers trying out. Also I wanted to cultivate more resilience and break through my fear of being rejected. That year for Halloween I was a Laker Girl, and my husband, Nick, a loyal Lakers fan, dressed as shooting guard Kobe Bryant.

One evening while we were watching the show together, Nick dared me to audition for the team. At first I thought he was joking, and then I realized he wasn't. The Laker Girls had open trials coming up. Because I loved the show so much, I decided to go for it.

I only had two weeks to prepare, so I asked my dance teacher,

Allan Avendano at Equinox West Hollywood, what I needed to do to get ready for the audition. He told me to take three to four hours of dance classes daily. He explained that since the Laker Girls dance routines were jazz-based, it would be best for me to take classes at two of the best dance studios in Los Angeles, the Millennium Dance Complex and the EDGE Performing Arts Center.

I had a plan, and I was nervous and excited. I'd never danced professionally before, only for fun on the stage of various night-clubs. It was a different experience to be in class alongside Broadway dancers. I had to face many of my fears. Among other things, I also learned that dance is a challenging art form. My brain struggled to follow the choreography.

The day before the Laker Girls audition, I had my last two classes. My husband dropped me off at EDGE dance studio for a turns class, after which I planned to go straight to Millennium for a jazz class. At the time I was forty years old and our son, Dominick, was three years old. When I walked into the turns class, my heart sank. The class was full of eleven-to-fourteen-year-olds with more training than I had. It was an intermediate class, which means it has an advanced curriculum for someone who isn't a professional dancer.

The moment I felt the greatest discomfort was when the teacher instructed us to do a series of pirouettes while traveling from one side of the studio to the other. There was a glass window at the other end of the room where a bunch of parents stood looking into the dance studio. As I spun and got dizzy, I felt a massive surge of embarrassment and shame sweep over me. I wanted to leave the class, but I didn't. When the class finished, Nick and Dominick were waiting for me outside the studio door.

"How was it?" Nick asked as I got in the car.

"Horrible," I said and burst into tears.

"Are you okay to go to the next class?" he asked.

"I can't quit. Let's go to Millennium," I said.

The next morning was audition time. There were already hundreds of girls lined up outside the Toyota Sports Center in El Segundo when we pulled up. TV cameras were everywhere. Nick turned to me and said, "You may not be able to dance, but you're a bloodhound for a camera."

That resonated. I held the image of being a bloodhound in my mind, and I was ready. Within a couple of minutes, the crew heard my British accent and interviewed me. By the time I got inside the building, I was determined to have my story featured on the show. I wanted to become part of Lakers history for my husband, who is a massive fan. I used my TV production knowledge and thought about what could make an interesting story line. Then I pulled out my angel cards and did a reading for a dancer who'd traveled all the way from Colorado. We sat in the splits on the floor with the angel cards between us, and a camera crew descended. I felt great, in my element as an intuitive, but didn't realize that my confidence was about to be very short-lived.

The basketball court where we were to perform our dance routine was several times larger than any dance studio in which I'd practiced. When it was my turn to go, my mind went blank the moment I saw the director of the Laker Girls, Lisa Estrada (whom I admire and had watched many times on TV), three hundred dancers, and the camera crew in front of me. I was terrified, but I remembered Nick's words, "Bloodhound to the camera," and made myself do the routine as well as I could. It felt like one of the most humiliating moments of my life, as I bombed the routine, but in retrospect it was actually not as bad as taking the turns class with the little kids the day before.

I didn't make it past the first round, of course. As I crossed the floor, I saw Lisa give her assistant a look as if to say, "What was she thinking of, auditioning?" but I stuck to my deeper purpose, which was to get outside of my comfort zone. I called Lisa's office after the audition to thank her and let them know that I'd always loved dancing and I'd auditioned because I wanted to inspire others with the knowledge that it's never too late to follow your dreams. I was invited to an after-dance camera interview, where I shared that message, and when Season 2 premiered, I was featured on the first episode for over two minutes of screen time.

Nick couldn't believe it! When he saw me bomb the dance routine on TV, he rolled around on the floor crying with laughter. I had fulfilled the dare and moved far beyond my comfort zone, which led me to feel courageous enough to reopen the issue of my childhood dream of acting. Creatively, seeing myself up on screen liberated me and helped me make the decision to sign up for acting classes with Howard Fine. I broke through so many fear barriers in auditioning for the *Laker Girls* that I was able to put myself out there in a bigger way professionally as well, and I ended up having my first $100,000-plus income-generating month. I also helped several clients experience great breakthroughs too.

Getting outside your comfort zone is doing something you're scared to do. It happens anytime you think you're going to fall flat on your face and get laughed at—but do it anyway. After all, what's the worst thing that could happen? Will you die? When you go outside your comfort zone, your attachment to other people's opinions of you and the ways you've held yourself back in response become very clear. If you stick with the activity, whatever it is, you will quickly discover the fear you thought was unbearable isn't. Once you experience this, fear no longer has power over you. That's why fear is really an angel whose message is, "Reclaim your power!"

There is a purpose to the pain and challenges you will experience when you go beyond your comfort zone. But it's usually only after you've stretched your limits that the purpose becomes clear. When you reach beyond places that feel safe or comfortable, the discomfort you experience will bring to the surface the fearful parts of yourself. At that moment, you'll be able to see who you are without a mask or excuses. When we allow ourselves to remain in complacency so we can pretend everything is fine and we aren't scared of anything, we can fall into procrastination and end up never giving our secret desires a shot.

Build Resilience

You have untapped resilience within you. What's the worst thing that can happen when you go for your dreams? Someone could reject you if you reveal your heart. You could lose all your money if you take a financial risk, but you could risk even more by never pursuing your dream and living an uneventful life in a job you dislike and a relationship that you've settled for. You can start over; many people have. You could face ridicule if you test a new skill, but the more you practice, the better you'll get. How bad might the rejection, loss, and shame be? Not as bad as you imagine, because after the critics' initial judgment their focus moves back to their own problems. They don't care about you or your failure as much as you do. If someone rejects you, use it as motivation to move in a new direction or try something else. If you persist, you'll eventually succeed.

Think about something you really want, but haven't given yourself permission to pursue. If you were on your deathbed and hadn't done it, how do you think you would feel? This is a good way to gauge how important doing a new thing is to you. Create a bucket list and make a plan to fulfill those dreams.

I loved dancing from a young age. When I tried out for the Laker Girls, I knew it was too late to become a professional cheerleader. Nonetheless, the experience of challenging myself to study with amazing dance teachers, learn choreographed jazz routines, and go through the audition process made me feel so alive. I was constantly pushed outside of my comfort zone. Being a total beginner crushed my ego and overrode my need to look good. That was humbling.

When I returned to my work as a spiritual coach, I had a fresh perspective, a beginner's mindset, and a willingness to learn, which made me a better teacher. It also gave me the courage and confidence to reach out to people who are more successful than I am.

If you commit to getting outside of your comfort zone, you'll develop resilience far beyond that of most people and you'll radiate a star quality. Perhaps there's someone you'd like to date who you think is out of your league—smarter, better looking, or more successful. Growing up I remember hearing adults make comments like, "Nice body, shame about the face." I was horrified, and it made me paranoid about how I looked. On the London club scene I was surrounded by models, and I felt terribly insecure. When those I liked paid attention to me, because I felt I was below them I thought they might be playing a practical joke on me. However, I eventually overcame my fear of rejection and found my inner well of resilience. Whatever your fear, use it as fuel to break through. If your heart desires it, you deserve it.

Happiness, joy, and freedom lie beyond your comfort zone. If you knew how much good was waiting there for you, you'd summon the courage you need to move beyond your comfort zone. The idea of public speaking could feel very scary when you see thirty people in an audience in front of you. But in truth, if you're focused on spiritual growth, in the faces of those people you'll see thirty opportunities to change someone's life for the better. This will override your fear.

Remember the distinction between living a small life and living a simple life. You certainly don't need to move to a bigger home if having a big house isn't one of your goals. A bigger life takes different forms. Be true to your own vision for a better life and admit it if you aren't challenging yourself to follow through on manifesting it. Fear can only control you as long as you believe it can.

If someone says you don't have the skill to do something, you have the power to decide to study how to do it and to practice until you are great at that skill. Fear would have you believe that you aren't capable even of studying. Fear wants you to buy in to other people's limiting beliefs. If you agree with a fear, it will paralyze you.

Overcoming Fear with a Miracle Box

As long as your head is full of fear and resentment, it will be hard for you to focus on your vision. Creating a Miracle Box—your personal mailbox to Spirit—will free up space in your mind where you can dream big. Let Spirit take away your worries and transform them into miracles.

Your Miracle Box can be as big or as small as you like and any color. You could buy a beautiful box or craft your own. Feel free to decorate it with messages of inspiration. My Miracle Box is violet and covered in sparkles. I drew angels in gold ink and stuck these on top and inside the box. I also pasted a label on the lid that reads MIRACLE BOX and two on the sides that read SPIRIT IS MY EMPLOYER and SPIRIT PROVIDES MY ABUNDANCE. I keep this box by the side of my bed, next to a notepad and gold Sharpie. I write messages to Spirit and place them in the box before I go to sleep and the first thing after I wake up, because I feel such a strong connection with Spirit while I'm dreaming.

Whenever you find your mind overwhelmed with fear or negativity of any kind, write a note describing the thing that's bothering you and put this message to Spirit in your Miracle Box. For example, to release fear you might write:

Dear Spirit,
Please help me release my fear about how I will pay rent
this month. Release my blocks so I can take action to gener-
ate income.

_____

[your name]

To get an answer, ask a question. For example:

Dear Spirit,
I want to start my own business. Is now the right time to
leave my job or is it best to wait?

_____

[your name]

I suggest that you write the date on each of your messages, so you can look back at them and see the amount of
time it took for things to work out. Fold up the note you've
written and put it in your Miracle Box, and then get on with
your day or night as you normally would. This quick ritual is
very powerful. It loosens the grip of fear and opens you up
to spiritual guidance and solutions.

Over time your Miracle Box may fill up, depending on
how many messages you send to Spirit on a daily basis.
Once your box is full, tip out your folded-up notes and
read them. It's fun to look back over the last few months
and see the miracles you received by demonstrating
faith. You may be surprised to see that so many things
you worried about have worked out well. Answers will
be delivered. Things that you wanted, but didn't know

how to do or to get, will have miraculously manifested for you.

Over the years, I've prayed to Spirit to help me find a beautiful home, get me booked on TV appearances, find my ideal clients, generate more income, heal relationships, create my best body, and so much more. Seeing what has worked out has helped me build my faith in Spirit and come to truly believe, down to my bones, that the universe conspires to support our dreams. Anytime I've had writer's block when I needed to write a blog post or a newsletter, I've gone right to my Miracle Box and requested that Spirit use me as a spiritual vehicle. If I turned to unhealthy eating, I made a request to Spirit to help me stop craving sugar and other tempting foods.

If a prayer you put in your Miracle Box has not yet manifested by the time you tip out and read the messages, put that message back in and reaffirm your request for clarity or guidance in reaching for a goal. Keep messages in the box until you get the results you want. If you're traveling away from home, you could use a velvet bag or cloth pouch to hold your notes to Spirit.

Bust Out of Your Comfort Zone

There is a critical point in your life when you can set in motion your heart's desire or settle for a life of mediocrity. This is when you really want something, but hold yourself back. Busting out is required to go beyond your limitations or you'll only experience short-lived success. It seems that there is always a point when we want to stop as we get close to a big miracle breakthrough. We have an impulse to compromise our dreams as we get uncomfortable. Fear can consume courage, and pain can outweigh enthusiasm. People who are successful understand that if they don't feel this discomfort, it's a sign that they aren't learning or growing.

If you want to bust out of your comfort zone, you must make a painstaking search for the false stories you've created in your mind that make you think you're in danger. At some point you convinced yourself that these stories were real. At the moment when you become certain that you must stop, you must recommit to your miracle (Rule 3).

When you come up against the edges of your comfort zone, the fear you feel will be intense. This is how you'll know you've reached your border. To go any farther will feel utterly wrong. This is where Rule 1 is also imperative. Align with Spirit, so that you can get a clear read from your inner guidance system on what you're meant to do next.

Your comfort zone has a strong defense system in place, set up by your ego. Your ego will do everything possible to deter you from aiming high and stepping forward. As soon as it senses you are moving beyond the limits it finds acceptable, it sets off a warning that triggers fear in your body, insisting that there will be severe consequences if you take any additional action in this area.

To make matters worse, you may see others pursuing a vision similar to yours, but failing to realize their goals or crashing and burning around you. This can seem like evidence that the false story your ego is telling you is real. Even though there may be no physical danger involved in your activities, it can feel as though your very survival is being threatened. The impression of danger can feel incredibly real.

Struggling salesman Chris Gardner had to bust out of his comfort zone after he was evicted from his apartment, his girlfriend left him, and he had to raise his five-year-old son alone while jobless and homeless. Similar events might have crushed another individual. But Chris's response to the pressure of his circumstances was so inspiring that his memoir, *The Pursuit of Happyness,* became a *New York Times* bestseller and was made into a movie starring Will Smith. Chris's dream was to become a stockbroker on Wall Street, so he could provide his son with a good life. Against the odds, he was accepted into an unpaid internship in a brutally competitive stockbroker training program, where only one in twenty interns would make the cut. Because of his incredible work ethic and no-fail sense of purpose, he ended up being selected and going on to become a Wall Street legend.[1]

The movie is a must-see if you're serious about busting out of your comfort zone, even though it's highly unlikely that you'll ever have to endure as much hardship as Chris did. Every time you feel too uncomfortable and imagine that you can't continue, watch a few minutes of the movie to refocus on doing what needs to get done to achieve your goals and aspirations.

When you feel threatened by an action you need to take, revisit your original motivation for doing it. Focus on your connection to this action in your body until you begin to feel that not following through on it will cost you more than giving up will. You have to convince yourself of this in order to break through.

Once you've pinpointed where you're stopping in your mind and life, clarify why. Ask yourself:

- "Have I moved outside my comfort zone in the past and failed?"
- "What were the consequences of busting out of my comfort zone?"
- "Did I lose money, a relationship, friends, or respect when I did?"
- "Did I lose my confidence?"
- "Is there a time in the past when I went outside my comfort zone and succeeded?"

- "What doors opened for me?"
- "What were the rewards of my persistence?"
- "What could I do in service to my dream to get outside my comfort zone?"
- "What do I fear could go wrong?"
- "What is the likelihood I will succeed vs. the likelihood I will fail?"
- "What is the worst thing that could happen?"
- "Do I know where my beliefs are causing me to stop?"
- "If I could secure my big vision, what would I do to bust out of my comfort zone?"

Take a Calculated Risk

A calculated risk is when you've done a satisfactory amount of research before making a decision and acting upon it. There is no guarantee of the outcome you desire, but when you have a repeated urge to move forward, that is your intuition guiding you and the risk is worth taking. For example, if you've repeatedly experienced heartbreak in a relationship, you may be scared to date; but if you take time to learn your date's viewpoints, values, and dreams, you will quickly be able to see if there is potential for the relationship to work. Taking a calculated risk means there is a stronger likelihood that you'll succeed than that you'll fail. Putting a plan in place for your career can help you to identify what to focus on first. When you find something doesn't work, you may need to make a simple adjustment that leads to your desired outcome, rather than discarding your plan altogether and starting over.

You will reap the rewards of your labor even when others are sure you'll fail, if you do proper investigation. When you are considering hiring someone for a service, speak to three people before making a commitment, rather than going with the first person. Invest in learning as much as possible about the industry you are interested in succeeding in. Then you'll be prepared for opportunities to be involved in exciting projects, because you've demonstrated that you're smart and resilient. Others may wonder, *Why her and not me?* The reason is that you were willing to take a risk, and they were not.

The time and money you invest in taking a calculated risk won't be wasted if you've truly done your due diligence. Taking a calculated risk means that even if you lose money or spend time on a speculative project, you still benefit. Learning about a new industry or more about your current assignments will pay off eventually if you don't give up.

Risk an adventure. My client Brenda had a long-standing dream of traveling to the Great Wall of China. But in her mind it was never the right time, the cost was extravagant, and it was too scary to travel alone in a foreign country without being able to speak the language. When Brenda switched jobs, she unexpectedly found herself with several weeks between her former job and her new one. When I suggested she use this window of time to finally travel to the Great Wall, she froze up. However, as we talked through it, her fear eased because we discussed the steps she'd be taking and addressed the likelihood of her fears coming to pass. She did research and found a tour she liked so she could travel with a group. She bought a Chinese dictionary. Later she told me it was the best vacation of her life. What is something you'd love to do, but feel is too risky?

Risk being first in your field. Regardless of the outcome, you'll learn a lot about your business by being the first to market with a new product or service. Even if your results aren't spectacular, you'll have a head start the next time you do something similar—and you'll now be aware of the pitfalls. You'll clarify the areas you need more skill or knowledge in, and you'll get equipped to handle whatever challenge comes along. You'll have the ability to quickly get done what needs to be done and make informed decisions.

Businessman Richard Branson said, "You've got to take risks if you are going to succeed. I would much rather ask forgiveness than ask permission."[2] When the British postal strike happened in 1971, he could have cut his losses and dissolved his mail-order record company. Instead, he increased his risk by leasing a physical store in a prime London location to establish Virgin Records. This was a groundbreaking business for the U.K. music industry as it didn't have record stores back then. His company evolved into Virgin Music Group and eventually sold for $1 billion.

If you don't know what to do or how to do what is necessary, there's a high probability someone else can guide you to minimize your risk. But you must be prepared to fail and try again to arrive at the big miracle you desire. And what if there isn't a person around you who has done it before? Like other people who didn't know what to do, you can pray for spiritual guidance about what you should do next.

Examples can sometimes be found in nature. When the ultimate innovators, the Wright brothers, had the idea that there was a way for humans to fly, they watched large gliding birds in the sky for guidance as to their next steps. They researched and tested their ideas relentlessly before achieving their first flight. From their study, they discovered that Kitty Hawk in North Carolina was an ideal spot to test their ideas, because its consistent high winds off the ocean were perfect for kite flying. When an experiment didn't work, they found a new way to test their theories. Eventually they were able to translate what they found worked in nature and make a breakthrough that resulted in human flight.

Your desire for the things you want must be greater than the fear you have in pursuing them. You must toughen up your heart to withstand the barbs and judgments from others who are watching from the sidelines. This means having a learning mindset, warrior spirit, and courageous heart. Calculated risks are the way to move from your current circumstances to a life filled with joy by focusing on research and being flexible when things don't work out so you can course-correct your life. As you gain the relevant information and take more actions, eventually the fear will dissolve. Expect to always be faced with new challenges; it means you are experiencing spiritual growth. If you stop taking risks, you stop growing. If success were guaranteed, there would be no risk or growth. A risk has a higher reward.

Risk revealing your heart. If you are shy, reserved, or guarded and wait for another person to speak more openly, you could miss out on a very special connection in a relationship. Have you ever met someone and sensed that you've known the person before, perhaps in another life? If you have an urge to talk to someone, follow through on that feeling, even if you don't know where it will lead you. Perhaps it will lead to mentorship, marriage, children, or a dear friendship. Who knows? If you don't act boldly, you'll never know.

Will you choose a small life in a box where your routines become barriers to adventures? Or will you get outside your comfort zone and reach for an abundant life? Spiritual growth occurs and courage is developed anytime you step outside your comfort zone and say *yes*. Ignore those around you who only want to step up when it's a sure thing, because their opinion doesn't matter.

Seven Ways to Build Your Confidence

The more you practice going outside your comfort zone, the easier it will get. Those initial feelings of awkwardness, fear, or embarrassment subside. Most times you'll discover that the rejection or failure you feared does not turn out to be real. What was once uncomfortable will become exciting for you.

The more confident you are, the more willing you'll be to get outside your comfort zone. Here are seven ways to build that confidence through stretching yourself. These are the types of actions that can lead to miracles. I challenge you to pick one idea from the list below and put it into practice. You can begin with a simple challenge and as your confidence increases move on to something that causes you more discomfort, but you know in your heart will ultimately be good for you.

1. Speak to a stranger in an elevator or the supermarket checkout line. Ask how the person is.

2. Strike up a conversation with the person next to you on a flight and reveal something personal about yourself to elevate the conversation beyond small talk for an authentic connection.

3. Research a conference or workshop that's out of state and get a ticket to it to get you out of your daily routine and home environment. When you invest more, you're more likely to implement what you learn to get a return on your investment.

4. Take a class in something you've never done before, for example, a foreign language, computer coding, golf, improvisational comedy, or survival training.

5. Visit a new country and learn about its culture.

6. Host a party and invite old and new friends.

7. Set a challenging fitness goal, like running a marathon, and use it to raise money for a good cause.

What You Can Expect as You Move Beyond the Fear Barrier

When you get serious about your dreams and begin taking actions to manifest them, it's common to feel overwhelmed as the reality of the gap between where you are and where you want to be grows clear. If you don't feel overwhelmed, then you haven't reached your fear barrier yet.

"How are you going to break through your fear?" the ego asks. Because you don't know, you'll wonder if the ego has a point. Every cell in your being feels a discomfort that you thought (and hoped) you could avoid. Your unevolved ego is clear that it wants you to go no farther. Right before breaking through your fear, you may feel a tugging sensation in your belly. If you've never felt this before, it could scare you when it happens. That's okay. Stay true to your spiritual path, and the sensation should subside very soon. I have experienced this sensation many times in my own life, and I can assure you that beyond your fear barrier life will feel so much better.

Be willing to take bold action beyond your comfort zone. Practice speaking your mind and matching your actions to your values when you feel resistance. Remind your ego you don't need to be right in your relationships; you need to be free from doing things that would put you out of spiritual alignment and compromise your values. Whenever you feel overwhelmed by resistance, get centered in the present and then take small diligent steps. Live one moment at a time, and remember to breathe. When we look into the future through the eyes of fear, it will always seem overwhelming. But eventually we can get everything our hearts desire, as long as we keep moving toward it in increments.

*

Embrace Humility

Life is always testing us, which means you have an opportunity to express more of your potential. Embrace humility, and it will serve you well in reframing the challenges you face to break through to your big miracle. When you embrace getting out of your comfort zone on a regular basis, you'll find yourself graced with new opportunities.

A Letter from the Future You

Write a letter to yourself from the future you. Imagine that you've already created your big miracle and you're living beyond the fear barrier. You've overcome the majority of your inner demons and external obstacles. From this perspective, what wisdom can your future self impart to you? Using stream of consciousness, put down those thoughts from the future you in your Miracle Journal.

Live your future possibilities in your mind first and then in your body, knowing that you're in the process of manifesting miracles right now.

Many years ago I lost everything I owned and had to start over again. I thought I was humble, but really I was often fearful of Spirit. I'd pray to be a spiritual vehicle, and then I'd put a lot of conditions on the type of spiritual vehicle I was willing to be. If I didn't get what I wanted, I thought I was forsaken and became angry. When I surrendered the unevolved parts of my ego, my life quickly began to turn around. As I stopped clinging to what was keeping me uncomfortably comfortable, miracle upon miracle flowed into my life.

Expect Miracles

As you get outside your comfort zone and move beyond fear, you'll align with miracles. Miracles come to those who expect them. Before they come into physical form, you can feel them in the air. It's as if the space around you is charged with electric energy. This dynamic sensation is caused by your energy streamlining itself in anticipation of receiving what you've imagined in your mind. When the mind is no longer contained or restricted by fear, it is a powerful conductor for creation.

Get outside your comfort zone to make yourself receptive to miracles now. The energy you require to break through is available to you, if you have the courage to claim it.

12

BREAK THROUGH TO YOUR BIG MIRACLE

Having read the eleven rules you now have a strong foundation to create your ultimate success. You may find yourself being particularly drawn to certain rules, because they are reflected in your life, and you'll see how the application of those rules will assist you in breaking through your barriers. As you exercise each rule, you'll feel when you've reached a certain level of mastery. You'll also see evidence of your big miracle taking shape. This will give you confirmation that the rule is integrated in your daily behavior, and you can amplify your breakthrough by adding the practice of an additional rule.

Breaking through to your miracle means you have accepted the idea that you have a direct connection to Spirit and that the resources you require to create your big miracle are available to you, even if you don't see evidence of them. If you focus solely on Rule 1, Align with Spirit, on a daily basis, all that is necessary to break through will be clear to you, and you'll find the resilience to stay the course for the realization of your big-picture vision. But if you circle through the eleven rules and commit to their application, you can be confident that what you desire will come to fruition.

As a miracle worker, you have the ability to inspire others through your actions. People love being around miracle workers, because they feel so much better in our presence. People will often tell a miracle worker, "I was feeling awful today, but being around you has made me start to feel like everything is going to work out. I feel better." Has that happened to you yet?

Interestingly, one of the best ways to increase your energy to experience more miracles is to imagine seeing miracles wherever you go. Develop the habit of acknowledging miracles in your life and thanking Spirit for them. As you do, you'll find your direct connection to Spirit strengthening and confidence in your decisions building.

Eleven Everyday Miracles

Here are some miracles that are easy to see. Practice expressing gratitude for these everyday miracles to increase your momentum toward your breakthrough.

1. *Your body is a miracle.* If you are faced with a health challenge, you could choose to believe you are limited and give up on your dream or see the miraculous vehicle you live in through clear eyes. Your body is constantly performing a multitude of tasks and doesn't require your attention. The force of nature that pumps blood through your heart does not complain that it doesn't get to have a rest. If it did, you'd be dead!

When Lewis Howes, former world record holder for achieving the most receiving yards in a football game, got a terrible injury, his dream of playing professional football was shattered. He fell into depression and could have stayed on the couch, as he did not have another vision for his life. Then, by following a practice of expressing daily gratitude for his body, Lewis was able to turn away from fear and focus his attention on aligning with Spirit. As he did this, a new vision came to him. He went on to become an Olympic athlete playing for the American men's handball team, while simultaneously running a multimillion-dollar business and becoming a *New York Times* bestselling author.

Miracle workers treat their bodies with love and respect. Even if they have pain or physical challenges, they appreciate their bodies and don't let their physical limitations stop them from pursuing their heart's desires. The Special Olympics is filled with children and adults who are miracle workers.

2. *A meal is a miracle.* One thing none of us can avoid spending money on is food. For people struggling financially, getting a meal can seem like an obstacle to freedom. Many simply do not have the finances to afford nutritious food, which can lead to poor health. A number of years ago, I visited the Navajo Nation and worked with a local medicine man. I was shocked that the closest grocery store was over sixty miles away from his home and the only nearby retail food choices available were Burger King and Kentucky Fried Chicken. I remember ordering corn on the cob and as I took a bite discovering that the corn was soggy and tasted sugary.

The experience was a humbling reminder that so many of us take our abundant food choices for granted. In Los Angeles or New York, I can walk outside my house and eat at an array of healthy restaurants or shop at a number of grocery stores bursting with fresh produce.

Miracle workers are grateful for the miracle of a meal whether they're eating at a gourmet restaurant or sharing a simple home-cooked meal. They take a moment to acknowledge the food source: the elements from nature that helped the food to grow, the workers who transported the food, and the people who supplied it. They are aware of the food's miraculous journey from farm to table. They view a meal with loved ones and friends as an opportunity to share the blessing of life and appreciate each other.

3. *A home is a miracle.* Do you ever feel trapped in your environment or look negatively at your living space? Do you find yourself focusing on the crack in a wall, the annoying drip of a leaky tap, or a noisy neighbor? If you want to be a miracle worker, you must make your home your headquarters for manifesting miracles and see it as a springboard to your big miracle. It doesn't matter whether your home is big or small or if you're between homes and staying in a hotel. There was a time when I didn't have a home and stayed with friends or did housesitting. I've slept in presidential suites at five-star hotels, in a sleeping bag under the stars in the Peruvian desert, and on a blow-up mattress in a friend's garage. Wherever I lay my head, I am simply grateful to have a place to sleep. The idea that I can break through to a big miracle is possible, as I can feel the encouragement of Spirit surround me. I can gain a clear perspective of my environment and that it serves a purpose to move me forward.

4. *Family is a miracle.* Family is a social unit that teaches you, for better or worse, how to give and receive in relationships. As we grow up, we have the opportunity to create our own families. Whatever your circumstances—whether you come from a toxic family or a loving one—if you're a miracle worker, you see the miracle of family.

Many people I've met say they feel like the black sheep in their family. A miracle is that many black sheep find each other and end up living very happy lives together. Miracle workers know that what doesn't kill them makes them stronger. They seek close relationships with Spirit and focus on making themselves spiritual vehicles for their family members. Miracle agents can look back upon difficult times they've experienced, forgive, and feel compassion for relatives who have hurt them, also demonstrating mindful forms of interaction and communication through their examples.

5. *A friend is a miracle.* Miracle workers are true friends. They are happy to give emotional support to others, so that they can find their way back to their spiritual center. True friends also love serving as

compasses to truth. They don't give advice, unless they're asked. They listen, they love, and they accept others for who they are. Miracle workers make awesome friends. They're the best friends to have, because no matter what is happening in your life, good or bad, they are like bright rays of sunshine breaking through the clouds of a gloomy day. Miracle workers have healthy boundaries and have a circle of friends who are miracle agents too. This makes for a powerful community full of miraculous resources everyone in the circle can use to move forward with their own visions of how to serve and be a spiritual vehicle.

6. *Money is a miracle.* Although money is an inanimate object, it can bring out the worst behavior in people. Some will lie, cheat, steal, and kill to get their hands on money. But miracle workers understand that money is a symbol of the respectful exchange of energy. Money's real purpose is to demonstrate a value for a product or service. This value is in the eyes of those who sell it and those who buy it.

Miracle workers know they can increase their value by believing they are valuable and offering something wonderful to their customers and clients that helps, heals, inspires, creates, fixes, or entertains. They are grateful for money, but not attached to it. They know not to fixate on money, because this will cost them their freedom. A miracle worker's core value is freedom. Miracle workers understand that the money needed to live an abundant life presents itself when needed.

7. *A job is a miracle.* Oh, the complaints people have about their work! Miracle workers understand that the jobs they do make other people's lives richer and more satisfying—and in some cases regularly save lives. What if no one wanted to be a pilot, doctor, nurse, chef, accountant, singer, plumber, or electrician? Miracle workers love to be of service, so they take or do jobs because they enjoy them. Some miracle workers can afford to lie on a tropical beach all day, but prefer to spend just enough time on the beach to feel great. The rest of the time they go about inspiring and teaching others how to create prosperity and happiness.

8. *Meditation is a miracle.* Some people's minds are so filled with negative and fearful thoughts that there's no room in them for joy. They wake up gloomy, expecting the worst, and if the day does go well, they begin searching for a problem. Crazy, right?

The miracle of happiness is inside you, and meditation will give you access to it. Miracle workers know the miracle of meditation well and make it a daily priority. Even if they're extremely busy, they start the day with a couple of minutes of meditation and if time permits, do more. Meditation is like a vacuum that can clean unhappy thoughts from the carpet of your mind. Spirit loves to assist miracle workers in doing their mental housecleaning.

9. *Today is a miracle.* People often look to the future with fear and worry or feel regret and sadness about the past. They miss the miracle of the present moment, because they're so caught up in their minds. Though they have dreams, they don't act upon them. They say they'll "get to it tomorrow," but then tomorrow becomes today and they still don't do what needs to get done.

Miracle workers seize the present moment and get excited about what they can create. They recognize that anything is possible if they maintain an open heart and mind. Miracle workers choose one activity and start there. Then they watch as a miracle unfolds before their eyes, which fills them with happiness that gives them the energy to take additional actions. They recognize that they have the time to do what they want if they give themselves real permission to do it. If a miracle worker wants to publish a book, she begins her day with writing. If he wants to open a cafe, he begins his day with cooking or fine-tuning his recipes. If a miracle worker wants to be a healer, she commits to making herself whole and being of service to others, starting her day with a prayer of gratitude.

10. *The song of your heart is a miracle.* Some people cannot hear the sound of Spirit's music. Instead, they're tuned in to the radio station of the inner critic, the judgmental parent, the jealous sibling, the

gossiping friend, or the backstabbing coworker. If you accidentally turn your dial to one of these stations, quickly change the channel. Don't listen. There is a song in your heart, and it wants to be heard and sung. Sing it.

Miracle workers know that the songs in their hearts are meant to be expressed and shared. When you listen for yours, you'll be guided to miracles and understand how to create them too. In my experience, there's always a sound that precedes a big miracle break-through, which is the sound of Spirit singing to us. Miracle workers also know to listen carefully when they're in a natural setting for signs of guidance.

11. *Spirit is a miracle.* The world is not against you. Life is not trying to punish you. Nor is Spirit. To people who are suffering, de-pressed, or overwhelmed it often seems as though Spirit doesn't exist or is neglecting them. These people have heard of Spirit and heard stories of others experiencing miracles, but they just don't see how a miracle could ever happen for them. In the presence of a miracle agent who suggests Spirit could perform a miracle, these people may say something like, "You don't understand." They're often more comfortable using unhealthy habits to numb their pain. What they may be failing to realize is that miracle agents have suffered at some point too. Everyone does. Life includes pain.

Before miracle workers experience miracles, many of them have had bad habits, which may have included engaging in toxic relation-ships, borrowing and spending money they didn't have, eating in excess, living for the moment without regard for the needs of others, and abusing their bodies with alcohol and drugs. For some, a miracle came when they were in a state of despair. They sensed Spirit sur-rounding them, and as soon as they saw a tiny gleam of sunlight in their darkness, they were able to find their way to a door that opened to miracles. When they stepped beyond their bad habits and chose to leave them behind, they were transformed into miracle agents.

Miracle workers have received the message that they are Spirit and therefore are miracles.

The Breakdown Before the Breakthrough

Often, just before we break through to a big miracle, it can suddenly feel as though things in our lives are falling apart. This can cause us to revert to bad habits—to put a foot on the brake of our spiritual vehicles when we really need to keep our foot on the accelerator. This "breakdown before the breakthrough" happens because, from the ego's viewpoint, we are dying. It is like a spiritual "die-off syndrome." The physical die-off syndrome (technically called the Jarisch–Herxheimer reaction) occurs when we take antibiotics, and the body reacts to the large number of toxinlike products released by the death of harmful microorganisms by experiencing flulike symptoms; it is the "feeling worse before feeling better" syndrome. Your bad habits, which were created by your unevolved ego, share the same energy signature as harmful microorganisms.

A bad habit starts as a one-time action that is repeated until it becomes second nature. Then it seems as though you have no power to release yourself from the struggle, pain, and suffering the bad habit brings with it. Ironically, the first time you took the action, it brought you pleasure, comfort, or relief, which was what drew you to form the habit. Of course, there's a positive behavior that can supersede every bad habit. But before you can embrace these positive actions, it's also helpful to focus on what *not* to do, so that you won't sabotage your efforts to change.

Once you make a decision that you're ready to release a bad habit and replace it with a good one, it can feel as though a weight has been lifted from you. However, when you're focused on breaking the bad habit, your ego can return with a vengeance. Because you don't know what lies on the other side of the breakthrough, fear can push you out of the driver's seat of your spiritual vehicle and hijack you, taking you in a direction opposite to the one you want to be going in.

Fear hates the unknown, and the ego gets angry and bossy when it's not in control of you. Ego and fear will gang up on you just before you have a breakthrough and unanimously say, "You have no proof that you'll get what you want, so what makes you think now is the time it will happen?" That is the cue for doubt to enter and fill your mind with all the reasons why you should keep doing things the way you've always done them, why you should play it safe.

Bad habits will skew your thinking, leading you to expect pain, danger, and stress as normal parts of your life. So if you ever hear people say, "I always have bad luck," or "Life is the school of hard knocks," you can be certain that they have bad habits that are keeping them stuck in a narrow way of living.

You are a spiritual vehicle. However, your bad habits will create potholes, diversions, and delays in your life. Sometimes they cause someone wonderful to live in obscurity or end a life too soon due to addiction. You can succeed in a job with bad habits, but it is unlikely you will be happy, because you'll always be trying to disguise the truth. Just remember, people can look like roaring successes to the outside world, bragging in their social media posts, at public events, and in the press, but when they go to bed at night they cannot escape the painful thoughts. Unhappiness and anxiety will keep them up at night. As Buddhists say, everywhere you go, there you are.

Bad habits are a way to mask overwhelming feelings. The energy it takes to defend and justify them could be channeled into having more happiness and doing more good in your community. But no amount of bribery can make you give up a bad habit; you have to come to the conclusion yourself that you want to transform your life by embracing more positive behavior. As you overcome bad habits, you'll free your mind, and this will allow you to further align with Spirit.

To prepare yourself for a breakthrough, it's essential to look at the reality of what your bad habits are doing to your life, relationships, health, and finances. Many times we can't see when we're engaging in a bad habit, even if it causes us and others harm. When you align with Spirit, you'll be able to see through the illusions you've created for yourself about your bad habits. No one consciously chooses to live in denial. But when you're not spiritually aware, denial slips into your mind and settles in without opposition.

Creating a big miracle breakthrough for your life will take commitment and diligence. The whole process can be overwhelming, if you think you need to make every change at once. If a woman is significantly overweight and has been eating bowls of pasta, hamburgers, and large desserts on a regular basis without doing any exercise for years, making a sudden change to doing a green-juice cleanse for ten days and spending an hour on the treadmill every day is an enormous undertaking. If she fails in her attempt, it could not only cripple her belief in herself; it could be dangerous for her to ramp up the new exercise regimen too quickly. For the woman, the ultimate goal is feeling great, living a healthy lifestyle, and being strong and toned. She has to become a new version of herself who can sustain a lifestyle where those goals are not only possible or probable, but inevitable. A big miracle breakthrough is a permanent transformation related to consistent patterns of behavior that change our identities and our lives.

Eleven Don'ts for Breaking Through

When we're working toward a breakthrough in any area of our lives, what we *don't* do is just as important as what we do, because our negative choices can cancel out our positive ones. The eleven don'ts for breaking through will empower quick and noticeable changes in your life that will help you build your confidence and strengthen your commitment to transforming the bigger picture of your life. As you read them, one or two will likely jump off the page at you, begging to be implemented.

1. *Don't make assumptions.* People who make assumptions have closed minds. Because they're sure they're right, they miss valuable information that would contribute to making better-informed decisions. If you tend to make assumptions, then you may waste your energy thinking someone is upset with you, wants to hurt you, dislikes you, or is trying to make your life difficult. You'll arrive at conclusions that aren't true and hold yourself back from having loving relationships and career advancement.

People who make assumptions also often act without thinking. One time a pharmacist was curt and aloof with me when I was picking up a prescription at the drugstore—or that's how I perceived her demeanor. Instead of being offended, I stopped and asked how she was. Her energy softened, and she confided that it was hard for her to focus on work that day as her husband was in the final stages of cancer.

I was in my twenties when my maternal grandmother died. I remember an incident that occurred when I was walking down the street feeling the loss. A building contractor called out to me, "No need to look so grumpy. It wouldn't harm you to smile a little!"

"My grandma just died," I told him, feeling slightly violated.

"Oh," he said in an apologetic tone.

We often don't know what's going on with people. If they aren't cheerful or friendly, it's easy to assume that they have negative feelings toward us, when most of the time that isn't the case. Even if someone does have bad feelings toward you, those feelings are more about that person than you. Don't assume you'll be disliked or be rejected. Allow your heart and mind to be open. Fill them with compassion.

2. *Don't blame others.* When you blame people, you are abdicating your responsibility. If you are late to a date, meeting, or appointment,

don't blame it on a spouse, child, roommate, friend, client, or traffic; take responsibility and apologize sincerely. Of course, if your flight is delayed because of the weather, it's not your fault. Acts of God are beyond your control. If you make a mistake, admit it. If you're honest, other people will respect and accept your apology. If you ordered the wrong food for takeout, don't blame the server on the other end of the phone. You may have misspoken. If you put on weight, don't blame your boyfriend for keeping ice cream in the freezer. You didn't have to eat it. Don't blame a lack of money for stopping you from pursuing your dreams. Get a second job if you need money to invest in your business and you're serious about going after your dreams. When you blame someone else, it allows you to stay angry. It doesn't leave you open and ready for miracles.

3. *Don't resist uncertainty.* If you're focused on spiritual growth and pursuing your dreams, you'll be faced with much uncertainty, but feeling uncertain doesn't mean things won't work out for you. One thing that is certain is that we'll all eventually die. It can feel scary and unsettling to think about our imminent death, especially if we're diagnosed with a serious illness and have a spouse and children who need us. Sometimes death can come unexpectedly, but living each day in fear limits our access to happiness.

What if you were to dive into your life and surrender your need to know exactly what's going to happen next? If there's something you want to do, but you're uncertain about the outcome, what's the worst that can happen? If you feel passionately about what you want to do, from a spiritual perspective it's clear that you must pursue it. There's no guarantee that any relationship will work out—or last permanently. If you've had your heart broken many times before and you fall in love with someone new, you may feel uncertain, but that doesn't mean you should close the door on a relationship. One of my girlfriends is a widow. She has often told me how lonely she is, but for many years every time she was asked on a date, she said no.

She was terrified that she would go through another tragic loss. Her discomfort with uncertainty caused her to forfeit the opportunity to have children.

4. *Don't go for the quick fix.* Anyone who says you can get what you want quickly is either lying, doesn't have the life experience to know better, or is leaving out important details about the amount of work that needs to be done to get fast results. One of my friends underwent liposuction, but returned to her prior weight in just a few months. She could have avoided the surgery and recovery time and saved herself thousands of dollars by working with a nutritionist and getting a gym membership. Hiring a personal trainer to keep her motivated in the early stages of working out, when it's the hardest to make the commitment, would have been a good protocol too.

Magazine articles with headlines that read "Lose Ten Pounds in Ten Days" won't get you the quick results you want unless you weigh 240 pounds and would like to get down to 230 pounds. I've known many people who dieted, yet I've never met anyone who weighed 150 pounds and got down to 140 pounds in ten days. In the final stages of losing the last unwanted pounds and stubborn fat, it is healthy to only lose roughly 1 pound per week.

If someone tells you that you can get out of debt fast with a special loan, ask yourself, "Who has to eventually pay back that loan?" You! There may be a very high rate of interest or a finance fee on the loan that could create even more debt you will have to deal with in the future.

Quick fixes do not work for problems that have been brewing for a while. Next time you feel the urgency to get rid of a problem, take a step back and give yourself permission to opt for a more realistic timeline so you can get long-lasting results.

5. *Don't wait for others to get it done.* What you want may be a priority for you, but unless people want exactly what you want too or you are paying them a good sum of money, they aren't going to act

within your desired time frame. If you live with messy roommates or family members, don't wait for them to tidy up. Get it done yourself or hire a maid and have your roommates contribute to the expense. In a more extreme case of untidiness, you may need to hire a professional organizer or move.

If you're waiting for a decision maker to get back to you on a project, don't wait for the answer. Be proactive. What else can you do to motivate the person to make your request a priority? Or who else can you approach who will respond in a more favorable time frame? Perhaps there's another way you can get your project moving, independent of the decision maker.

If you've been in a relationship for a long time and your partner isn't stepping up in the way you want, tell your partner what you want and need. Be specific. Don't be passive-aggressive or expect your beloved to be a mind reader. Communicate clearly and do everything you can to make yourself happy. The next step will then become clear to you.

6. *Don't compare yourself to others.* If you compare yourself to others, you'll probably find yourself rationalizing why you think you're better than they are or feeling resentful when you mistakenly determine you don't measure up. Comparing will suck up your time and prevent you from taking the actions that would move you a step closer to your breakthrough.

Remember, there will always be someone with more money and someone with less money in your world. Comparison puts you on an unhealthy scale. Even for an A-list Hollywood star it is dangerous to compare, because it is a subjective view of reality. Feeling good that you recently fit into a size 8 when your best friend is a size 14 won't help you feel good after you meet someone who wears a size 4. When you compare yourself to others, you are looking for faults in them to make yourself feel better. Focus on yourself and create goals. Whenever you feel you're in competition with others, you could be closing the door on friendships and career opportunities because of fear and unworthiness.

7. *Don't gossip.* Not only is gossiping mean; it's unproductive. Almost everyone has gossiped at some point in their lives and if you've engaged in it, you already know that it usually comes back to haunt you or hurt you. If someone confides in you and tells you not to repeat something, don't repeat it. If you don't want the responsibility of the secret, tell the person you'd prefer not to be privy to it.

If you're centered in your heart and grounded in your body, you can sense when someone is asking sincere questions rather than fishing for information to use against you later or to report back to someone else. Those who have an ulterior motive may give you a piece of gossip in the hope that you'll open up and share more of your feelings. Try not to fall for this trick. There's an important distinction between gossiping and sharing a story with a friend or loved one. If you're listening to or divulging information to gain a greater perspective, learn from it, and figure out what you need to do next; that is different from criticizing another person.

One of my friends wasn't invited to our mutual friend's dinner party, and she said she felt hurt. She went on to tell me that she feared our friend was jealous, and she didn't want to feel that way herself. I could have easily engaged in a negative way, by gossiping, but I chose simply to listen to her express her feelings instead. Once my friend had processed the upset and sense of rejection aloud, her feelings passed, and we were able to enjoy the rest of our time together. All three of us met up at a future gathering, and there were no uncomfortable feelings.

8. *Don't check out mentally.* When a person experiences challenges, checking out mentally with a few glasses of wine and sugary foods can seem like the easiest option. There's a clear difference between having many things to do that you need to prioritize and having commitments and responsibilities that you're ignoring. You don't

want to check out if you've got important actions to take or have made promises.

People want things when they want them, and you shouldn't drop what you're focused on to meet someone else's demands. Be realistic about what you can get done in the time frame available. Taking on too many commitments could result in wanting to check out, so don't take on commitments if you can't complete them in a reasonable amount of time. If in the past you've engaged in bad habits that created a lot of fires you had to put out, checking out mentally is not going to make them go away—in fact it will make those fires spread.

Look at the entirety of what needs to be done and then commit to addressing each thing on your list in the order of urgency and value. Checking out won't get things done. Commit to doing one thing per day if you feel overwhelmed, and soon enough you'll become more productive and feel good about your day ahead.

9. *Don't settle.* Compromising is different from settling. Sometimes you need to compromise if you want to be in a relationship, maintain a friendship, or do a business deal. Compromising is making sure that everyone's needs are met. Settling is when you don't see your value, fear abandonment, or don't put healthy boundaries in place. If you know your value and others expect you to do things their way without consideration for you, walk away. You may say, "I can't," but what that means is that you're choosing not to engage in toxic relationships or abusive behavior.

If you accept or engage with someone whose actions are negative toward you, you will be both continuing this cycle of behavior and harming yourself. Energy needs to be invested by all parties for abuse to occur. When you settle and give up on meeting your needs, things never turn out well. Even if you do what another person demands, it won't be enough; in such a dynamic the person will still find fault in you and your actions. You deserve better. You're entitled to get your needs met. If you've settled throughout much of your life, asking for what you want will feel challenging at first. But in time you'll learn to ask for what you want with conviction and fairness.

One of my friend's didn't see her value as an account executive in an advertising agency. The longer she stayed at her job, the more responsibilities she accepted, and she worked longer hours too. She was an asset to this award-winning team. When she asked for a pay raise, her boss gave the excuses that she needed more experience and they didn't have the budget for it. She settled for being underpaid for several years. A miracle happened when she was headhunted by an agency that offered her more than she'd requested in her current job. She happily accepted and made a request for a bonus to kick in after she had proved her value when her annual contract came up for renewal.

10. *Don't squander money.* Lottery winners are notorious for burning through their winnings. Similarly, people who are given an allowance and don't have to earn a living can fail to recognize the value of money. As they haven't had to work for it, they tend to spend it quickly. For those who work as entrepreneurs or freelancers, cash flow can be unpredictable. When they are cash rich, they may forget that their earnings can go from feast to famine and that they need to plan for the times when the tide of abundance temporarily recedes. Even the best businesses go through highs and lows. Other businesses make plenty of money, but their employees may be working in jobs they don't like. To reward themselves and to compensate for doing work they don't like, they buy expensive meals and clothes. They rationalize spending more.

Some people are insecure and feel the need to keep up with the Joneses, so they'll squander money they don't have and buy things on credit. Low self-esteem can lead some to spend money on partying and gambling. They feel that if they act like a big shot without a care in the world, they can keep the feelings of pain suppressed.

You can learn to be smart with your money. You don't have to be an accountant or a wealth manager to understand how to make your money work for you. Look at what you need, then at what you want. Needs come first. And remember, just because you can't afford to buy something now doesn't mean you can't have it several months from now. Interestingly, at that point you may not even want the thing you want so much today. If you do, when you get it, you'll value it much more because you patiently waited to have it.

11. *Don't let fear stop you.* Remember, your goal is a big miracle, and you have every right to it. Some people will say you can't do what you want. Some will say that you shouldn't. Search inside yourself. Are your motivations selfish? Are you being unrealistic? Are you okay allowing someone else to dictate the way your life unfolds? What is your reasoning for putting your dreams on hold? If you're passionate about something, why do tomorrow what you can do today? If you don't do it today, then it means that you don't want it that much.

If you keep telling others you want something but you push your dreams aside, you will need to admit that either you don't want your big miracle or you don't believe it is possible. You must find what motivates you to take action.

Believe in Miracles

Keep moving toward your miracles, even when you don't have evidence that the things you want are being manifested. Don't stop doing what needs to be done! Regroup when you hit a bump in the road and then move forward again. If you expect miracles, they will come. They always do for people who believe in them.

If you have any doubt that a big miracle breakthrough is possible for you, take a look around you. Miracles exist. They're happening to people all around you every day. Go back to Rule 1, Align with Spirit. This is the most important rule to follow to create the breakthroughs you are seeking. Make a commitment to integrate Rule 1 into your daily life. If you do, you'll find yourself getting into a flow of abundance.

It doesn't necessarily mean that things will get easy. Remember, if you're focused on spiritual growth, you'll always be moving through resistance. However, the idea of breaking through will no longer scare you, if you practice aligning with Spirit every day. You'll soon find yourself moving forward with courage, excitement, and gratitude for the opportunity to break through. You'll recognize that you're in control of your circumstances, with Spirit's love and support.

A big miracle breakthrough is the result of a series of many small miracles. So keep looking for miracles and telling yourself that the big miracle breakthrough you desire is within reach. As you look back a year from now on how you've applied the eleven rules, if you've been diligent with them you'll see that your life has become everything your heart desired, and more.

Acknowledgments

Thank you, Spirit! I've felt your love and support in creating this book and guiding me to the people who've been a crucial part of its creation.

Thank you to my husband, Nick: I love creating big miracles with you. To my son, Dominick, the joy of my life.

A huge thank you to Claudia Riemer Boutote, Senior Vice President and Publisher, and Libby Edelson, Senior Editor, at Harper-Elixir, for believing in me and for your depth of vision and heartfelt care with this material. The first time we sat down for lunch together in San Francisco was a very special day. I also want to thank Lisa Zuniga, Suzanne Wickham, Julia Kent, Adrian Morgan, Anissa Elmerraji, and everyone else at Elixir who worked to bring this book to life. I am so grateful to be part of the HarperElixir family.

An eternal thank you to my dear friend, guardian angel, and book midwife Stephanie Gunning. I appreciate you raising the bar for me and getting the book out of my head and onto the page.

A special thank you to JJ Virgin for introducing me to my agents, Sarah Passick and Celeste Fine, of Sterling Lord Literistic. I appreciate your taking such good care of me.

To my father-in-law, Richard Garzilli, for being my legal counsel and a great support, and to my mother-in-law, Jane Garzilli, for encouraging me to reach for the stars.

To Diana Maxwell, Robert Quicksilver, and the Conscious Life Expo team, thank you for putting me on the right stage at the right time.

My gratitude also extends to my social media manager, the talented Heather Catania.

A special thank-you to Vanessa Marcil, Kia Miller, Lewis Howes, Ted McGrath, and Manny Diotte. Your contributions have made this book richer and more filled with Spirit.

To my mom, for keeping me grounded and motivated. I love you.

Notes

CHAPTER 1

1. Clients' names have been changed to protect their privacy.

CHAPTER 3

1. Jeff Haden, "Seven Inspiring Steve Jobs Quotes That Just Might Change Your Life," Inc.com, March 19, 2015, http://www.inc.com/jeff-haden/7-inspirational-steve-jobs-quotes-that-will-change-your-life.html.
2. Rhett Herman, "How Fast Is the Earth Moving?" *Scientific American,* October 26, 1998, http://www.scientificamerican.com/article/how-fast-is-the-earth-mov/.
3. Gary Baum, "L.A.'s Soho House Turns Five: Membership Rejections, Success Secrets Revealed in Oral History," *Hollywood Reporter,* March 27, 2015, http://www.hollywoodreporter.com/news/las-soho-house-turns-5-784025.
4. From a lecture by Paul Haggis given at Soho House Los Angeles on October 23, 2010.
5. Matthew Jacobs, "A Decade after 'Crash,' Paul Haggis Reflects on the Polarizing Racial 'Fable' That Stormed the Oscars," *Huffington Post,* May 6, 2015, updated June 6, 2015, http://www.huffingtonpost.com/2015/05/06/paul-haggis-crash_n_7216026.html.

CHAPTER 4

1. Ivan Pavlov's classical conditioning experiment is described in detail in Saul McLeod, "Pavlov's Dogs," *Simply Psychology,* 2007, updated 2013, http://www.simplypsychology.org/pavlov.html.
2. David Ropeik, "How Risky Is Flying?" *Nova* blog, PBS.org, October 17, 2006, http://www.pbs.org/wgbh/nova/space/how-risky-is-flying.html.
3. Napoleon Hill, *The Law of Success* (New York: Tarcher/Penguin, 2008).

CHAPTER 5

1. "Hands Across America," kenkragen.com, March 1, 2016, http://www.kenkragen.com/HandsAcrossAmerica.html.
2. "Hands Across America."
3. "Hands Across America."
4. Elissa Goodman, "Elissa's Story," elissagoodman.com, March 1, 2016, https://elissagoodman.com/about.
5. From a one-on-one interview with Ted McGrath conducted on March 7, 2016.
6. "Mother Teresa of Calcutta (1910–1997)," Holy See Press Office, the Vatican, http://www.vatican.va/news_services/liturgy/saints/ns_lit_doc_20031019_madre-teresa_en.html.
7. "Mother Teresa of Calcutta."
8. "Mother Teresa of Calcutta."

CHAPTER 6

1. Tim Ferriss, "How to Live like a Rock Star (or Tango Star) in Buenos Aires. . . ." *Tim Ferriss Experiment,* March 30, 2007, http://fourhourworkweek.com/2007/03/30/how-to-live-like-a-rock-star-or-tango-star-in-buenos-aires.
2. "Celebs Who Went from Failures to Success Stories" (slideshow), *CBS Money Watch,* March 16, 2016, http://www.cbsnews.com/pictures/celebs-who-went-from-failures-to-success-stories/7.
3. Posted by Chris Pratt (prattprattpratt) in February 2016, Instagram, https://www.instagram.com/p/BBCS7PoDHMX.
4. *Whiplash,* written and directed by Damien Chazelle (2014).

CHAPTER 7

1. Armen Keteyian, "Where Does Mega Millions Money Go After the Jackpot?" *CBS News,* March 30, 2012, http://www.cbsnews.com/news/where-does-mega-millions-money-go-after-the-jackpot.

CHAPTER 8

1. http://ronfinley.com/meet-ron-finley/.
2. From a one-on-one interview with Vanessa Marcil conducted on February 8, 2016.
3. *The Rock,* screenplay by David Weisberg, Douglas Cook, and Mark Rosner, directed by Michael Bay (1996). Production details available at the Internet Movie Database website: http://www.imdb.com/title/tt0117500/?ref_=ttfc_fc_tt.
4. *Las Vegas,* created by Larry Scott Thompson (2003–2008). Production details available at the Internet Movie Database website: http://www.imdb.com/title/tt0364828/?ref_=nm_flmg_act_12.
5. Amanda de Cadenet, "Episode 6: Ariana Huffington, Crystal Renn, Olivia Wilde, Sarah Silverman," *The Conversation,* June 1, 2012, http://theconversation.tv/videos/catch-up-on-last-nights-conversation-watch-episode-6-in-full.
6. *Inside Out,* screenplay by Pete Docter, Ronnie Del Carmen, Meg LeFuave, and Josh Cooley, directed by Pete Docter and Ronnie Del Carmen (2015).

CHAPTER 10

1. "What We Give," Toms.com, http://www.toms.com/what-we-give.
2. Recovery 2.0 Retreats, http://recovery2point0.com/retreats.
3. From a one-on-one interview with Kia Miller conducted on February 4, 2016.

CHAPTER 11

1. *The Pursuit of Happyness,* screenplay by Scott Conrad, directed by Gabriele Muccino (2006).
2. Posted by Richard Branson, Google+, April 10, 2013, https://plus.google.com/+RichardBranson/posts/ZGH5yF4xvSQ.